Interviewing and Diagnostic Exercises for Clinical and Counseling Skills Building

Interviewing and Diagnostic Exercises for Clinical and Counseling Skills Building

Pearl S. Berman
Indiana University of Pennsylvania

with

Susan Shopland

LEA
2005

LAWRENCE ERLBAUM ASSOCIATES, PUBLISHERS
Mahwah, New Jersey   London

Lawrence Erlbaum Associates, Inc., Publishers
10 Industrial Avenue
Mahwah, New Jersey 07430

Cover design by Kathryn Houghtaling Lacey

Library of Congress Cataloging-in-Publication Data

Berman, Pearl S., 1955–
    Interviewing and diagnostic exercises for clinical and counseling skills building / Pearl S. Berman, with Susan Shopland.
        p. cm.
Includes bibliographical references and index.

ISBN 0-8058-4640-9 (pbk.)
1. Mental health counseling—Problems, exercises, etc. 2. Psychotherapy—Problems, exercises, etc.
    3. Clinical competence.   I. Shopland, Susan.   II. Title.
RC466.B47   2004
616.89'14'076—dc22   2004055152
                                                                                         CIP

Books published by Lawrence Erlbaum Associates are printed on acid-free paper, and their bindings are chosen for strength and durability.

Printed in the United States of America
10 9 8 7 6 5 4 3 2 1

Contents

PART III: CHILD AND TEEN PROFILES FOR USE
IN INDIVIDUAL SESSIONS

Acknowledgments

We would like to thank the following individuals for their advice and support in writing this book: Ms. Sarah Dietz, Dr. Renu Garg, Dr. Beverly Goodwin, Dr. Kimberly Husenits, Dr. Dasen Luo, Ms. Binal Purohit, Dr. Constantine Vaporis, and the doctoral students in the Psychology Doctoral program of Indiana University of Pennsylvania.

Preface for Instructors/Supervisors

This book contains twenty client profiles to use in practicing interviewing and diagnostic skills. Ten profiles are of adult cases ranging in age from eighteen to seventy (chapters 3–12). Ten profiles are of child or teen cases ranging in age from seven to seventeen (chapters 13–22). In addition to age, the twenty profiles vary in terms of ethnicity, gender, national origin, religion, socioeconomic status, presenting problems, and level of problem severity.

The instructor can have students simply read through these profiles and then complete the three sets of exercises that follow them. These exercises help students develop diagnoses using the *Diagnostic and Statistical Manual of Mental Disorders Fourth Edition* (*DSM–IV–TR*), deepen their interviewing skills, and practice responding to important clinical issues as they relate to the client. Students can develop their skills more quickly if the clinical profiles are also used in role-play practice with interviewing skills.

In basic role playing, students are divided into teams of two. Before each practice session, one student reads a client profile and prepares to take on the role of "client." The profile contains information about the feelings, thoughts, actions, and interpersonal patterns of the client as he or she participates in a diagnostic intake or initial interview. This allows the student to realistically portray the client and thus be an effective partner for the student taking the interviewer role.

WHY USE ROLE PLAYS?

Interviewing and diagnostic skills are complex and students will make mistakes. The major advantage of role plays is that the focus is on the interviewer's skill building and not client welfare. Thus, you are not faced with any ethical dilemmas if one of your students does, for example, an ineffective screen for suicide. You don't have to take over the session, as you might, with a truly suicidal client. Instead, you can put the interview on temporary hold while you coach your student on how to conduct an effective suicide assessment. Once the student understands what to do, you can have the role playing begin again. Real clients, who have already undergone an inadequate or inappropriate screen, may alter their responses the second time around; you may remain unclear about the validity of the assessment which raises ethical concerns. In a role play, however, the role-play client can simply be instructed to start over again as if the first suicide screen did not occur. This gives the interviewer a fresh start. At the end of this second screen, the role-play client can give the interviewer feedback about both the first and second experience of being screened for suicide. This type of immediate feedback, from both the instructor and the role-play client, can help solidify skill building so that the student is prepared when a real suicidal crisis arises.

Another advantage of role plays is that client confidentiality is not an issue. Thus, students who are not taking on either the client or interviewer role can watch the role-play interview and learn from observing. Although you can have your students watch interviews with real clients, many clients will not want to be observed. Even when they agree to be watched, they may be uncomfortable with, or unwilling, to disclose all the information that might be gained in a more confidential setting.

Finally, role plays can serve as a gatekeeping device. Students who appear to be progressing well in role plays can be assigned real clients to interview; these students are unlikely to jeopardize clients' welfare through a lack of sufficiently honed skills. Those students who seem to be struggling can be given additional role-play practice before being assigned real clients.

WHAT COURSES WAS THIS TEXT DESIGNED TO SUPPORT?

This text was designed to supplement a variety of master's and/or doctoral level courses that cover diagnosis, interviewing, crisis intervention, and/or diversity issues in clinical work. The clinical material within the profiles should be relevant to students in clinical psychology, counseling psychology, counselor education, school psychology, psychiatry, psychiatric nursing, and other allied professions.

WHAT IS THE TEXT'S APPROACH TO INTERVIEWING?

As the case profiles provide information on a client's behaviors, thoughts, emotions, and relational patterns, the student will be able to practice interviewing skills that stem from a variety of theoretical orientations including behavioral, cognitive, dynamic, humanistic, transtheoretical, and eclectic. Each client profile is unique from the others in terms of demographics and presenting issues so that the students are presented with a variety of interviewing challenges. The client information is comprehensive enough that students should be able to gain an in-depth understanding of the client's strengths, weaknesses, and life situation. If your course objectives go beyond preparing students for an intake or initial interview, the profiles can also be used in role-play sessions of (a) helping the client identify personal goals, (b) helping the client identify problems that need to be solved, (c) collaborating on a treatment plan, and (d) carrying out intervention sessions.

Each client chapter contains exercises covering three or four of the text's highlighted interviewing skills of attending, open-ended and closed questions, reflective listening, responding to nonverbal behavior, empathetic comments, summarizing, redirecting, supportive confrontation and process comments. The client profiles in the beginning of the adult and child/teen sections provide practice in the more basic skills of nonverbal attending, responding to nonverbal cues, open-ended and closed questioning, summarizing, reflective listening, and making empathetic comments. The client profiles starting in the middle of the adult and child/teen sections add practice with the more complex skills of redirecting, supportive confrontation, and making process comments.

Although these highlighted skills are just a selection from a vast arena of other available techniques that you might have your students practice, they are comprehensive enough to help the student interviewer build an effective working relationship with the client, define the issues that need to be worked through in treatment, and bring the client's attention to issues of importance when and if the interviewing session gets off course. Once this basic list of skills is mastered, the students can easily add other skills to their interviewing and intervention repertoire. If you wish your students to have a brief review of these highlighted interviewing skills, assign them to read chapter 1 of this text along with any of the worksheets in the Appendix that you consider appropriate. Otherwise, direct them to skip chapter 1 and proceed to the client chapters to begin practicing their interviewing skills.

PROVIDING FEEDBACK ON INTERVIEWING

Live supervision of students during their interviews can be a powerful learning experience. First, it allows you to give immediate feedback to them while the session is still fresh in their minds. Second, you know your feedback is accurate because you saw what happened in the interview. Students may not accurately perceive problems that occur in the interviews. For example, they might believe a client is paranoid rather than recognizing that the client was angry with them because of a mistake they made in interviewing. If you didn't see the interview, you might end up giving the student feedback on how to assess paranoia rather than on how to respond to client anger.

In addition, beginning interviewers often have trouble actively listening to their clients because they are too busy wondering what they should say next. They can more actively listen to their clients when they know they can rely on feedback from others to guide them if a problem arises in the interview. For all of these reasons, live supervision can help students develop their interviewing skills more quickly.

If you plan to provide live supervision of real or role-play interviews, you might want to review the supervisory feedback worksheet (p. 253). This worksheet tracks all of the interviewing skills highlighted in this text. It also gives you the opportunity to comment on the interviewer's areas of strength and weakness. Finally, it provides you with a section for giving interviewers feedback about their clients' issues, including areas that ought to be covered in future sessions with the client.

WHAT IS THE TEXT'S APPROACH TO DIAGNOSIS?

Following each client profile, the text provides a set of exercises to help students develop *DSM–IV–TR* diagnoses that accurately balance the impact of individual, situational, and biological factors on the client's behavior. Exercises first ask the student to work methodically from Axis I to Axis V considering what diagnostic choices are most appropriate for the client. Then, the student is asked to review in reverse their choices from Axis V to Axis I. This reverse review is to help the student reconsider whether a proper balance of individual, situational, and biological factors has been reflected in the diagnostic choices. Once this reverse review is conducted, the exercises prompt the student to complete a second reverse review. In this review, the student takes the client's point of view and considers how this individual might react to the diagnostic choices that have been made. The intent of this three-pronged approach is to make students aware of potential biases that may have entered into their diagnoses and correct them before they can lead to negative consequences for the client.

Chapter 2 of this text provides a brief review of issues related to diagnosis and guides students through a basic understanding of Axes I–V. If your students do not need this review, tell them to skip chapter 2 and proceed to the client profiles in chapter 3. Students will need a copy of the *DSM–IV–TR* (2000) to support their work with the diagnostic exercises. The clinical profiles provide students with a wide range of experience in formulating diagnoses. Some of the clients present students with relatively straightforward choices. For example, students are asked to compare the accuracy and utility of classifying Erica's behavior, following a death, as more representative of an Adjustment Disorder or Bereavement (chapter 18). However, other clients provide complex diagnostic choices. For Aaron (chapter 6), students need to consider whether his symptoms are best explained through a diagnosis of Schizophrenia, a Substance Abuse Disorder, or if he is a dual diagnosis case.

WHAT IS THE TEXT'S APPROACH TO DIVERSITY?

The clinical profiles expose the interviewer to issues in human diversity and how these issues might influence the interviewing and diagnostic processes. Assessing a client who differs from the intended interviewer in terms of age, ethnicity, gender, national origin, socioeconomic status, religion, and so forth can be used as an eye-opener to students, driving home the point that effective interviewing must be flexible if it is to adequately address the needs of diverse people.

The student is exposed to the feelings, thoughts, actions, and interpersonal styles of diverse clients and how these factors might influence the course of the interview. For example, Jie (chapter 4), a Taiwanese university student, comes to the interview asking for help with academic problems. The profile explains that Jie will be embarrassed and confused if the interviewer asks any emotionally focused questions because he considers it immature to express or discuss emotions. Raoul (chapter 17) is living in a community that holds many prejudices against Mexican Americans. As a result, Raoul is highly suspicious of how the interviewer may view Mexican Americans. His client profile indicates that he will only begin to open up during the interview situation if the interviewer demonstrates respect for his heritage. If the interviewer does not, Raoul will stay quiet, noncommunicative, and subtly hostile. Raoul is not paranoid. The detail provided in his profile helps students, who are unfamiliar with the types of experiences that Raoul has been through, recognize that his behavior reflects a realistic response to past prejudice.

Mary (chapter 7), of European-American heritage, is struggling to grieve for her husband after his sudden death. Her profile reveals that her cultural and religious beliefs dictate self-sufficiency, emotional control, and altruism to one's children. These beliefs keep her from asking for the help she needs during this tragic period in her life.

The personal details provided for Jie, Raoul, Mary, and the other clients give students an opportunity to understand the worldview of clients who may be very different from themselves. In the exercises that follow each profile, students are guided to seriously reflect on what differences might exist between themselves and the client. First, they write down what they think might be most difficult about establishing rapport with the client based on their own age, ethnicity, gender, socioeconomic status, sexual orientation, religion, physical characteristics, and personality style. Then, they are asked to consider what specifically might happen between themselves and the client as they begin the interview process. Finally, they are asked to consider what they could do to enhance their ability to establish an effective working relationship with the client.

Chapter 1 of this text provides a brief introduction to how diversity issues might influence the interviewing process. Chapter 2 provides a brief introduction to how diversity issues might influence the accuracy of *DSM–IV–TR* diagnoses. If you want your students to have more background in these issues, you can refer them to Suggestions for Further Reading (p. 251).

WHAT IS THE TEXT'S APPROACH TO CRISIS INTERVENTION?

Clinical profiles and exercises provide students with challenges/crises that may arise during an interview with clients who are psychotic, violent, suicidal, or difficult to work with for a variety of other reasons. For example, the exercises will help them practice assessing for suicide risk using the case of Mary (chapter 7) and violence risk using the case of Gary (chapter 12). Is a client psychotic or under the influence of drugs? Students will have an opportunity to assess this using the case of Aaron (chapter 6). Students will also gain practice responding to many other "tough moments" in treatment such as David's sexual overtures (chapter 10) and Sabina's questions about their knowledge of Islam (chapter 20).

WHICH CLIENT PROFILES ARE OF VALUE TO YOU?

You may not have the interest or class time available to cover all of the available client profiles. The Table of Contents provides you with a brief overview of every chapter. You can use this to make strategic selections to meet the needs of your course. Tables 1–3 can also be used to select chapters. They organize the material covered in chapters 3–22 in three different formats for easy reference. If you want your students to practice particular interviewing skills, you can consult Table 1 to get a quick reference to the chapters that provide practice exercises in these skills. You can then also select matching skill-building worksheets from the Appendix. If you want your students to gain practice thinking through specific diagnostic issues, Table 2 provides a quick reference for which diagnoses are covered within each chapter. Finally, Table 3 summarizes which chapters cover special topics in interviewing such as aggression, culture, psychosis, substance abuse, suicide, and so forth. This table also indicates the cultural background of each client. These three tables are located directly after the Preface for Students/Trainees.

WHERE DID THE TEXT CLIENTS COME FROM?

The profiles represent composites of case information collected over years of clinical practice and do not represent any real person seen currently, or in the past, by Dr. Berman or Dr. Shopland. The authors have a combined total of thirty-one years of clinical practice. Many of the people they came in contact with, during this time, served as inspiration for certain details contained within the profiles.

Preface for Students/Trainees

This book contains twenty client profiles to use in practicing interviewing and diagnostic skills. Ten profiles are of adult cases ranging in age from eighteen to seventy (chapters 3–12). Ten profiles are of child or teen cases ranging in age from seven to seventeen (chapters 13–22). In addition to age, the twenty profiles vary in terms of ethnicity, gender, national origin, religion, socioeconomic status, presenting problems, and level of problem severity.

You can simply read through these profiles and then complete the three sets of exercises that follow them. These exercises help you develop diagnoses using the *Diagnostic and Statistical Manual of Mental Disorders Fourth Edition* (*DSM–IV–TR*), deepen your interviewing skills, and practice responding to important clinical issues as they relate to the client. You can develop your skills more quickly if you use the clinical profiles in role-play practice with interviewing skills.

In basic role playing, students are divided into teams of two. Before each practice session, one student reads a client profile and prepares to take on the role of "client." The profile contains information about the feelings, thoughts, actions, and interpersonal patterns of the client as he or she participates in a diagnostic intake or initial interview. This allows the student to realistically portray the client and thus be an effective partner for the student taking the interviewer role.

WHAT COURSES WAS THIS TEXT DESIGNED TO SUPPORT?

This text was designed to supplement a variety of master's and/or doctoral level courses that cover diagnosis, interviewing, crisis intervention, and/or diversity issues in clinical work. The clinical material within the profiles should be relevant to students within the fields of clinical psychology, counseling psychology, counselor education, school psychology, psychiatry, psychiatric nursing, and other allied professions.

WHAT IS THE TEXT'S APPROACH TO INTERVIEWING?

As the case profiles provide information on a client's behaviors, thoughts, emotions, and relational patterns, you will be able to practice interviewing skills that stem from a variety of theoretical orientations including behavioral, cognitive, dynamic, humanistic, transtheoretical, and eclectic. Each client profile is unique from the others in terms of demographics and presenting issues so that you are presented with a variety of interviewing challenges. The client information is comprehensive enough that you should be able to gain an in-depth understanding of the client's strengths, weaknesses, and life situation. If the course you are taking goes beyond the intake or initial interview, the profiles can also be used in role-play sessions of (a) helping the client identify personal goals, (b) helping the client identify problems that need to be solved, (c) collaborating on a treatment plan, and (d) carrying out intervention sessions.

Each client chapter contains exercises covering three or four of the text's highlighted interviewing skills of attending, open-ended and closed questions, reflective listening, responding to nonverbal behavior, empathetic comments, summarizing, redirecting, supportive confrontation and process comments.

Although these highlighted skills are just a selection from a vast arena of other available techniques that you might want to practice, they are comprehensive enough to help you build an effective working relationship with the client, define the issues that need to be worked through in treatment, and bring the client's attention to issues of importance when and if the interviewing session gets off course. Once this basic list of skills is mastered, you can easily add other skills to your interviewing and intervention repertoire. If you want to have a brief review of these highlighted interviewing skills, read chapter 1 of this text and fill out any of the worksheets in the Appendix that you consider appropriate to your skill building. Otherwise, skip chapter 1 and proceed to the client chapters and begin practicing your interviewing skills.

WHAT IS THE TEXT'S APPROACH TO DIAGNOSIS?

Following each client profile, the text provides a set of exercises to help you develop *DSM–IV–TR* diagnoses that accurately balance the impact of individual, situational, and biological factors on the client's behavior. Exercises first ask you to work methodically from Axis I to Axis V considering what diagnostic choices are most appropriate for the client. Then, you are asked to go in reverse from Axis V through to Axis I. This backward review is to help you reconsider whether a proper balance of individual, situational, and biological factors has been reflected in the diagnostic choices. Once this first reverse review is conducted, the exercises prompt you to complete a second backward review. In this review, you take on the client's point of view and consider how this individual would react to the diagnostic choices that have been made. The intent of this three-pronged approach is to make you aware of potential biases that may have entered into your diagnoses and correct them before they can lead to negative consequences for the client.

Chapter 2 of this text provides a brief review of issues related to diagnosis and guides you through a basic understanding of Axes I–V. If you do not need this review, skip chapter 2 and proceed to the client profiles that begin at chapter 3. You will need a copy of the *DSM–IV–TR* (2000) to support your work with the diagnostic exercises. The clinical profiles provide you with a wide range of experience in formulating diagnoses. Some of the clients present you with relatively straightforward choices. For example, you are asked to compare the accuracy and utility of classifying Erica's behavior, following a death, as more representative of an Adjustment Disorder or Bereavement (chapter 18). However, other clients provide complex diagnostic choices. For Aaron (chapter 6), you need to consider whether his symptoms are best explained through a diagnosis of Schizophrenia, Substance Abuse Disorder, or if he is a dual diagnosis case.

WHAT IS THE TEXT'S APPROACH TO DIVERSITY?

The clinical profiles expose you to issues in human diversity and how these issues might influence the interviewing and diagnostic process. Assessing a client who differs from you in terms of age, ethnicity, gender, national origin, socioeconomic status, religion, and so forth can be used as an eye-opener. You need to learn to respond flexibly to clients so that you can address the needs of diverse people.

To help you gain this flexibility, you are exposed to the feelings, thoughts, actions, and interpersonal styles of diverse clients and how these factors might influence the course of the interview. For example, Jie (chapter 4), a Taiwanese university student, comes to the interview asking for help with academic problems. The profile explains that Jie will be embarrassed and confused if you ask any emotionally focused questions because he considers it immature to express or discuss emotions. Raoul (chapter 17) is living in a community that holds many prejudices against Mexican Americans. As a result, Raoul is highly suspicious of how you view Mexican Americans. His client profile indicates that he will only begin to open up during the interview situation if you demonstrate respect for his heritage. If you do not, Raoul will stay quiet, noncommunicative, and subtly hostile. Raoul is not paranoid. The detail provided in his profile helps you, if you are unfamiliar with the types of experiences that Raoul has been through, recognize that his behavior reflects a realistic response to past prejudice.

Mary (chapter 7), of European-American heritage, is struggling to grieve for her husband after his sudden death. Her profile reveals that her cultural and religious beliefs dictate self-sufficiency, emotional control, and altruism to one's children. These beliefs keep her from asking for the help she needs during this tragic period in her life.

The personal details provided for Jie, Raoul, Mary, and the other clients give you an opportunity to understand the worldview of clients who may be very different from yourself. In the exercises that follow each profile, you are guided to seriously reflect on what differences might exist between yourself and the client. First, you write down what you think might be most difficult about establishing rapport with the client based on your own age, ethnicity, gender, socioeconomic status, sexual orientation, religion, physical characteristics, and personality style. Then, you are asked to consider what specifically might happen between yourself and the client as you begin the interview process. Finally, you are asked to consider what you could do to enhance your ability to establish an effective working relationship with the client.

Chapter 1 of this text provides a brief introduction to how diversity issues might influence the interviewing process. Chapter 2 provides a brief introduction to how diversity issues might influence the accuracy of *DSM–IV–TR* diagnoses. If you want to have more background in these issues, consult Suggestions for Further Reading (p. 251).

WHAT IS THE TEXT'S APPROACH TO CRISIS INTERVENTION?

Clinical profiles and exercises provide you with challenges/crises that may arise during an interview with clients who are psychotic, violent, suicidal, or difficult to work with for a variety of other reasons. For example, the exercises will help you practice assessing for suicide risk using the case of Mary (chapter 7) and violence risk using the case of Gary (chapter 12). Is a client psychotic or under the influence of drugs? You will have an opportunity to assess this using the case of Aaron (chapter 6). You will also gain practice responding to many other tough moments in therapy such as David's sexual overtures (chapter 10) and Sabina's questions about your knowledge of Islam (chapter 20).

WHICH CLIENT PROFILES ARE OF VALUE TO YOU?

You may not have the interest or class time available to cover all of the available client profiles. The Table of Contents provides you with a brief overview of every chapter. You can use this to make strategic selections to meet your needs. Tables 1–3, which follow this preface, can also be used to select chapters. They organize the material covered in chapters 3–22 in three different formats for easy reference. If you want to practice particular interviewing skills, you can consult Table 1 to get a quick reference to the chapters that provide practice exercises in these skills. You can then also select matching skill-building worksheets from the Appendix. If you want to gain practice thinking through specific diagnostic issues, Table 2 provides a quick reference for which diagnoses are covered within each chapter. Finally, Table 3 summarizes which chapters cover special topics in interviewing such as aggression, culture, psychosis, substance abuse, suicide, and so forth. This table also indicates the cultural background of each client.

TABLE 1:
Interviewing Skills Across Chapters

Skills	Chapter and Case
Empathetic Comments	CH 6: Aaron, CH 7: Mary, CH 8: Mark, CH 12: Gary, CH 13: Cynthia*, CH 14: Jeffrey*, CH 15: Melissa*, CH 17: Raoul*, CH 19: Joseph*, CH 20: Sabina*, CH 22: Cathy*
Nonverbal Attending	CH 4: Jie, CH 6: Aaron, CH 7: Mary, CH 12: Gary, CH 18: Erica*, CH 20: Sabina*
Open-Ended and Closed Questions	CH 3: Monisha, CH 6: Aaron, CH 7: Mary, CH 10: David, CH 13: Cynthia*, CH 15: Melissa*, CH 16: Edward*, CH 18: Erica*, CH 20: Sabina*
Process Comments	CH 11: Lisa, CH 12: Gary, CH 17: Raoul*, CH 20: Sabina*, CH 22: Cathy*
Redirecting	CH 8: Mark, CH 9: Sarah, CH 10: David, CH 18: Erica*, CH 21: Alex*
Reflective Listening	CH 5: Brenda, CH 6: Aaron, CH 7: Mary, CH 8: Mark, CH 14: Jeffrey*, CH 15: Melissa*, CH 17: Raoul*, CH 19: Joseph*, CH 20: Sabina*
Responding to Nonverbal Behavior	CH 3: Monisha, CH 4: Jie, CH 9: Sarah, CH 14: Jeffrey*, CH 15: Melissa*, CH 16: Edward*, CH 18: Erica*, CH 19: Joseph*, CH 21: Alex*
Summarizing	CH 4: Jie, CH 5: Brenda, CH 11: Lisa, CH 13: Cynthia*, CH 21: Alex*, CH 22: Cathy*
Supportive Confrontation	CH 10: David, CH 12: Gary, CH 17: Raoul*, CH 19: Joseph*

*Represents a child or teen case; CH stands for chapter.

TABLE 2:
Diagnoses Across Chapters

Diagnosis	Chapter/Client
Adjustment Disorder	CH 3: Monisha, CH 4: Jie, CH 9: Sarah, CH 11: Lisa, CH15: Melissa*, CH 18: Erica*
Anxiety Disorder	CH 4: Jie
Bereavement	CH 7: Mary, CH 18: Erica*
Bulimia Nervosa	CH 13: Cynthia*
Child or Adolescent Antisocial Behavior	CH 20: Sabina*
Conduct Disorder	CH 17: Raoul*, CH 19: Joseph*
Eating Disorder NOS	CH 13: Cynthia*
Identity Problem	CH 20: Sabina*
Intermittent Explosive Disorder	CH 12: Gary
Learning Disorder	CH 16: Edward*
Major Depressive Disorder	CH 5: Brenda, CH 7: Mary, CH 14: Jeffrey*
Oppositional Defiant Disorder	CH 14: Jeffrey*, CH 21: Alex*
Parent–Child Relational Problem	CH 21: Alex*
Phase of Life Problem	CH 11: Lisa
Posttraumatic Stress Disorder	CH 8: Mark, CH 22: Cathy*
Schizophrenia	CH 6: Aaron
Separation Anxiety Disorder	CH 19: Joseph*
Sexual Abuse of Child	CH 22: Cathy*
Substance-Related Disorders	CH 6: Aaron, CH 10: David, CH 12: Gary, CH 17: Raoul*

*Represents a child or teen case; CH stands for chapter.

TABLE 3:
Thought Issues Across Chapters

Issue	Chapter and Case	Cultural Background
Absent Father/Single Parent	CH 13: Cynthia*	European-American
	CH 16: Edward*	African-American
Aggression/Violence	CH 12: Gary	European-American
	CH 14: Jeffrey*	European-American
	CH 21: Alex*	European-American
Bereavement	CH 3: Monisha	African-American
	CH 7: Mary	European-American
Confidentiality	CH 15: Melissa*	European-American
	CH 17: Raoul*	Mexican-American
Culture	CH 4: Jie	Taiwanese
	CH 7: Mary	European-American
	CH 13: Cynthia*	European-American
	CH 16: Edward*	African-American
	CH 17: Raoul*	Mexican-American
	CH 19: Joseph*	Biracial: European-Puerto Rican
	CH 20: Sabina*	Bangladeshi-American
Custody	CH 15: Melissa*	European-American
	CH 19: Joseph*	Biracial: European-Puerto Rican
Development	CH 5: Brenda	European-American
	CH 13: Cynthia*	European-American
	CH 18: Erica*	European-American
Gender	CH 5: Brenda	European-American
	CH 11: Lisa	European-American
Health	CH 9: Sarah	European-American
	CH 11: Lisa	European-American
Individual vs. Family Treatment	CH 15: Melissa*	European-American
Medication	CH 5: Brenda	European-American

(Continued)

TABLE 3
(*Continued*)

Issue	Chapter and Case	Cultural Background
Narrow vs. Wide Treatment Focus	CH 3: Monisha	African-American
Poverty	CH 16: Edward* CH 17: Raoul* CH 19: Joseph*	African-American Mexican-American Biracial: European-Puerto Rican
Psychosis	CH 6: Aaron	African-American
Personal boundaries	CH 9: Sarah CH 18: Erica*	European-American European-American
Racism	CH 17: Raoul*	Mexican-American
Reaction to Trauma	CH 8: Mark	European-American
Religion	CH 7: Mary CH 18: Erica* CH 20: Sabina*	European-American European-American Bangladeshi-American
Self-Awareness of Interviewer	All chapters	
Sexual orientation	CH 7: Mary CH 22: Cathy*	European-American European-American
Sexual overtures	CH 10: David CH 22: Cathy*	European-American European-American
Substance abuse	CH 6: Aaron CH 10: David CH 12: Gary	African-American European-American European-American
Suicide	CH 7: Mary CH 14: Jeffrey*	European-American European-American

*Represents a child or teen case; CH stands for chapter.

I

INTRODUCTION

Interviewing Skills Highlighted in the Text

If you feel confident that you are ready to practice your interviewing skills, skip this chapter and proceed to the client profiles in chapters 3–22. If you prefer to review some basic interviewing skills before you begin to practice, then read the following descriptions of interviewing skills. They are only a small selection from a vast arena of useful interviewing skills. It is a bias of this text that intensely covering a small group of skills may produce a more competent beginning interviewer than briefly covering a larger set of skills. After mastering this short list, students can increase their repertoire fairly easily through direct instruction or further reading. The short list highlighted in this chapter will help the interviewer achieve the goals of the intake or initial interview, which include gaining an in-depth understanding of both client strengths and client weaknesses or areas of difficulty; and identifying, with the client, appropriate goals if treatment is recommended.

WHY WERE CERTAIN SKILLS SELECTED?

The skills of open-ended and closed questioning are introduced because they help interviewers engage clients in a review of their lives so that intake or initial interview goals can be achieved. Nonverbal attending, responding to client's nonverbal behavior, reflective listening, empathetic comments, and summarizing are introduced to help interviewers demonstrate not only interest, respect, and caring for their clients, but also accurate understanding of their clients' lives. Finally, because the intake process can sometimes get off track with difficult clients, the skills of making process comments, redirecting, and supportive confrontation are introduced. These skills help interviewers respectfully re-engage clients in a discussion of relevant issues. These interviewing skills are now discussed in more depth.

WHAT IS ATTENDING BEHAVIOR?

If you show attending behavior, it means you are using verbal and nonverbal behavior that allows the client to see that you are listening carefully and trying to understand fully what is being said. This type of behavior will help your clients develop trust in you, open up and reveal their concerns to you, and thoughtfully explore issues that are relevant to their problems with you (Egan, 1994, p. 91).

What Is Verbal Attending?

Verbal attending behavior includes things such as your tone of voice, rate of speech, sighs, and uhums. Verbal signs of interest, such as the classic "uhum" also encourage a client to keep talking. Accurate summaries, reflections, and empathetic comments also show the client that you are listening carefully and understanding the importance of what is being said.

What Is Nonverbal Attending?

Nonverbal attending behavior can include things such as eye contact, orientation of your body vis-à-vis the client, body posture, facial expressions, use of pauses in the conversation, your attire, and your autonomic behavior (breathing rate, perspiration rate). Clients react to their interviewer's nonverbal behavior. When the interviewer's tone of voice and nonverbal behavior indicate warmth and genuineness, rapport is enhanced because the client feels respected and valued. If verbal and nonverbal behaviors are incongruent, the client is likely to trust the nonverbal message over the verbal one. For example, if the interviewer's tone of voice and nonverbal behavior indicate boredom, the client will not feel listened to or valued no matter how much the interviewer expresses caring thoughts.

There are no universal criteria for what is appropriate or inappropriate nonverbal attending. Nonverbal attending behavior varies across ethnic and racial groups as well as across individuals within an ethnic or racial group. Thus, while it is valuable to be aware of differences that might be present in a group's nonverbal attending, don't assume these differences will exist for a specific client. Sue and Sue (2002, chap. 5) and Ivey, Gluckstern, and Ivey (1997, pp. 19–20) strive to educate helpers about the nonverbal behaviors that might vary between different cultural and ethnic groups. The basic European-American model, which they believe pervades many training programs, suggests that providing direct eye contact is a sign of respect. These authors stress that this model does not hold for many individuals from other ethnic and cultural backgrounds. For example, Ivey et al. (1997) indicate that some Southwest Native Americans may consider eye contact a sign of aggression. The fact that you may not be familiar with the attending behavior of some of your clients and they may not be familiar with yours may cause a subtle barrier to clear communication. To try and prevent these misunderstandings from happening, work to become aware of your own attending behavior and how it might be influenced by differences between yourself and others. Then, openly discuss with your clients any differences that might exist in nonverbal attending behavior before any misunderstandings occur. The only way to know if there is the potential for nonverbal miscommunication is to directly discuss the issue with the client. Cardemil and Battle (2003) caution helpers not to assume they can tell, by looking at a client, if such ethnic or racial differences exist.

As an example of how this might be addressed in an intake, assume you know that you give a lot of eye contact during an interview to show clients that you are interested in what they are saying. Assume again that you are interviewing a client who comes from an ethnic or racial group where direct eye contact is considered rude. As you introduce yourself to your client, at the beginning of the interview, you might say something like, "I always look people in the eyes when they are talking to me to show respect for them and to show interest in their lives. If this is uncomfortable for you, I will try not to do it." This comment opens up a conversation between you and the client that can be a useful tool in building rapport. This particular client may or may not find it problematic that you give eye contact. Only by raising the issue can the client have an opportunity to discuss it with you.

If the client tells you that eye contact is offensive, you should try to avoid giving it. It may be difficult to avoid giving eye contact if it is one of your engrained habits. However, because you discussed this behavior pattern at the beginning of the interview, your client might be more understanding of your intent to show respect even if she or he normally views eye contact as disrespectful. Later, if your client is showing signs of discomfort, you will be prepared to recognize that this may be because of something YOU are doing (giving eye contact) rather than it being caused by something else.

During an interview, you might find yourself matching a client's body posture, facial expression, and tempo and intensity of speech. This matching tends to occur automatically and unconsciously when two people are intently communicating with each other and is called *nonverbal mirroring*. In some cases, this is a nonverbal signal to clients that you understand them. In these cases, mirroring may increase the client's comfort with you and further deepen rapport. However, when this is not experienced by a client as genuine behavior on your part, it may be perceived as "mocking" and cause client alienation (B. Goodwin, personal communication, December 10, 2003). Thus, nonverbal mirroring doesn't always build rapport.

Even when the client does view the mirroring as a sign of rapport, it is not always a sign of positive movement in the interview. Sometimes your client is using nonverbal behavior to minimize something. For example, assume that your client is laughing while talking about a serious event. If the interviewer mirrors this, then it sends the message to the client that minimization is appropriate. In this situation, verbally commenting on the incongruency between the client's nonverbal and verbal behavior may be more appropriate than mirroring. This may help the client more deeply explore his or her experience in relation to this serious event. The interviewer could also choose to communicate about the seriousness of the situation through intentionally using nonverbal behavior that is opposite that of the client. Take the previous example: In response to the client laughing, the interviewer could look grave and speak in an intense voice. This would send a nonverbal signal to the client that the topic is not a laughing matter. In a different situation, imagine that your male client is slumping in his chair and speaking softly and slowly because he is depressed. You could intentionally sit up in your chair, look at him intently and speak with energy to see if your energized, nonverbal behavior could lead him to mirror your energized behavior. This can serve as an indirect assessment of how deeply depressed the client is. As with all other interviewing techniques, rapport will only be enhanced if the client views your behavior as respectful and caring.

RESPONDING TO NONVERBAL BEHAVIOR

Interviewers can increase their awareness of what their clients are thinking and feeling by noticing their nonverbal behavior. At times, the interviewer might simply note these signs for his or her own knowledge. At other times, the interviewer might choose to comment on these nonverbal cues to help the clients themselves recognize more fully how something is influencing their lives. Clients may not recognize that their nonverbal behavior can serve as an important source of information about how they are really experiencing things. In learning to become aware of their bodily signs of thoughts and emotions, clients may gain a deeper understanding of themselves. For example, assume a client says that her recent divorce proceedings are going smoothly but, in fact, her nonverbal behavior suggests agitation. If the interviewer comments on her physical signs of agitation, the client may recognize that something she had cognitively labeled to herself as unimportant was in fact very important. Clients may develop a deeper understanding of the nature of their strengths, as well as their problems, when they learn to tune in to their nonverbal behavior.

Interviewers also provide cues about their own thoughts and feelings to clients through their nonverbal behavior. Clients are likely to recognize incongruence between what helpers are saying and how they are behaving.

Identifying Nonverbal Behavior

When commenting about nonverbal behavior to clients, you can simply direct their attention to their own nonverbal behavior. For example, if a female client looks away while you are talking to her, it might mean she is angry with you, she is anxious about what you are saying, she is bored with what you are saying, and so forth. You might say to her, "I noticed that when I brought up your mother, you looked away and I was wondering what this meant." The client's attention is then drawn to this nonverbal behavior and she can use it to understand herself and her situation more completely.

Identifying Feelings

When commenting on nonverbal behavior, you can help clients identify their feelings. Some adults and teens have cut themselves off from their emotions. You can help them reconnect to their emotional experience by encouraging them to label the feelings that are reflected in their nonverbal behavior. Young children often need this help because they have little experience recognizing and identifying feeling states. You can support their emotional learning by helping them tie their nonverbal behavior to potential feeling states.

When you identify feelings from nonverbal behavior, you are making an inference or interpretation; you may be wrong. Thus, expressing your inference tentatively may show the client that you are open to being corrected when you are mistaken. Not all comments on nonverbal behavior represent equally deep inferences about clients' thoughts and feelings. The deeper the inference, the less clearly it is tied to the immediate nonverbal behavior of the client. Thus, you should gain a great breadth of knowledge about a client before making deep inferences.

To illustrate how you might help a client identify feelings from nonverbal behavior, assume you are talking to a male client who has serious academic difficulties and has been referred for an intake with you by his college adviser. You have noted that whenever you ask him about his academic progress he slumps in his chair, looks down, and mumbles. In the earliest stage of the interview, when you don't know much about the client, you might just comment on his nonverbal behavior by saying, "I noticed that when I asked you about your grades, you began to slump in your chair" (all nonverbal behavior). This comment allows the client to see that you are carefully attending to him and are aware that something has changed within him. It might also help the client be more aware of his own experience. As you only commented on nonverbal behavior, you are not making any inferences; thus, the client is unlikely to react negatively to what was said or reject the comment.

If rapport is developing well, you may consider making a comment that identifies a potential feeling state (an inference) to his nonverbal behavior. In response to the same nonverbal cues as before, the interviewer could say, "I noticed that this is the second time that when your grades came up, you began to slump in your chair. I wondered if you are feeling sad?" (nonverbal behavior plus low level and tentatively expressed inference). This comment invites the client to think about the meaning of his nonverbal behavior and consider whether it indicates sadness. Because the feeling state was expressed tentatively, the client might feel comfortable telling you if your interpretation of his nonverbal behavior was wrong. Whether you were right or wrong about the feeling state, the client will have had an opportunity to gain a deeper awareness of his emotional experience. Your rapport with him may increase because he feels understood.

When your rapport with the client is deep, you may feel confident that you understand the meaning of your client's nonverbal behavior. In this case, you might make comments that identify feelings without including the evidence of the nonverbal behavior. For example, in response to the client slumping in the chair you might say something like, "I wonder if you are feeling sad right now." It is important to remember the differential power between the client and the interviewer (Feminist Therapy Institute, 1995). This may make it difficult for clients to correct their interviewers. Thus, whenever you comment on nonverbal behavior, you need to be attentive to the verbal and nonverbal reactions of the client to your comment. If the client shows any signs of discomfort, you may need to say something like, "I wonder if I misunderstood how you were feeling." This further comment might help clients feel comfortable enough to correct your misunderstanding of their experience.

WHAT ARE OPEN-ENDED AND CLOSED QUESTIONS?

Interviewers ask questions in order to gain an understanding of the strengths and weaknesses of their clients as well as to gain an understanding of which issues, concerns, or goals to address with the client in greater depth. Open-ended questions are questions that tend to draw complex information from the client and allow the client a great deal of scope in determining how to respond. Clients who are given opportunities to think about an open-ended question are likely to give detailed information to the interviewer. Closed questions tend to draw out very brief and specific responses from the client. These questions may be more useful when the interviewer needs some specific pieces of information and less useful when the interviewer wants in-depth information.

Using Open-Ended Questions

Open-ended questions can provide the basic structure for an intake interview. For example, to gain a broad perspective on a client's life, the interviewer might plan to ask open-ended questions in the areas of reasons for referral, client concerns, client strengths, client's educational history, client's employment history, client's medical history, and so forth. There are many levels of openness to questions. Some open-ended questions may be widely focused such as, "Tell me about your life?" Other open-ended questions may be more narrowly focused such as, "Tell me what happened last Saturday night?" An interviewer often begins discussion of a topic area by asking a widely focused, open-ended question. As the client responds to this question, it may be appropriate for the interviewer to follow up with several more narrowly focused, open-ended questions that help the client delve deeper into his or her experience. For example, if the interviewer wants to gain knowledge of a client's use of alcohol, a widely focused open-ended question such as, "Tell me about the role alcohol plays in your life?" gives the client a great deal of latitude in how to respond. If the client responds with a brief comment such as, "Well, I always drink on the weekends to help myself relax," the interviewer might follow up with several more narrowly focused, but still open-ended, questions. For example, during the course of a discussion the interviewer might say things such as, "How did you use alcohol last weekend? What happened on Saturday that made you feel the need to relax? How well did the alcohol help you relax?"

Using Closed Questions

There are times during the interview when you want very specific information from the client. For example, in listening to a client talk about his or her alcohol use, there may come a time when you want to know specifically how much a client is drinking. In this instance, a closed question such as, "Tell me how many drinks you had last Saturday night?" will help determine precisely how much alcohol the client used on a specific occasion.

Closed questions may also be useful when talking to a client who tends to go off on tangents, is evasive, or tends to become overly detailed in his or her answers. In these cases, a closed question can serve to direct the client back to the topic at hand. Assume that you asked a male client about how much alcohol he had at a party last weekend. He responded by going off on a tangent giving you lots of details about the jazz music played at the party. You could say, "How many drinks did you have while you were listening to that jazz CD?" This closed question brings an unfocused answer back to the issue of alcohol consumption.

Further Examples of Open-Ended and Closed Questions

A client has been referred for an intake interview with you after admitting to her teacher that she has been binging on food. The following are examples of open-ended and closed questions that might be appropriate to ask during an intake:

Open-Ended: 1. "What is a binge like for you?"
2. "Could you explain to me how binging is helpful to you?"
3. "How has your binging caused problems for you?"

Closed: 1. "How many pizzas did you eat on Saturday night?"
                  2. "What food do you prefer to eat when you binge?"
                  3. "How hard was it for you to throw up?"

WHAT ARE REFLECTIVE LISTENING COMMENTS?

A reflective listening comment focuses the client's attention on the thoughts or feelings he or she is having in response to certain events or issues that are being discussed. A reflective listening comment stays very close to the information the client has just related. It may simply reflect back what the client has said or it may tie expressed or hypothetical emotions or thoughts that the client is experiencing to the information that was disclosed. In adding feelings to a reflective listening comment, you are not making interpretations of why the client is having an emotion or a thought. You are simply reflecting back what you heard the client saying.

Reflective listening comments demonstrate to clients that you are listening to them. It is important for your tone of voice to be congruent with the message in your reflection. Otherwise, the reflection will seem mocking rather than genuine. When making a reflection, your comment can include the feelings the client expressed, the thoughts, or both. If a client expresses more than one feeling, or expresses ambivalent feelings, then the reflective comment could do the same.

Examples of Reflective Listening

Client: It's unbelievable how ideal things are at this point. My new teaching job is going well. I like my students and they seem to like me too. I have begun to make some friends among the other teachers. Things with my husband Jose are going much better than I expected. He isn't just tolerating this new thing in my life, he actually seems to be proud of me. I overheard him telling his mom on the phone how impressed he is that I got this job. What a change! He used to just criticize me to her. We both seem to be putting more effort into our marriage and even into our sex life. I just never expected this! But, because of all the horror we have been through in the past, part of me is just waiting for the explosion that tears us apart again.

Interviewer:

1. You seem to be feeling excited because so many things are going well since you started your new job. (reflecting the good feelings)
2. You are thinking a lot about the changes that you have made in your life and how this has changed your relationship with your husband. (reflecting the thoughts)
3. On the one hand you feel things couldn't be better since the job started, but on the other you worry that something has to go wrong. (reflecting both the positive and the negative feelings)

WHAT IS AN EMPATHETIC COMMENT?

Many of the skills that have been discussed previously may show clients that you care about them and are trying to understand their experiences. Even a nod, if given at the right moment, can make the client feel understood and cared about. However, nods are not communications that necessarily impart any information beyond that you are listening. Empathetic comments are attempts to directly tell clients that their perspective of their situation is understood and valued. Empathetic comments give the client emotional support. A reflective listening comment that focuses on feelings starts the process of empathy. However, it is a restatement of what the client has already said. An empathetic comment goes beyond what the client says and adds something more to demonstrate that the listener understands the meaning behind the words the client used. The interviewer derives this greater meaning from the context of what the client has said, the words the client has used, and the client's nonverbal behavior. There are three main uses for empathetic comments.

Empathetic Comments That Show Clients You Understand Them

One use for empathetic comments is to simply communicate to the client that you really understand the meaning behind what they are saying. For example, assume you have a client whose husband died last month. She says to you in a mournful voice, "He died last month. I should be getting on with my life. I am alive in some ways and dead in others. I don't want to betray him but I can't go on being half dead." Based on what the client has just said to you, her nonverbal behavior as she made this statement, and her prior comments, you believe that in addition to grieving, she is struggling to decide if she has the right to continue living without her spouse. Empathetic comments might convey to the client that you understand the pain of her loss as well as the dilemma she finds herself in as she tries to build a life without her husband. Examples are, "He was the one who died, not you. But, it is hard to go on. You feel driven to prove to yourself that you have a right to live even though he is dead." To truly convey empathy with these statements, you need to make them using a genuine and emotionally congruent tone of voice.

Assume that rather than grieving, your client is trying to cope with the recent loss of her husband by minimizing it. She may be trying to prematurely end or avoid the grieving process by just "getting on with her life." If this is the case, assume she responded to the empathetic comment expressed above with, "Well, maybe I am just a little thrown by the death." You might make a further empathetic comment in response to this such as, "You don't want to feel devastated by what has happened; you just want to be a little thrown by it because otherwise how will you get on with your life?" This says to the client that you understand what she is trying to do but, by shifting the words from "a little thrown" to "devastated," you may help her get back in touch with the reality of how she is feeling inside. In this way, empathetic statements can emotionally support this client and also help her develop new insight or meaning from what she is experiencing.

Empathetic Comments That Validate Clients' Experiences

A second use for empathetic comments is to validate clients' reactions to their experiences as acceptable, normal, or understandable. A validation tells the client that their reaction is "normal" or "to be expected" or "appropriate" in light of what their experience was. To make a validating comment to the previously described client, you might respond to her "a little thrown" remark with, "For most people, losing a spouse is one of the most difficult situations they face in life and it may take two years or more for a person to really fully accommodate to this type of loss." This type of empathetic comment gives the client validation that it is not unreasonable to need a lot more than a month to cope with the loss of a spouse.

Empathetic Comments to Support Emotional Control

Finally, empathetic comments may be used to help clients regain control of their emotions when they are feeling overwhelmed by them. Assume that rather than trying to control her emotions, the bereaved woman discussed earlier has spent the past month alone crying in her apartment. Over the course of your session with her, she has said, "I can never get over this. My life is shattered forever. No one can understand how devastated I am. My family pushes at me constantly to take care of myself. I am incapable of taking steps to help myself. I need to just collapse. Maybe I could do something else in a few weeks." By making a series of empathetic comments to the client, that show you have understood the complexity of her experience, she may feel more supported and less overwhelmed. An example of such an empathetic series would be, "You feel immobilized and trapped in pain and you wish people would understand this and not try to make you cope. You feel so overwhelmed. You have lost all hope. You don't feel you can find a way out of your intensely traumatic world. You need to be shattered for a while. You could pick up the pieces . . . eventually . . . if people would just stop pressuring you."

Further Examples of Empathetic Comments in Response to Client Information

A client who was recently in a very serious accident says, "When I think about how things are going, I can hardly bear to get up in the morning. I am still having flashbacks of the accident when I dream. It is always the same thing. The other car crosses the midline again, but it takes hours in the dream for it to hit me. I try to maneuver my car away from it, but somehow it is always right in front of me and then the glass splinters are everywhere and I see that my husband is unconscious and bleeding and I wake up in a lurch. Then, the alarm goes off and I have to get dressed and drive twenty minutes to work. Every little thing that happens on the road sends me into a panic. Yesterday, a child ran in front of my car as I turned the corner. I had plenty of time to stop, but my heart beat so fast I thought it would burst. When anyone gets in my car, I just freeze until they are secured in the seat belt."

This client has provided you with a context for understanding her current driving experiences. In response to each of her next comments, an example is given of one of the three uses for empathetic comments.

1. **Client:** "I am afraid to get into a car since the accident."
   Interviewer: "The terror of the accident is still with you." (Interviewer demonstrates understanding.)
2. **Client:** "I found the accident so terrifying and I can't get it out of my mind."
   Interviewer: "Having a car come at you head on is terrifying!" (Interviewer validates the client's reality.)
3. **Client:** "I don't know if I can stand living with all that has happened. I feel out of control. I'm running around in a panic and yet doing nothing." (Client is sweating, breathing heavily, and seeming close to a panic attack as she says this.)
   Interviewer: "You have been through a traumatic event. You try to change the situation while you sleep so that your car won't get hit and your husband won't die. You wouldn't drive if you didn't have to because then you couldn't be responsible if someone did get hurt. You wonder if you can ever control things so that no one will get hurt. Bad things can happen without our having any control over them and this can be hard to live with." (Interviewer provides a series of empathetic comments to support the client and aid client self-control.)

WHAT IS SUMMARIZING?

Summarizing can be used to review with clients the information they have given you. Clients then have the opportunity to tell you if you have understood them. This may build rapport because clients hear that you have listened to what they have said and have a real desire to understand them accurately. In summarizing, you don't repeat back exactly what the client has said to you; this might seem like you are mocking the client. When you summarize, you cover the client's key points in a succinct and compelling manner. Summarizing may be useful for four related tasks.

Summarizing to Demonstrate Listening

The first use of summarizing is to simply demonstrate you are listening. Assume that your client says, "I am so angry. My children are always misbehaving. They swear at me all the time. Yesterday my oldest son called me a bitch. They all swear at me, even the youngest who is only eight. Furthermore, they always refuse to do their chores. I actually felt a surge of hate for them this morning when I realized they had all gone to school without making their beds. After a few moments of this, I started blaming myself. This situation must be my fault. If I had been a better mother, they wouldn't be so selfish." An example of summarizing would be to say, "Your children are doing a lot of things that make you so angry that this morning you actually felt hatred for them. At other times, you wonder if their bad behavior is really your fault. You wonder if they would be more helpful if you had somehow done things better."

Summarizing to Highlight Themes

A second use of summarizing is to highlight themes that reoccur as clients relate their experiences. Assume that over a fifteen-minute time frame, your female client has said many things about her work situation and then ended with, "My boss is so demanding. He never has anything good to say." She then goes on to talk about her children and ends with, "My children seem to take and take and take and never be satisfied or appreciative." You recognize that your client is expressing a theme of being unappreciated. You then might summarize by saying, "You feel that you are working very hard both at home and at work but feel no one appreciates what you do."

Summarizing as a Transition

A third use of summarizing is to provide a transition from one topic area to another. For example, assume that the client discussed above has given you a thorough understanding of her parenting concerns and now you would like to move on to her husband's view of the issues. You might say, "If I understand correctly, you are concerned because your children are misbehaving constantly and while some of their behavior is their responsibility, you wonder if some of it may be yours. What is your husband's take on all of this?"

Summarizing to Decrease Emotional Intensity

A final use of summarizing is to decrease emotional intensity when the level in the interview is too high for the client to work effectively. When clients are in reaction to feelings mode, summarizing the experiences they have related to you and encouraging them to think can put them into a reflective thinking mode. For example, the woman described previously is so angry that she can't think through how she would like things to change. You might help her decrease her level of anger by saying, "I can hear how angry you are that your children didn't do their chores. I can hear the anger in your voice as you relate how they swear at you. You sound at the end of your rope as you say they don't appreciate all the hard work you do for them. Have you thought about what you specifically want from them?" This series of comments may help the client go from being overwhelmed with anger to being angry but able to think.

WHAT IS REDIRECTING?

When you interview clients, you spend much of the time following their comments without interruption because you are getting a feeling for their style and trying to understand their experiences. However, there are some circumstances when interrupting the client's flow, and redirecting it, may be helpful or even critical. A redirection is most successful if it starts with a respectful and emotionally supportive comment prior to changing the direction of the conversation. For example, if you ask a client how much they drank on Saturday and they respond by telling you about how much they enjoyed the party, you might say, "You really enjoyed your time with other people at that party" (supportive piece), and then add, "How much did you drink?" (redirection back to topic of concern). Redirection can be offensive if the supportive piece is left out. For example, a negative example of redirecting would be to say something like, "You didn't answer me when I asked how much you drank. Now, please tell me how much you drank last Saturday." This type of redirecting is likely to be perceived as criticism or hostility.

When clients perceive the interviewer as being critical or hostile, it may damage the therapeutic relationship and may even cause psychological harm to the client (Beutler, Machado, & Neufeldt, 1994). Warmth, genuineness, and a caring attitude from the interviewer are critical to building an effective therapeutic alliance (Beutler et al., 1994; Whiston & Sexton, 1993). Thus, even when interrupting a client, you need to maintain a caring attitude. There are several uses for respectful and supportive redirecting.

Redirecting for Clarity

Redirecting can be used to signal to clients that you are confused by what they are saying. For example, assume that a female client is giving you a lot of confusing information about her personal relationships. You don't understand how all the information fits together. Early on in the interview, she said that she was an active member of a sorority and always busy doing projects with her sorority sisters. However, now, she is talking in detail about how she is planning to transfer to another school because she feels so socially isolated where she is now. An example of redirecting for clarity would be to say, "I am sorry to interrupt you. Your decision to transfer is an important one and I do really want to understand what you are going through" (supportive piece). "However, we need to back up a moment because I am confused. Earlier you told me that you belonged to a sorority and were always busy with social engagements. But, now you are talking about transferring because you say you spend too much of your time alone. Could you help me more clearly understand your social situation?" (redirecting back to topic of concern).

Redirecting to Prevent Avoidance

Sometimes the very topics you believe are most in need of discussion are those the client seems to be avoiding. Avoidance can come through the client changing the subject or going off on a point only tangentially related to the subject. For example, assume you asked a client to talk about why he was fired from work last week but he quickly went off on a tangent to discuss the great fishing trip he went on because he was fired and didn't need to go to work. Redirecting might include saying something like, "I know it is hard to discuss being fired. It is understandable that you prefer to talk about something enjoyable like fishing" (supportive piece). "However, I really want to help you. I think to help you, I need you to go back and talk about your experience of being fired" (redirecting back to topic of concern).

Redirecting to Change the Subject

Finally, you might redirect a client who is extremely talkative. Such a client may give you a great deal of detail about everything whether it is an important topic or a tangential detail. This client may flood you with unnecessary information. In addition to being unnecessary, this excess detail also stalls the process of gathering relevant information. In this situation, you might use a redirecting comment whenever you consider that you understand topic A thoroughly enough to move on to topic B. For example, assume that a client has spent fifteen minutes describing his recent fight with a friend over the weekend. You now feel you have a clear understanding of the situation and you want to move on to other areas so that you can gain a comprehensive view of the client's life. You might wait for a natural pause in the client's stream of talk and say, "Thank you so much. I really feel that I have a good understanding of the conflict you had with your friend. You have really thought a lot about this conflict and how it influenced the two of you" (supportive piece). "Could you now tell me about how things are going at work?" (redirecting to next relevant topic).

WHAT IS SUPPORTIVE CONFRONTATION?

In a simple confrontation, you bring your clients' attention to their problematic behavior or situation and the need for them to consider changing. Your confrontation may evoke careful thought from clients, or it may lead the client to avoid further contact with you because they don't want to change. A supportive confrontation tries to prevent this type of avoidance by preparing clients to listen to your point of view before you ask them to consider changing. You do this preparation work by interweaving your confrontational statements with client-affirming statements. These affirming statements can include statements that show you recognize the client may not want to change, acknowledgment of the positive benefits the client is getting from the problematic behavior, acknowledgment that change can be stressful, and acknowledgment that the client has the right to decide not to change. When clients are supported in their desires to continue their problematic behavior, they may be more open to really thinking about reasons why change might be useful.

In addition to affirming statements, a supportive confrontation includes confrontational remarks that bring clients' attention to the negative consequences of their behavior. Your supportive confrontation may have more impact if both your affirming and confronting comments are specific and concrete. For example, if a client tells you he loves the free feeling he gets from taking drugs, an affirmation might be, "I can hear in your voice, and see in your facial expression, how much that free feeling means to you" (specific and concrete affirmation). The confrontational step would be to add, "Unfortunately, besides this free feeling, the drugs are harming your kidneys. You said your last medical screen of kidney functioning indicated they were damaged. If you keep taking drugs, you may go into renal failure and die" (specific and concrete confrontation). An example of a less specific supportive confrontation would be to say, "I know drugs feel good to you. But, if you keep taking drugs your health will be impaired." It may be easier to ignore this type of general information than the specific information given earlier.

A supportive confrontation may be needed when clients are engaged in a dangerous behavior such as unprotected sex, drunk driving, borderline parenting behavior that might become abusive or neglectful, and so forth. Another time supportive confrontation may be needed is when clients are engaged in behavior that, while not dangerous, has led to serious negative consequences in the past and is likely to continue to lead to serious consequences in the future if it continues. Examples of serious consequences include job loss, divorce, loss of property, expulsion from school, and so forth. Supportive confrontation is needed because the clients are unaware or underaware of the negative consequences of what they are doing.

When Do You Make a Supportive Confrontation?

You are most likely to help clients with a supportive confrontation if you use it only after establishing a trusting relationship with them. Affirmations are not likely to be taken seriously if given by a "stranger" who clients don't perceive as really caring about them. Similarly, the negative consequences you describe from continuing the behavior are more likely to be discounted if the client doesn't have a positive relationship with you or doesn't have respect for you. However, there may be times when client behavior within the intake situation, or immediate life circumstances, is so serious that a confrontational comment is necessary despite the fact that rapport is not firmly established. For example, if clients are an immediate danger to themselves or others, the interviewer has to emphasize safety needs over attempts to develop rapport. While this may be necessary, this early confrontation is unlikely to help clients maintain real change and may inhibit or prevent the development of rapport.

How Do You Make a Supportive Confrontation?

Confronting clients, without alienating them, can be a significant challenge. Four styles for trying to do so are described here. Each contains an affirming or supportive part and a confrontational part. These styles are adaptations of techniques described in the book *Motivational Interviewing* by Miller and Rollnick (1992). The examples of each style will be based on the following scenario:

The client is married and has an eight-year-old son. He has been abusing cocaine for the last four years. Last week, his wife moved out of the house, taking their son with her. This move was precipitated by the client being fired from his third job in the past year. As the wife stalked out of their home, she said to her husband, "Your boss and I agree that you are a drug addict. Unless you come to your senses, our marriage is over." After his wife left, the client rushed back to his office and beat the pulp out of his boss. The client comes in to the session complaining about how unjust his boss and his wife are to call him a drug addict. He states he can't live without his wife. He says beating up his boss was justified because the boss fired him and because the boss encouraged his wife to walk out on him.

Strategy 1: De-emphasize the importance of the client accepting a label of "drug addict," "violent," or "irresponsible," and so forth. Instead of labeling the client's behavior, describe what is going on in the client's life.

Example of supportive confrontation: I can hear how frustrated you are by your fights with your wife and boss over whether or not you are a drug addict (affirmation). What is important for us to discuss is how your drug use led to your wife moving out. You may need to make a choice between having her or having your drugs (confrontation).

Strategy 2: Emphasize that the client has personal choice and responsibility for deciding what his future behavior will be and that neither you nor anyone else can control him.

Example of supportive confrontation: Whether you take drugs or not is up to you (affirmation). However, you need to realize that your drug use does affect your wife and your son, not just you (confrontation). I was impressed with how much you were able to help your son with his school work last Thursday. It seems that you have a lot to offer him when you aren't high or hung over (affirmation).

Strategy 3: Demonstrate that you have listened to what the client says he needs and wants and show how changing the problem behavior may help him attain what he wants.

Example of supportive confrontation: You are under a tremendous amount of stress with the loss of your job and your concerns that your wife will divorce you. You deserve support in dealing with these problems (affirmation). While cocaine may make the problems seem to go away, in fact, cocaine has stolen your job and your wife from you (confrontation). Beating cocaine may help get them back.

Strategy 4: Be honest with the client. Don't pretend not to see problem behavior because you are trying to emotionally support him and develop trust. Not all life choices are acceptable to others and/or are equally likely to help the client in the long run.

Example of supportive confrontation: You are right when you say everyone gets depressed and angry sometimes. I would have been angry too if my boss had fired me and the immediate result was my spouse walked out on me (affirmation). But, it is not going to help that you beat your boss up. It is just going to make it harder to get the next job and convince your wife that you want to make things work (confrontation). I want to help you succeed in getting what you want both at home and at work (affirmation). But, you won't succeed as long as the cocaine is controlling you (confrontation).

WHAT IS A PROCESS COMMENT?

There are two levels to an interview. One level is the content. The content of an interview is the actual topic or topics that are being discussed. For example, if you were asking a client about any stresses she was currently under and she indicated a recent death in her family, an impending divorce, and escalating conflict with her teenage son, these would all be the content of the interview. The second level of the interview is the process that is occurring between the interviewer and the client. The process of the discussion refers to the "how" of the interview. While at times it is most appropriate to focus on the content of what the client brings to the interview, at other times, it is the process of how the client is presenting the information and the process of how the client is relating to significant others and/or to the interviewer that is of most importance.

Teyber (1997, p. 40) recommends two steps to making a shift from the content of the interview to the process of the interview. First, he recommends that the interviewer describe, ask about, or make overt whatever may be occurring at the process level at a given moment in the interview. Second, the interviewer should encourage the client to explore the meaning of this interpersonal process. In making process comments, it is important not to sound critical or judgmental. Your intent is to bring the process of what is going on into clients' awareness so that they can evaluate what it might mean. When process comments are used to help clients focus inward, they may discover new and important concerns that they weren't aware they had. They may also develop a deeper meaning from their experiences. This new learning may allow clients the freedom to change constructively in how they relate to others (Teyber, 1997). Process comments may be valuable in two related situations.

Describing a Client's Interpersonal Pattern Across Relationships

It may be helpful to make a process comment when you perceive that your client is showing a pattern of problematic interpersonal relating across many of her significant relationships. Pointing out the pattern, and then asking the client to consider its effect on her relationships, is making a shift from the content of what is happening in different relationships to the process that may be occurring across relationships. This may help the client resolve a problematic relational pattern rather than continuing to reenact it.

For example, assume that in describing her current life circumstances, a client speaks very critically about her best friend, her boss, and her son. You might hypothesize that the client has an interpersonal pattern of being highly critical in her relationships. If you make a content-to-process shift, you would make the criticalness the topic of the discussion rather than a particular relationship per se. An example might be to say, "I notice that you are disappointed with your friend, your son, and your boss. I wonder how this disappointment is influencing your relationships with them."

This type of process comment may help the client see herself through the eyes of the other people she is trying to relate to. She may learn that her critical style of communicating is having the effect of pushing people away from her.

Describing the Interpersonal Process Between Client and Interviewer

You might also make a process comment to describe the interpersonal pattern that is occurring between the client and yourself in the immediacy of the intake interview. This allows the client the opportunity to practice relating in a different way. For example, assume a female client has a pattern of first asking for help from significant others but then criticizing the advice they give her. Assume that the client has now repeatedly asked for your advice about how to improve her relationships. Whenever you try to suggest ways she could work on these relationships she says, "Yes, but I really don't think that could possibly work." A content-to-process shift might be for you to say, "I have noticed that whenever we start discussing a problem you have, you ask for advice. However, then you find my advice unhelpful and I feel that I have let you down. It's important for us to figure out why this keeps happening." This type of comment helps the client to focus inward to explore her interpersonal pattern rather than focusing outward on a power struggle with the interviewer. While perhaps feeling criticized by the client, the interviewer is not responding by being defensive; instead, the interviewer is inviting the client to focus inward and explore the meaning of the interaction. In this way, the interviewer is behaving differently than the people the client has related to in the past. As a direct result of this new reaction from the interviewer, the client has the opportunity to break out of a rigid pattern of relating and learn a new way to interact in a personal relationship (Teyber, 1997).

ISSUES IN HUMAN DIVERSITY DURING INTERVIEWING

In a successful intake interview, the interviewer listens carefully to what the client says through both verbal and nonverbal behavior. At the end of the interview, the client leaves feeling respected and understood. The interviewer leaves with an understanding of the needs and goals of the client. This type of successful ending is not a result of mechanically using the interviewing skills that were highlighted in this chapter. Keep in mind that any particular interviewing skill will not be equally useful for every interviewer and every client. You need to select the skills that fit you best as an individual and then be prepared to modify your interview to fit the uniqueness of each client. Professional organizations, such as the American Psychological Association (2000, 2003), consider it an issue of both professional ethics and professional competence to learn to modify services to the unique needs of individuals. These issues are discussed here briefly; to examine them in more depth, see Suggestions for Further Reading (p. 251).

When might you need to shift your interviewing strategy? It may be more necessary when there are significant differences between you and the client that make mutual respect and communication more of a challenge. It is not necessarily obvious or easy to determine if significant differences exist between the interviewer and the client because identity is a complex concept. Hays (2001) considers identity to be composed of the multidimensional cultural influences of age and generational influences, disability, religion and spiritual orientation, ethnicity, socioeconomic status, sexual orientation, indigenous heritage, national origin, and gender. Furthermore, Hays takes the position that an individual's identity is not static. At any given point in a person's life, and any moment of a person's day, some of these cultural influences may have more or less impact on identity. From this perspective, the context of the interview situation, as it consists of a specific person interviewing a specific client within a specific interview context will have an impact on the identities of the individuals involved and how similar or different the individuals view each other to be.

For example, assume that two unemployed adults, one male and one female, are attempting to relate to each other. If they are both Protestants, and they are in church praying together, they may view each other as similar. On the other hand, if instead they are in a vocational class together and discussing job opportunities that might put them in competition with each other, their gender difference might make them feel dissimilar. One year later, assume one of these individuals is in the position of interviewer and one is in the position of client: How then might these individuals view each other? There is no simple answer to this question. Hays recommends that you discuss, within the interview session, all areas of identity where differential power might exist between you and your client. This process of discussing identity may help build trust between you and your client.

How important is this process of building a trusting relationship? In research on the common factors of effective treatment and the factors that predict positive outcomes in treatment, a critical factor that always emerges is the presence of a strong working alliance (Grencavage & Norcross, 1990; Lambert & Bergin, 1994; Whiston & Sexton, 1993). Can any interviewer develop an effective working alliance with any client? This is unlikely. Beutler et al. (1994) found that matching the client with the helper on cultural variables and personal style can help in the development of an effective working alliance. However, when this is not possible or would not be appropriate for important reasons, they recommend that the helper work to create a "pseudo-match."

In attempting to create such a match, an important step is for you to educate yourself about issues that might be relevant to your clients about which you might currently be unaware or underaware. Sue and Sue (2002) is an example of one of the many texts currently available that highlights issues in human diversity. Although educating yourself about diversity is valuable, remember the information in these texts is often based on groups of people, not individuals. Cardemil and Battle (2003) caution you to avoid assuming that all clients from a given cultural or ethnic group have identical experiences; heterogeneity is to be expected. In addition, they consider it vital that you ask clients how they identify themselves rather than making assumptions about their culture or ethnicity (Cardemil & Battle, 2003).

A second step in trying to create an interviewer–client match is for you to recognize that clients are experts on their own unique cultural issues. Ask your clients to educate you about their identities. Finally, ask clients how they perceive you and what differences they perceive to exist that might hinder the development of a good working relationship. Differences in communication styles can hinder your ability to help the client. Admitting this may lead clients to perceive you as more knowledgeable and trustworthy (Sue & Sue, 2002). This attempt to match clients must involve genuineness and personal honesty from the interviewer or it may be perceived as mocking, unacceptable, or a sign of incompetence to some clients (B. Goodwin, personal communication, December 10, 2003).

One of the important goals of this text is to give student interviewers the opportunity to practice adapting their skills to fit the uniqueness of clients. The clients in chapters 3–22 differ in terms of age, country of origin, ethnicity, gender, religion, socioeconomic status, and so forth. After each clinical profile, exercises are provided to encourage the interviewer to reflect on differences that may exist between him- or herself and the profiled client. The interviewer is encouraged to consider how these differences may or may not influence the development of a strong working alliance and what he or she might do to try to increase the likelihood of developing such an alliance. Additionally, sometimes the interviewer has the opportunity to reflect on how changes in an aspect of the client's identity might influence the course of the interview. For example, in chapter 7, Mary is grieving over her husband's death. In the thought questions, the interviewer is asked to reflect on how it might change the interview, for the interviewer, if Mary were grieving over the loss of her long-term, lesbian partner.

Highlighted Diagnostic Practice

This text is intended to provide students with practice in developing diagnoses using the *Diagnostic and Statistical Manual of Mental Disorders* (4th ed., rev. [*DSM–IV–TR*]; American Psychiatric Association, 2000). If you feel ready to start practicing your diagnostic skills, skip this chapter and move on to the client profiles in chapters 3–22. If a brief review of the diagnostic process would be of help to you, read on.

The first step in practicing diagnostic skills is to conduct a thorough intake interview. In this interview you need to ask appropriate mental status questions, recognize problematic behavior, and determine the degree of impairment caused by these problematic behaviors. In doing this, you want to avoid both over- and underpathologizing behavior. For example, you need to consider issues of normal development as they are influenced by what Hays (2001) calls the multidimensional cultural influences on identity, including age and generational influences, religion and spiritual orientation, ethnicity, sexual orientation, indigenous heritage, national origin, and gender. It is important to keep these cultural influences in mind because you need to be able to tell the difference between someone showing behavior that is culturally different from what you expect, based on your own identity, and an individual showing problematic behavior. Developing a diagnosis is a complex process. You need to examine the psychological, social, and biological influences on an individual and attempt to determine the most likely causes for the behavior that you are considering maladaptive.

It is assumed that the student will work through the diagnostic exercises in chapters 3–22 using the *DSM–IV–TR* manual itself or a training guide to the *DSM–IV–TR*, such as Reid and Wise (1995), Rapoport and Ismond (1996), or House (2000). It is beyond the scope of this book to review the complex diagnostic support offered by these training guides. Rather, this chapter provides only a short description of how the student might want to proceed to practice diagnosing clients using the clinical profiles provided in chapters 3–22.

START THE DIAGNOSTIC PROCESS
WITH A THOROUGH INTAKE INTERVIEW

During the intake interview, you need to ask open-ended and closed questions that will give you a comprehensive view of your client's areas of strength and weakness. It is critical for this to include a mental status evaluation. Morrison (1995) provides detailed suggestions for carrying out a mental status exam. Critical questions the interviewer wants to resolve by the end of the intake interview include: Does the client have organic problems such as brain damage or dementia? Is the client psychotic? Does the client have an anxiety or mood disorder? Is the client suicidal or homicidal? Is the client abusing substances? Is the client a victim or perpetrator of violence? The interviewer wants to gain a comprehensive view of how a client's present functioning may be influenced by psychological, biological, and situational influences. While asking relevant questions of the client, you need to assess whether the interpersonal process occurring between you and the client is appropriate. Is the mood and behavior of the client congruent with the topic being discussed? Does the client seem to be responding to your questions or to something occurring from within himself or herself?

Be Aware of the Limited Nature of Your Information

If all of your knowledge of a client is contained within a forty-minute interview, then your diagnoses will need to be more tentative than if you interviewed the client for two hours, conducted formal testing, interviewed family members, and collected collateral information from relevant sources. The more you know about a client, the more accurate your diagnoses can be. In confusing or complex situations, formal intelligence and personality testing may be necessary before accurate diagnosis is possible. In this case, the interviewer will only be able to use provisional or deferred diagnoses until this testing has occurred.

Ask Questions That Would Rule Out Diagnoses

During the intake, it is important to ask follow-up questions that could confirm as well as disconfirm the presence of a disorder. Assume that in screening for the presence of hallucinations, your client admits to seeing her deceased husband's face wherever she goes. She sees him as she walks through crowds, as she enters rooms in their home, and in walking through the park. Is this woman schizophrenic? Might she be having hallucinations due to substance abuse? Do her religious or spiritual beliefs include the view that deceased relatives become guardian angels? Are there other explanations? Asking both potentially confirming and disconfirming questions is vital to making the correct diagnosis. For example, if you ask the woman how long she has been having these experiences, and she says they began last month after the woman's husband was killed in an automobile accident, then you have data that may suggest the "hallucinations" represent grieving behavior rather than the hallucinations of schizophrenia. However, don't assume this means the client is not schizophrenic; go on and ask even more follow-up questions. It is possible, for example, that the client is "seeing" her husband because she is abusing substances. You don't want to miss this important diagnostic information because you prematurely assume you understand her situation. In addition, it is possible to be both grieving for a spouse and schizophrenic. Just as you do not want to overdiagnose this client, you also do not want to underdiagnose her.

Assume that during a screen for delusions, a male client expresses a lot of suspicious thinking. In asking follow-up questions, the man expresses suspicions of his boss, his four coworkers, and his two subordinates. Your client states that all of these individuals are intentionally doing things to undermine his work. This behavior may reflect paranoid delusions. However, ask questions that might disconfirm this possibility. Assume that the client is not paranoid and ask him why these individuals are behaving this way toward him. Assume he then tells you that he is the only Latino American in a company peopled by European Americans and he believes they hold racist views of him. In this situation, you are gaining data that may disconfirm the idea that he is delusional and confirm the idea that he may be the victim of bigotry. However, as with the above example of hallucinations, accurate diagnosis requires detailed follow-up questions to insure that you are not jumping to conclusions. Make sure to ask if the client has reasons to be suspicious of anyone else beyond the people at work. If he indicates that he is not "suspicious" at home, at church, and in his local community, then you have further data to suggest that his suspiciousness does not reflect delusional thinking.

What domains should follow-up questions cover? You want to conduct a thorough assessment of the situational, biological, and psychological influences on your client's functioning.

CONSIDER YOUR DIAGNOSTIC CHOICES

Once your intake interview with a client from chapters 3–22 is complete, it is time to use the exercises that follow the case to support the development of a diagnosis or diagnoses for the client. The exercises prompt you to consider one axis at a time starting with Axis I and proceeding through to Axis V. After this is completed, you are encouraged to look back at your work, starting at Axis V, to consider whether the level of importance you have given to situational factors over individual factors has been appropriate. This strategy of looking back is adapted from recommendations in Hays (2001) for preventing bias in your diagnoses.

If you follow this step-by-step approach, will your diagnoses represent the "truth" about your clients? If you look at the cautionary statement written at the very beginning of the *DSM–IV–TR*, it warns users that the criteria offered for each disorder are to serve only as guidelines to understanding clients. They are not offered as the truth about clients. The criteria for each disorder are in a state of periodic reevaluation and revision as research hones our knowledge of diagnosis.

Remember that the goal of diagnosis is not to "label" a client correctly. The goal is to describe, as accurately as possible, the client's functioning.

Be Stringent in Your Use of *DSM–IV–TR* Criteria

Multiple diagnoses are encouraged by the multiaxial system. However, do not give a diagnosis if the client does not fully meet the criteria, and do not give multiple diagnoses where the guidelines say it is inappropriate. For example, if you examine the criteria for Oppositional Defiant Disorder in the *DSM–IV–TR*, the guidelines specifically state that this diagnosis should not be given if the client meets the criteria for Conduct Disorder or Antisocial Personality Disorder. Furthermore, the guidelines for Antisocial Personality Disorder indicate that this diagnosis is not appropriate unless the client is 18 years or older.

Consider the Benefits and Risks of Different Diagnoses. Whereas correct labels may help clients receive the most appropriate treatment, labels can also have negative implications for clients. Social psychological research has demonstrated in many domains the power of labels to influence people's perceptions of others. In his classic study, Rosenhan (1973) demonstrated that once an individual received a label of schizophrenic in a mental health facility, all the behaviors of this individual were interpreted through the lens of psychopathology. Similarly, Langer and colleagues (1974, 1980) found that observers rated interviewees differently depending on whether they were labeled as job applicants, psychiatric patients, or cancer patients. Snyder (1984) found that teachers viewed student behavior differently when the student had previously received a label of gifted versus hostile. Thus, labels have tremendous power to affect the course of a client's life, so we need to use them cautiously.

Remember That a Client Is Not a Diagnosis. A client has a life that includes many things including, sometimes, the presence of a psychological disorder. The disorder describes problems the client may be experiencing it does not define the client. As a result of this, when you provide a diagnosis for a client, be aware that not all clients who have the same disorder have identical symptoms, have symptoms at the same level of severity, or have the same duration to their difficulties. The *DSM–IV–TR* provides some additional descriptors to add to your diagnostic choices to help individualize them to your client's current situation. Descriptions include information about potential subtypes of the disorder, severity of the disorder (Mild, Moderate, Severe), and clinical course of the disorder (in partial remission, full remission, prior history, age of onset, mode of onset, progression).

Differential Diagnosis Problems.   Symptoms can occur in more than one disorder. Furthermore, some disorders have a significant overlap in their symptoms. This creates unclear boundaries between some of the disorders and makes accurate diagnosis difficult. If you are having difficulties with differential diagnosis, Appendix A of the *DSM–IV–TR* provides six decision trees that can be used to help within the categories of (a) Mental Disorders due to a General Medical Condition, (b) Substance Induced Disorders, (c) Psychotic Disorders, (d) Mood Disorders, (e) Anxiety Disorders, and (f) Somatoform Disorders.

Sometimes the Correct Decision Is Not to Diagnose.   At the end of the intake, it is possible that you will determine that the correct label on Axis I or II is No Diagnosis. At other times, the client may need services but you aren't clear what the appropriate diagnosis would be. In these cases, remember that the statistical manual allows you to make diagnoses that include qualifiers such as "provisional" or "unspecified." If you are unclear about what the correct diagnosis is, but you are clear that a diagnosable condition exists, then the correct temporary label is Diagnosis Deferred.

Axis I

The first chapter exercise asks you to consider what might be appropriate diagnostic choices on Axis I. It encourages you to consider several different diagnoses and then select which is most appropriate. On Axis I, you code what the manual calls Clinical Disorders, Adjustment Disorders, and Other Conditions That May Be a Focus of Clinical Attention. There is an implied continuum of severity of Axis I codes with the Clinical Disorders being the most severe, followed by the Adjustment Disorders which are defined as time-limited reactions, followed by Other Conditions That May Be a Focus of Clinical Attention but which do not represent the presence of a psychological disorder within the individual.

Axis II

The exercises for Axis II ask you to consider if your client meets any of the criteria for a Personality Disorder and/or Mental Retardation. If the client does not meet the criteria for an Axis II diagnosis, the diagnostician can still use this axis to report any personality traits or maladaptive mechanisms that might be relevant for treatment. *DSM–IV–TR* allows the diagnosis of most of the Personality Disorders for adults, teens, and children. However, each disorder presents the caveat that the behaviors need to be long term and represent entrenched patterns that differ from what is expected by the individual's culture. How can you determine if a client's interpersonal behavior reflects a disorder or culturally sanctioned but different behavior? Hays (2001) cautions helpers that this may be difficult to determine. She recommends that helpers develop a comprehensive understanding of the cultural influences on their clients' interpersonal styles before considering if a diagnosis on Axis II is appropriate or not. Rapaport and Ismond (1996) express a similar caution about diagnosing Personality Disorders in teens and children, as the research base supporting such diagnoses is sparse. In response to these cautions, the chapter exercises direct you to be as specific as possible in describing the reasons you chose, or decided not to choose, a diagnosis on Axis II. As with Axis I, you can make a provisional diagnosis, no diagnosis, or indicate that a diagnosis is deferred on Axis II when this is appropriate.

Axis III

On Axis III, you report any general medical conditions that you feel are relevant to the management of the client's Axis I or Axis II condition. These medical conditions may have played a causal role in the development of the client's difficulties, may exacerbate the client's difficulties, or make the control of the client's condition more complex. Sometimes a client comes in for help specifically with a medical problem that has influences that are best understood as a Mental Disorder Due to a Medical Problem. When this is the case, you code this information on both Axis I and on Axis III. For example, *DSM–IV–TR* has an Axis I code for Personality Change Due to a General Medical Condition. This code would be appropriate to give a client with frontal lobe damage that resulted in things such as a lack of judgment or impulse control, inappropriately high mood, and so forth. On Axis III, you would use the International Classification of Diseases (ICD-10, 2000, as cited in *DSM–IV–TR*) to code this medical condition. If you need additional information to determine if a diagnosis is appropriate on Axis III, you can indicate that the diagnosis is deferred.

Axis IV

On Axis IV, you indicate any psychosocial or environmental problems that are relevant to the client's functioning. The *DSM–IV–TR* provides categories of problems for you to consider including problems with primary support group, problems related to the social environment, educational problems, occupational problems, housing problems, economic problems, problems with access to health care services, problems related to interaction with the legal system/crime, and other psychosocial and environmental problems. The manual provides a more detailed description of each of these categories in the introduction section called "Multiaxial Assessment."

Axis V

On Axis V, you indicate your global assessment of your client's functioning using the scale that is provided in the Multiaxial Assessment section of the manual. It is a straightforward process. For each numerical score from zero to one hundred on the scale, the manual provides a set of descriptors for how the individual is functioning at that level. The lower the score, the poorer the individual is functioning with the exception that a score of zero represents that you do not have adequate information to make a judgment about the client. One hundred represents the score you would give a client who is functioning in a superior way in all aspects of his or her life. Careful consideration should be put into determining the client's score. Do not simply defer to the client's own opinion because there may be reasons, such as psychosis, that the client's judgment is inappropriate. Collecting information from collateral sources can be helpful in verifying the level of the client's functioning.

After choosing a score that best represents your client's functioning, you put in parentheses the time period that it represents. For example, it might represent the functioning of the client at the time of intake, or, it might reflect their highest level of functioning in the past year. You can give them more than one score, with each score representing the client's functioning in a different, but specified, time period.

DOUBLE-CHECK YOUR CLINICAL JUDGMENT

After you have completed your initial judgments for Axes I–V, the chapter exercises will then ask you to reconsider all of your judgments in reverse order, from your own point of view. Have you overestimated or underestimated the impact of situational, biological, or individual psychological factors on the client's current functioning? If you have, correct your diagnoses. The exercises then prompt you to indicate why you did or did not decide to change your diagnoses after making this first reverse review.

Are you likely to have needed to change your diagnoses? Slattery (2004, chap. 1) suggests that due to the fundamental attribution error, interviewers may correctly recognize the impact of situational influences on their own behavior but be prone to underestimate the power of the situation on client behavior. This may lead to bias in the diagnostic process. For example, assume that a teenage girl is referred for an intake because of her verbally abusive treatment of teachers, her promiscuous sexual behavior with male teens, and her long-term academic underachievement. Additionally, this client has a history of being sexually abused by several male relatives. Does this client's behavior represent individual psychopathology? You could give her an Axis I diagnosis of Conduct Disorder, and then code her history of Sexual Abuse on Axis IV, as a situational stressor. Or, you could see her externalizing behaviors as "normal" for someone who has tried to survive in a sexually abusive environment. This stronger belief in situational influences might lead you to give this teen an Axis I diagnosis of Child Abuse from the category Other Conditions That May Be a Focus of Clinical Attention. Different diagnostic choices carry different implicit beliefs about the importance of individual and situational influences. The most appropriate diagnosis for this client may vary over time depending on the chronicity, severity, and frequency of her externalizing symptoms as well as changes, or lack of changes, in her living situation.

When are you most likely to misinterpret the individual, biological, or social influences on your client? You are most vulnerable to this when your client is significantly different from you in some way. The *DSM–IV–TR* has resources available to help you assess the impact of age, culture, and gender on the diagnostic process. Within the descriptions of each diagnosis, research relevant to these issues of difference is discussed. Appendix I of the *DSM–IV–TR* also contains the Outline for Cultural Formulation and Glossary of Culture Bound Syndromes. This appendix provides important information to help you take cultural considerations into account in making diagnoses. The *DSM–IV–TR* has also included, within Appendix I, some culturally specific diagnoses. Finally, you can indicate cultural influences on your client on Axis IV. Be careful and thoughtful in taking cultural issues into account trying to not overestimate or underestimate their importance.

Hays (2001) has expressed concern that the cultural information *DSM–IV–TR* provides is often too brief and nonspecific to give practical guidance in diagnosis. She suggests rectifying this situation by adding an Axis VI indicating the cultural factors relevant to the client's identity. She defines cultural influences to include age, disability, ethnicity, gender, indigenous heritage, national origin, sexual orientation, socioeconomic status, and religious and spiritual orientation. To diagnose accurately, Hays recommends you first complete Axis VI, then go back to Axis V, then IV, and so on. This reverse process may help prevent cultural bias in that it puts culture in the foreground of the diagnostic process (Hays, 2001).

Assume you have now completed a reverse review of your diagnostic choices, looking for your potential biases in diagnosis. Are you now done? Have you completed the process of making a responsible and thoughtful set of diagnostic decisions? Not quite yet. The chapter exercises ask you to review your decisions one more time. You make this final review from the client's perspective. Why consider your clients' point of view? First, clients are the experts on their lives not you. Second, clients do have legal access to their diagnoses. The choices that you make should support the discussions you have with your clients about their lives. Otherwise, these diagnostic differences may disrupt or prevent the development of a working alliance with the client.

Research has consistently shown that effective work occurs when the helper and client build a working alliance in which both parties treat each other with respect and actively work together to accomplish treatment goals (Grencavage & Norcross, 1990; Whiston & Sexton, 1993). Considering clients' own perceptions, when developing your diagnoses, also demonstrates to clients that you understand their viewpoint on their strengths and weaknesses. This may increase their motivation to change (Prochaska & DiClemente, 1986; Prochaska,

DiClemente, & Norcross, 1992). Thus, if you believe your client would have a strong negative reaction to your diagnostic choices, think seriously about what this might imply about the accuracy of your decisions; if appropriate, revise them.

CONCLUSION

Diagnosis is a complex process. Consider psychological, social, and biological influences in making your diagnoses. Be open to revising your diagnostic decisions based on any new information you receive. Treat your client as a partner in the diagnostic process. Consider not only the accuracy of your diagnostic choices but also their usefulness to the client. Will your choices help the client gain needed services? Will these choices help improve the services the client receives? Will the client, and the client's support system, be empowered by the information the diagnostic choices provide? If any one of these answers is no, then revise your diagnoses.

ADULT PROFILES FOR USE IN INDIVIDUAL SESSIONS

Preface to Part II

TAKING THE CLIENT ROLE

Read the following cases and try to put yourself into the client's life. Remember that you aren't to memorize the details that are provided in the profile. The details are provided to help you bring the client alive for your collaborator in the interview process. You may change any demographics or details about a case that will help you more actively portray it. If the case is of Cathy and you are a male, feel free to make it the case of Carl and change whatever details you need to fit this gender shift.

Before the official interview starts, tell the interviewer what your basic demographics are, the reason that you were referred for the interview, and the location where the interview is taking place; all of this information is provided in the first section of the case profile. At the end of the interview, both you and the interviewer should reread the case profile as it was written and then put yourselves in the role of interviewer in order to complete the exercises on diagnosis, deepening the interview, and reflecting on the client interview from the perspective of the interviewer.

TAKING THE INTERVIEWER ROLE

Remember that before you begin to ask questions about why the client is here, you need to explain to the client who you are, how your clinic works, how your work is being supervised, and what the limits of confidentiality are. If you are being watched through a mirror or over videotape or audiotape equipment, this also needs to be explained to the client. Make sure that you are comprehensive in explaining how all client information will be kept confidential before asking clients for their written consent to be interviewed or engaged in treatment. In some states, minors of certain ages can consent to certain types of inpatient or outpatient treatment but not to others. In other states, minors can not consent to any type of treatment. Therefore, the legal guardian of the minor is the one who needs to sign the consent form. You need to follow the Health Insurance Portability and Accountability Act (HIPAA) or your state confidentiality laws. It is recommended that you follow whichever code has the stricter standard (APA, 2002; Newman, 2003). This is all part of helping clients understand what your role is and what their role is. This process of role induction can improve treatment outcomes when carried out effectively (Whiston & Sexton, 1993).

WHAT WILL BE KEPT CONFIDENTIAL?

In most circumstances, the information gained during the interview will be kept strictly confidential within the confines of your training program with a few highly specific exceptions. Confidentiality will need to be broken in the following situations: if the client threatens to do bodily harm to himself or herself or to an identifiable other and if the client is the victim of child abuse or neglect. In these situations, you are required to put the safety of the client or others ahead of confidentiality and report the information to the appropriate authorities. Mandated reporting laws vary across states so you need to determine the exact parameters of reporting in your jurisdiction. For example, in Pennsylvania, a helper is only obligated to report to child abuse authorities if they have direct contact with a child who they suspect is being abused or neglected. In other states, if a helper hears about a potentially abused or neglected child from someone else, it is still a mandated report.

Confidentiality can also be broken if your clients want you to provide information to someone else such as a physician, school, the court, and so forth. According to the HIPAA privacy rule (1996), patients have specific rights, and practitioners have specific responsibilities in how they use and disclose confidential health information. For more information on how HIPAA relates to psychologists and other mental health providers, go online to www.APApractice.org.

In practical terms, if a client wants you to reveal information about themselves to someone else, they need to sign a release of information documenting what information they want released and to whom they want it released. In working with minors, issues of consent to treatment, confidentiality, and release of records are more complex because some or all of these rights are only in the hands of the minor's legal guardian.

DOES THE CLIENT DIFFER FROM YOU
IN IMPORTANT WAYS?

Adequate role-induction discussion at the beginning of the intake often needs to go beyond explaining who you are and the procedures of the setting in which you work. You may need to discuss the clients' expectations and perceptions for the intake. Both you and the setting procedures may be quite different from what the client expected. Discuss these differences with your client and listen carefully to what the client has to say. In addition to sharing your expertise with your clients, be prepared to discuss the limitations of your knowledge (Hays, 2001). Practice this during the role plays.

After the role play is complete, do not go directly to the didactic exercises. First, review the client profile to insure that you understand the client's thoughts, feelings, and patterns of relating. It is possible that the intake wasn't thorough enough to help you develop an accurate diagnosis, so let the client profile fill in any knowledge gaps you may have. As you complete the exercises that help you practice interviewing skills, try to adapt your thinking and the style of your comments to the client's cultural context in terms of age, ethnicity, gender, religion, socioeconomic status, and so forth. This can be a challenge. To help you with this challenge, each profile provides cues as to how a client might respond to different aspects of the interviewing situation. For some of the exercises, an example of how you might adapt your comments has been provided.

Case of Monisha

1. What are your basic statistics?

Your name is Monisha and you are an eighteen-year-old, African-American female. You are a freshman in college. You are the oldest of four children. Your siblings live at home with your parents in a city about three hours from the university you attend. Your parents work in a factory which manufactures upholstery for automobiles. You are the first one in your extended family to attend college. Both parents began working in the factory immediately after graduating from high school. You share an apartment with three other students and work part-time. You are carrying a heavy load of credits to try and get through the four years of college as quickly as possible so you can earn a decent income and help your family.

2. How do you behave in the interview?

Your clothing is neat and clean and your hygiene is good. You sit quietly with your hands in your lap and legs crossed at the ankles but keep jiggling one foot. You seldom make eye contact. Your attitude toward the interviewer is polite, cooperative, and deferential, but you do not volunteer much information and tend to speak in short sentences. Your speech rate is normal and your thoughts are well organized, but you are not particularly introspective and do not elaborate on the information you give to the interviewer.

When asked about what brought you to seek treatment, you focus primarily on symptoms (headaches, anxiety about tests and grades), but say little about your emotions. However, your foot-jiggling increases, you shift positions frequently, and you frown and rub your head as if in pain when asked more direct questions about your emotions or your internal experience. Although you have a lot of questions about how therapy can help with headaches and poor grades, you are unlikely to volunteer these questions unless the interviewer specifically solicits them.

If asked mental status screening questions, you do not exhibit any confusion, unusual thoughts, or delusional thinking. You deny feeling depressed or anxious, except when taking tests or thinking about your academic performance.

If asked about drug and alcohol use, you admit experimenting a little with marijuana and alcohol in high school. You sometimes go to bars on weekends with your roommates when they pressure you into taking a break from studying, but you deny drinking enough to get drunk. You are much too concerned with your academic performance to allow drugs or alcohol to interfere with your studying or class attendance.

3. Why are you being interviewed?

A nurse at the campus health center referred you after you sought treatment there for migraine headaches. You have had these headaches infrequently for several years, but they have become more frequent and intense since you came to college, and you feel that over-the-counter medication isn't effective anymore. The nurse at the health center asked about how you were doing in school and you admitted that you had performed poorly on several major exams recently and were feeling stressed about dropping grades. Although the nurse gave you a prescription for stronger headache medication, she also felt you might benefit from some relaxation or stress management training. She felt this might help you with your school performance and prevent some of your headaches from developing. You are skeptical, but the headaches are beginning to interfere with school work, and you are very worried about your grades.

4. How do you feel?

You do not volunteer information about feelings, but acknowledge feeling a bit uncomfortable in the interview if asked. If the interviewer probes further about these feelings, you admit that you are skeptical about how talking to an interviewer can decrease your headaches or help improve your grades. Adding to your skepticism is the fact that a younger brother has had some sort of emotional problem (you don't know what to call it) and has been in and out of the mental health system for some time. You are both curious and skeptical about psychotherapy because although you never participated in your brother's therapy sessions, you are under the impression that it didn't seem to do him much good. You are also used to being the strong one in the family and are uncomfortable with admitting any vulnerability. You are a bit anxious that the interviewer may try to get you to cry or express emotion, and this would embarrass you. If the interviewer specifically asks about anxiety, you admit that you become very anxious in testing situations, to the point that your heart pounds, your palms sweat, and you find it difficult to concentrate. These symptoms seem to occur regardless of how much you study before the exam, and you are frustrated by the fact that when you are feeling this way, you seem unable to recall information that you know you had learned.

5. How do you think?

You got A's and B's in high school and have been told by your teachers and guidance counselors that you have what it takes to succeed in college. Your goal is to become a teacher because you admired your teachers in high school and felt they were able to make a difference in your life and in the lives of other students. Your current difficulty with grades is puzzling to you because you always did so well in high school. You are beginning to wonder if your teachers made a mistake and you really don't have what it takes to succeed in college, but you do not volunteer this information unless the interviewer asks for it. You think a lot about disappointing your parents, who are very proud to have a daughter in college. You also worry about failing your siblings by not setting a good example. You pictured yourself getting through college quickly, getting a teaching job, and being in a position to help your younger siblings go to college as well. These thoughts are often foremost in your mind when you try to study for an exam or sit down to take an exam, and are part of what makes it difficult for you to concentrate.

6. What do you like about yourself?

You are proud of your success in high school and your role as the first member of your extended family to attend college. You may also describe yourself as responsible, dependable, and loyal, and if asked to give examples, you focus on your role as the oldest sibling in your family and the importance you place on living up to your parents' expectations for you and setting a good example for your younger siblings.

7. How have you been doing at work?

If asked about your part-time job at the grocery store, you admit that you don't really enjoy it and that you feel it takes time away from studying. However, you need the money to help with college expenses and you try to do a good job. Lately, you have had to call off a few shifts because of your headaches, and you are afraid your manager will perceive you as lazy or irresponsible, although she has been sympathetic and has not complained about the missed time as yet.

8. How have you been doing in school?

Your grades have recently dropped after you performed poorly on several major exams. You had solid B's in most classes until the most recent exams, but now have C's in a couple of classes and are in danger of failing your math class. You have missed a few classes recently because of your headaches. You have not sought out your professors for extra help, and you are embarrassed by the idea of receiving tutoring. You admit feeling worried about your grades and state that your plan is "just to study more and try to do better."

9. How is your health?

You have just been given a prescription for Imitrex from the campus health center. You are supposed to take this medicine whenever you begin to get a migraine. You have struggled with occasional migraine headaches since early adolescence, but until now you have been able to manage them with over-the-counter medication. You deny having any other real physical complaints. However, you only get five or six hours of sleep a night between classes, studying, and your part-time job at the local grocery store. You also have gained a few pounds since coming to college. You don't consider this a health problem. You just haven't had time to exercise.

10. How do you relate to others?

If asked about your social life, you laugh and say that you really don't have any. You always had friends in high school and people to hang out with on weekends, but classes, studying, and your job don't seem to allow much time for socializing since coming to college. If asked what you do to "unwind" or relax, you can say that you seldom do. Since coming to college, you have felt as if you were always "on," that there was really no time to relax or have fun. Your roommates tell you that you ought to make time for some fun, and they try to get you to go out and party with them. But you really don't see how other people manage to do that and still get their school work done. When you have tried to take time to just hang out with your roommates or go to a party, you find you feel guilty and distracted by thoughts of all the work you should be doing, and this gets in the way of enjoying yourself. You don't really see this as a problem. Friends just seem like a luxury you can't afford right now.

You are close to your family and talk with them on the phone once a week. You can't really call more frequently because of the expense. You and your mother, in particular, have been very close since the death of her mother (your grandmother) last year. She died of cancer. You and your mother were both very close to her and very involved in caring for her at the end of her life. You haven't really dealt with this because your role in the family is to be strong and competent. You don't really think of it as something unresolved, but once in a while you are surprised at the emotions that you feel when you think of her or are reminded of her in a dream or in conversation with your mother. Whether you share these emotions with the interviewer should depend on how comfortable the interviewer makes you feel. Remember, you think it would be embarrassing to cry in the interview and are trying to avoid this at all costs. However, when the subject comes up, you exhibit discomfort by shifting position in your chair, jiggling your foot, and perhaps rubbing your head.

11. How do you view your life?

Up until recently, you thought of your life as a challenge you could handle. You were proud of your success in high school and very proud to be the first member of your family to attend college. You were excited to be starting classes and hopeful about the future. Then the headaches began to get worse and you discovered that it was possible to fail a test despite hours of studying. Your confidence has been shaken and you now become anxious even when you anticipate taking a test. You thought if you worked hard and kept yourself focused on classes, you would succeed. But you seem to be caught in a never-ending cycle of trying harder and harder and performing more and more poorly. It is disconcerting to think of yourself as capable of failure and possibly in need of help. But you are beginning to recognize that you need to try something different to get out of this cycle. You are not sure that psychotherapy is that "something different" but are motivated to try anything at the moment rather than face giving up on your goals.

EXERCISES FOR THE INTERVIEWER

Exercise 1: Develop a diagnosis for Monisha

A. What criteria does Monisha meet for an Adjustment Disorder on Axis I?

_____

_____

_____

_____

Name two other Axis I diagnoses that you might want to rule out for Monisha, and indicate what additional information might be needed to differentiate between the diagnostic choices for her.

_____

_____

_____

_____

B. Does Monisha meet the criteria for an Axis II disorder, should a diagnosis be deferred, or is a diagnosis not needed?

_____

_____

_____

_____

C. What might you report for Monisha on Axis III (General Medical Conditions that are potentially relevant to a client's mental disorder)?

_____

_____

_____

_____

D. List all relevant categories of psychosocial and environmental stressors for Monisha and specify examples of each one on Axis IV. Indicate if each stressor is mild, moderate, or severe.

_____

_____

_____

E. What is your global assessment of Monisha's functioning for Axis V (current, highest in past year)?

_____

_____

_____

_____

F. Double-check your diagnostic choices starting at Axis V and proceeding in reverse order through Axis I to determine if you may have overestimated or underestimated the impact of the situational, biological, or individual psychological factors on Monisha's current functioning. Should you change anything? Be specific in describing why or why not.

_____

_____

_____

_____

G. Review your diagnostic choices again from Monisha's point of view. Do your choices support the discussions you have had with her? Would she be disturbed by your choices? Be specific in discussing why or why not.

_____

_____

_____

_____

Exercise 2: Practice deepening interview with Monisha

A. Monisha is working hard to be successful academically and to be an unfailing and strong source of support to her family members. She may be underaware of how this puts her under significant stress. Make comments on her nonverbal behavior that help her deepen her emotional awareness of these issues.

When Monisha speaks about the death of her grandmother, her voice drops and she speaks more slowly and haltingly, with long pauses. Write a comment that highlights her nonverbal behavior and encourages her to consider what emotional state or states it might reflect regarding her grandmother's death.

_____

_____

_____

_____

_____

When Monisha talks about her dropping grades, her concern that she might disappointing her parents, and her desire to set a good example for her siblings, she jiggles her foot, shifts position in her chair, frowns, and rubs her head as if in pain. What might you say to sensitively draw her attention to these nonverbal cues in order to increase emotional awareness of the pressure she feels to do well in school?

_____

_____

_____

_____

_____

B. Monisha is requesting stress management for presenting symptoms of migraine headaches and apparent test anxiety. In order to establish a baseline measure of her symptoms, you would need to obtain more detail about the specific times when these symptoms are present. Using open-ended and closed questions to gain information about the frequency, intensity, and duration of these symptoms will establish a way for you and for Monisha to evaluate her progress as treatment continues.

Make a list of questions you might ask to elicit specific examples of times when she has experienced headaches or test anxiety.

_____

_____

_____

_____

Make a list of questions you might ask to establish the frequency, intensity, and duration of these symptoms.

_____

_____

_____

_____

C. Make a list of questions you might ask to elicit specific examples of how she experiences a headache. Assess multiple dimensions of her experience (i.e., behavior, cognition, affect, imagery, sensation, etc.) that occur before, during, or after a headache or an episode of test anxiety?

_____

_____

_____

_____

D. What questions might you ask about exceptions to the above, for example, when Monisha is under pressure but doesn't get a headache or takes an exam without getting anxious?

_____

_____

_____

_____

Exercise 3: Thought questions related to Monisha

A. Consider who you are as an interviewer and write down what you think might be most difficult about establishing rapport with Monisha based on your age, ethnicity, gender, socio-economic status, sexual orientation, religion, physical characteristics, and personality style. What specifically might happen?

_____

_____

_____

_____

B. Is there anything you could do to enhance your ability to establish an effective working relationship with Monisha? Be specific and detailed in describing your ideas.

_____

_____

_____

_____

C. Given that Monisha has not indicated any connection between her grandmother's death and her current symptoms, is invested in maintaining her role as a strong, competent individual, and is somewhat uncomfortable with the idea of psychotherapy, how could you sensitively approach the task of obtaining more information about this event and her reaction to it?

_____

_____

_____

_____

D. Consider the pros and cons of focusing treatment on Monisha's presenting symptoms of headaches and anxiety versus expanding treatment to include exploration of possible unresolved grief.

_____

_____

_____

_____

E. What do you consider the optimal treatment choice for Monisha at this time? What factors led you to this choice?

_____

_____

_____

_____

F. Did your decision about optimal treatment for Monisha reflect your overall views about taking a narrow versus a wide focus to treatment, or did it reflect individual factors in Monisha's case?

_____

_____

_____

_____

Case of Jie

1. What are your basic statistics?

You are an eighteen-year-old, male Taiwanese student studying for your business degree at a university in the United States. Your immediate family consists of your paternal grandmother, father, mother, and three younger sisters. Your extended family includes three paternal and four maternal aunts and uncles and their children. Your family network is very close knit. Everyone works together to insure the success of a family manufacturing business that has been part of the family for many generations. You are fluent in spoken English, as well as your native Mandarin Chinese.

You have been in the United States for six months. You are living alone in the home of a Chinese family who is distantly related to a business associate of your father's. This family lives within walking distance of the northeastern university where you are studying. The mother of this family provides you with meals and takes care of your laundry. You are being interviewed at a university counseling center.

2. How do you behave in the interview?

You sit very quietly and look down most of the time. Your entire body stays very still throughout most of the interview. You do not kick your legs, cross your legs, or gesture with your hands unless you become extremely uncomfortable. The mental status questions raise your discomfort level to the point where your whole body becomes very noticeably tense. Your hands feel like gripping tightly to the arms of the chair or to your knees. You press your back against the chair, and your legs tremble with the pressure of being pushed into the floor. It is very important to you to present a mature appearance; this means that you need to maintain self-control at all times. Thus, while your body shows tension at times, your voice remains soft and controlled.

You are very embarrassed by any question that seems to infer you have an emotional problem. However, out of respect for the authority of the interviewer, you attempt to answer these questions. You believe that the interviewer has a bad impression of your mental health and you want to correct this. You try to do so by stating that the university physician felt your health problems would improve if you received suggestions for improving your academic performance. If asked for more information, you say that this is your first year at the university and it is very important for you to receive top marks. High marks will honor your family and earn you a place in business school after you get your undergraduate degree.

You have been told that coming in for this interview will help you succeed and so you are quite anxious to facilitate the interview and cooperate fully. If asked any "why" questions such as, "Why might you be stressed at school?", you answer that it is the result of external causes such as confusing exams, noise in the library, and a lack of family support because you are living far away from home.

If asked mental status questions that tap into memory and your ability to concentrate, you admit to a growing problem with focusing your attention on your school work and concentrating while you study. You also state that, despite long hours of study, during an exam you have trouble remembering what you have studied. Along with feeling very concerned and tense about these concentration problems, you have many somatic complaints. If asked about anger or aggression, you deny any feelings of anger or homicidal ideation. If screened for hallucinations and delusions, you become so embarrassed it will be hard for you to speak. Out of respect for the interviewer, you force yourself to respond by denying having any unusual thoughts or experiences and stating that no one in your family has ever had problems of this kind.

If asked if you have ever had suicidal thoughts, you admit to periodically having thoughts of suicide. If asked if you have a suicidal plan, you say no. You just indicate that if you can't succeed in school, you will have to kill yourself. You cannot shame and disappoint your family by returning home without your business degree.

3. Why are you being interviewed?

You have been sick throughout your six months at school. Your stomach has been the greatest source of consistent trouble to you. You have lost ten pounds in the last month. Your symptoms include a lack of appetite, heartburn, and stomach bloating. The physician at the University Health Center ran many tests on you before making the decision to refer you to the Counseling Center. He told you that your stomach problems and feelings of tension and anxiety are related to each other and that coming to the Counseling Center will help you take care of these problems so that you can succeed at the university. You find many opportunities to stress to the interviewer how important it is to your entire family that you succeed in school and how dedicated you are to fulfilling their expectations.

You admit to having had milder forms of these symptoms when you were younger, but family support always helped you overcome it. If asked for more details, say that your grandmother used family stories to help you. In each of these stories, a man in your family overcame a difficult obstacle through persistence and hard work. Your father also gave you a poem written by his grandfather that talks of family loyalty and obligations. This poem has always been very inspirational to you and you have read it every day since leaving home. If asked if you have any contact with your family now, say that you call long distance once every two weeks. During these phone calls, your mother and father remind you to work hard and bring honor to the family. Your aunts and uncles are sometimes available during these phone calls. They tell you about problems occurring in the family business and exhort you to find solutions to these problems.

You have never received counseling or psychotherapeutic services before and have not told your family that you were referred for it because you are certain this will shame them. You expect that the interviewer will give you some kind of medication as well as direct advice as to how to best succeed in school. If the interviewer is a female, or appears to be very young, you will be concerned that he or she doesn't have the knowledge needed to help you. You never directly mention this, but you indirectly inquire about the interviewer's credentials.

4. How do you feel?

You have trouble responding to feeling questions because you find them very embarrassing. You wonder if the interviewer is asking you these questions because he or she considers you immature and not in control of yourself. You try to respond to these questions but are hesitant and unsure of what to say because you are not at all used to being introspective about your emotions. The "feeling" questions you comprehend are those that deal with anxiety. You are able to talk of the long hours you spend pouring over your business texts and the way your stomach aches more and more as the hours go by. You mention how studying sessions only end when the pain in your gut is so great that you have to lie down. When lying down, you are flooded with ideas about how you will flunk your exams if you don't concentrate better and work harder.

If asked if you are disappointed enough with your performance at the university to actually kill yourself, you reiterate that killing yourself is your last choice if you can not succeed in school. The hopes of your family revolve around your being successful and you cannot live with the knowledge of disappointing everyone. As the eldest son of your father, who is the eldest living male of his family, it is your responsibility to insure the future success of the family and its business. Your voice slows down and you get choked up or you tear up as you discuss this. This loss of control is very embarrassing to you. You act confused if the interviewer says anything such as, "It is all right to let your feelings out. This is a safe place to express your feelings." You do not understand why the interviewer is encouraging you to behave childishly, but you defer to his or her authority.

5. How do you think?

You try hard to be logical at all times. If asked why you might be stressed, state that you have been thinking about it ever since you first met with the physician and believe it is because you are not doing as well in business classes as you expected. You have dedicated all of your time outside of class to studying. However, you have had trouble concentrating ever since you received a poor mark on a paper you wrote for your accounting class. You are concerned that this poor mark means you may not be successful at mastering the coursework you need to help your family.

If asked to explain how the family business is influencing your stress, state that your family's business grew rapidly about twenty years ago because it gained contracts from several companies in the United States. In the last five years, however, these companies have begun to do business with mainland China instead of with Taiwan because the labor is cheaper there. This has left your family with many more employees than they need for their current business demands. Your family needs to maintain their employees and has been struggling to do so. Sacrifices were made to send you to school in the United States in the hopes that you could develop new contacts and bring back new ideas to help the family out of trouble. A day doesn't go by when you don't worry about how you will help your family. As you read your textbooks, you struggle to apply what you are learning to the needs of your family. However, this is difficult and you find your mind freezing up; you stare at a page and can't understand what you are reading.

In the phone conversations with your father, he asks you how you are doing on homework assignments and exams. Your father has always had high expectations for you and you have never yet disappointed him. You do not intend to do so now. You argue with yourself over whether you should have told him you received a "C" on an accounting assignment. You worked hard on this assignment, but you haven't yet gained as good a facility with writing grammatical English as you have with speaking it. You did not tell your father about the poor grade because you didn't want him to lose face. However, not telling him has made you feel very ashamed and untrustworthy. If you can just get top marks on the rest of your work, you can reclaim your sense of worth.

You tell yourself each morning that you must work hard and improve yourself so that you will gain the knowledge that your family needs. You tell yourself to listen hard to your instructors because they have much to teach you. A small voice in your head responds with, "But what if I can't do it?" You expect the interviewer to have many ideas that you can use to be successful at your work. You may begin to feel cramps in your arms and legs from holding them tightly while you wait for these ideas.

6. What do you like about yourself?

This question is not easy for you to address. Your family places a high value on humility, so you always focus your attention on what you need to learn and not on what you can already do. You are more comfortable if you can talk about yourself in relation to your family. You are very proud of your family and its business record. The eldest son of your family has been in charge of this business for the past four generations. You are the fifth generation. Each son has improved and expanded the business. Your father was responsible for "Westernizing" the business enough to attract the attention of companies within the United States. Your father was able to make these contacts because of his excellent mastery of English. You have always greatly admired your father.

7. What have you been doing at work?

This question does not apply to Jie at this time.

8. How have you been doing in school?

In Taiwan, you went to school six days a week. After the school day was over, you would then go on to a cram school where different subjects were covered on different days. As a result, you have very fine work habits. Your teachers had no complaints about you. You always worked well and conformed to the group without any difficulties. They were never aware of your intermittent stomach problems. At the present time, you attend all of your classes and complete all of your work diligently. You have an "A" average in all of your introductory courses except for accounting. Accounting is the only course, so far, that has required you to write a paper. Your syllabi show you that you have to write papers in several other courses before the end of the term.

9. How is your health?

Your father sent you to the United States several months before school was to start. This was because of the advent of the SARS virus. Your father follows the international news carefully. Although no one in your vicinity had contracted SARS, your father decided that many schools outside of Asia might start refusing to allow students to travel to their country because of fear of SARS. Thus, your dad rushed you off before such a ban could take place. This did not give you enough time to say goodbye to your family.

You began to feel poorly almost immediately on arrival in the United States. You had a lot of respiratory problems but did not seek help out of fear that you would be deported for having SARS. You spent time alone in your room, afraid you might transmit it to the family you were living with. Fortunately, you were healthy by the end of your second week and you could forget about SARS. When you got the bad mark, your stomach problems became so intense that they kept you from listening in your classes for the rest of the week. This made you decide to go to the health center. You knew that you could not let your stomach decrease your ability to work hard at your studies.

The physician at the health center did a number of checks on you and found no serious medical problems. He did prescribe an acid blocker for your reflux problems. He recommended a diet that might reduce some of your stomach difficulties. However, it is hard to follow because Chinese food mixes many ingredients together and your doctor wants you to experiment with one food at a time. You cannot mention this to the woman who cooks your food; it would be an insult to suggest that her cooking could be making you ill. You decided regretfully that you had to ignore your doctor's instructions.

10. How do you relate to others?

You have always been a good son who worked hard and persistently at any task set for you by your parents and adult extended family members. You are very aware of your responsibilities as the eldest son of the house. In addition to learning everything that you can at school, you have done your best to encourage your younger sisters at school and you have helped them if they needed it. Your sisters see you as very strong and intelligent, and you have never shared with them any of your periodic concerns about being good enough to fulfill everyone's expectations.

If asked about peer relationships, you state that you have been meeting several times a week with a group of other Taiwanese students who are studying at your university. These meetings revolve around helping each other do well at school. You did not tell these students about your poor mark because you were too ashamed. However, you did mention to them that you were having some trouble with your written assignments. One of the other students recommended a grammar book to you that helps him check his written assignments before he hands them in. While this advice was helpful, it increased your anxiety because you see yourself as the least successful student in the group.

You intentionally keep at a distance from the non-Taiwanese students at your university. They are mostly European-American or African-American students. You avoid them because their behavior in the classroom seems immature to you. They seem to spend more time socializing with each other than paying attention to the instructor. You find this very disrespectful. At first, you were shocked by their behavior. Now, you just do your best to dissociate yourself from them. You are grateful that you have other Taiwanese students to associate with. Your Taiwanese group has heard that some international students get mistreated. This hasn't happened to you or any member of your group. The longer you live in the United States, the more you appreciate your life in Taiwan. You plan to return there as soon as you finish your education.

11. How do you view your life?

You feel that you are very fortunate to have been born into such a well-off and highly educated family where you can be in charge of the company rather than one of its employees. You are proud of your father and uncles and want them to be proud of you also. You seek their approval by your diligent cooperation and hard work. Sometimes, you have envied your sisters because the family expects less of them. You only share this information if a lot of trust has built up between you and the interviewer.

EXERCISES FOR THE INTERVIEWER

Exercise 1: Develop a diagnosis for Jie

A. What criteria does Jie meet for an Anxiety Disorder or Adjustment Disorder?

_____

_____

_____

_____

Name two other Axis I diagnoses you might want to rule out for Jie and indicate what additional information might be needed to differentiate between the diagnostic choices for him.

_____

_____

_____

_____

Does Jie meet all the criteria for an Axis I disorder? Should the diagnosis be deferred, or is a diagnosis not needed?

_____

_____

_____

_____

B. What criteria does Jie meet for an Axis II diagnosis (Personality Disorders and Mental Retardation)? Should a diagnosis be deferred, or is a diagnosis not needed? Explain and be as specific as possible.

_____

_____

_____

_____

C. Is there anything you might report for Jie on Axis III (General Medical Conditions that are potentially relevant to the client's mental disorder)?

_____

_____

D. List all relevant categories of psychosocial and environmental stressors for Jie and specify examples of each one on Axis IV. Indicate if each stressor is mild, moderate, or severe.

_____

_____

E. What is your global assessment of Jie's functioning for Axis V (current and highest in past year)?

_____

_____

F. Double-check your diagnostic choices starting at Axis V and proceeding back through Axis I to determine if you may have overestimated or underestimated the impact of the situational, biological, or individual psychological factors on Jie's current functioning. Should you change anything? Be specific in describing why or why not.

_____

_____

_____

G. Review your diagnostic choices again from Jie's point of view. Do your choices support the discussions you have had with him? Would he be disturbed by your choices? Be specific in discussing why or why not.

_____

_____

_____

Exercise 2: Practice deepening interview with Jie

A. Jie grew up in Taiwan and may show nonverbal attending behavior that is typical of his country and his status as the eldest son in his family. This may be different from your own typical nonverbal attending behavior. Behaviors that may differ include eye contact, orientation of body, posture, facial expressions, autonomic behavior and attire.

If this is so, what might you say to Jie to determine whether your nonverbal attending behavior is making him feel respected and listened to, or whether it is having some other impact?

_____

_____

_____

_____

_____

As you are an authority figure, Jie might not consider it acceptable to tell you directly that he is uncomfortable with your nonverbal attending behavior. What might you say to make it acceptable to him to give you feedback of this kind?

_____

_____

_____

_____

_____

B. In the situations that follow, you have asked Jie questions and have noticed him showing nonverbal signs of distress. Make statements to Jie that help him identify the emotions that may be fueling these nonverbal signs of distress. Because he considers it immature to show signs of emotion, choose your words carefully and explain to Jie that, in his current circumstances, recognition of his emotions is a critical step toward his gaining control over his physical symptoms. An example is provided for the first situation.

You have asked Jie a number of questions about his study habits. His facial muscles have tightened, and he has begun to surreptitiously rub his stomach.

Tensing your facial muscles and rubbing your stomach may be signs of anxiety. This anxiety may be a useful warning sign for you to learn to identify. When this sign comes, you may benefit from briefly stopping your studying and taking steps to care for your body so that your stomach problems won't intensify and prevent you from learning.

Jie has told you, in a halting voice, about his lack of success in studying for an exam over the weekend. He battled with this all weekend late into the night but had no success. There is a sheen of sweat on his face, and his hands are gripping his legs as he speaks.

_____

_____

_____

_____

_____

Jie has told you that he wastes a great deal of valuable study time thinking only of being a failure. These thoughts intrude on every study session and interfere with his progressing on his homework. As he says this, he is sinking deep into the chair, and his voice is getting difficult to hear.

_____

_____

_____

_____

_____

C. Use summarizing comments in response to the following remarks from Jie. You may use a summarizing statement to simply demonstrate that you are listening carefully, or you may use one to highlight a theme you believe pervades his experience or to serve as a transition to another topic or to decrease his emotional intensity. An example of summarization to highlight a theme is provided in response to Jie's first comments.

Jie says, "Since I received a poor grade on that paper, no matter what I do I will never be able to be the top student in my class. I have always been at the top. In my earlier years, I could always succeed by just trying harder. I don't understand why I can't do this now? I try over and over again, but this pain is too severe for me to ignore."

Theme: Needing to be the top student.

Being the top student is very important to you. You have always been able to achieve that by hard work and persistence, but now the pain is preventing you from concentrating, and the loss of this "top student" status is very confusing and distressing to you.

Jie says, "My sisters have many responsibilities at home, but they aren't responsible for the welfare of our family and all of the employees at our company. I think often about all the people who are depending on me. I do not want to let them down. I must not let them down. But sometimes I do think of my sisters and wonder why it must always be me. I am willing to do what is right, but it is so hard to be the eldest son."

_____

_____

_____

_____

Jie says, "The other students at school must all be so much smarter than I am because they seem to study so much less. I will be studying in the library in the afternoon and see them running around together outside playing as if they were young children. How can they be so relaxed when there is so much to do? I thought at first that they must work in the early morning or evening instead of in the afternoon, but I see them playing all day long. I find it hard to understand my classmates. Are they so smart, or are they young children?"

_____

_____

_____

_____

Exercise 3: Thought questions related to Jie

A. Consider who you are as an interviewer and write down what you think might be most difficult about establishing rapport with Jie based on your age, ethnicity, gender, socioeconomic status, sexual orientation, religion, physical characteristics, and personality style. What specifically might happen?

_____

_____

_____

_____

B. Is there anything you could do to enhance your ability to establish an effective working relationship with Jie? Be specific and detailed in describing your ideas.

_____

_____

_____

C. How will you explain your credentials to Jie so that he is most likely to perceive you as an expert who is trustworthy?

_____

_____

_____

_____

D. At the end of the first interview, you may not be ready to formulate a treatment plan. However, Jie may not return for a second session if he doesn't feel that he left today with something that will be a concrete benefit to him because he trusted his medical doctor enough to come but really wasn't sure if your services were useful. What might you say to him at the end of the interview that will make him feel it is worthwhile to come back?

_____

_____

_____

_____

E. Could Jie meet the academic goals he has set for himself without working through the feelings that relate to them? Be specific in discussing why or why not.

_____

_____

_____

_____

Case of Brenda

1. What are your basic statistics?

Your name is Brenda, and you are a thirty-one-year-old European-American woman. You are married to Bob, age thirty-four, who works as an engineer for a company located in a city fifty miles away. Bob commutes to work, leaving early in the morning to avoid rush hour traffic and often not coming home until 8:00 or 9:00 p.m. You are home with your two young children, Sarah, age two and a half, and Steven, three months old. You became a full-time homemaker when Sarah was born because both you and Bob felt it was important for you to be there with the children, and he made enough money to support the family. Before that, you worked as an editor for a local newspaper. You have a BA in Communications and an MA in Journalism. You are being interviewed in a private practice.

2. How do you behave in the interview?

You are casually dressed and apologize for your appearance, saying that you are long overdue for a haircut and really need to get some new clothes that fit your post-baby shape, but you haven't been out in public much lately and have gotten used to baggy sweat suits and oversized T-shirts. Besides, the baby tends to spit up or drool on you several times a day, and there doesn't seem to be a whole lot of point in dressing up for that. You speak clearly and express yourself well. However, you may make several disparaging comments about your brain having become "mush" since you seldom get to talk to adults and spend all day interacting with small humans with limited vocabulary. When the television is on, it is usually tuned to *Sesame Street* or some other children's program, so there isn't much intellectual stimulation there either. You sit on the edge of your seat as if you might jump up to leave at any moment, and you ask if the interviewer minds if you leave your cell phone on because you haven't left your kids with a babysitter very often and are a little worried that the babysitter might have questions or need to get in touch with you.

Your general demeanor is cheerful and talkative, but when the interviewer begins to ask about what brought you to seek psychotherapy, your voice wavers and you choke up and have to clear your throat several times before answering. You are apologetic about this, saying that you really didn't want to cry today, that you feel like a big baby yourself, and that you really should be able to "get it together" better. However, you continue to try to answer the interviewer's questions because you really do want to be cooperative and have the interviewer like you.

If asked about drug or alcohol use, you deny any usage explaining that you are breastfeeding your son. You also deny suicidal or homicidal ideation, but your voice wavers and you become tearful as you admit that you have found yourself wondering lately if your children would be better off without you. You admit that you find yourself crying several times a week, that the sad feelings seem to come out of the blue and overwhelm you when you least expect it, and that you worry a lot about your ability to be a good mother when you are "such an emotional basket case." You also admit that you have recently found yourself getting irritable with your two-year-old daughter and that she seems to be more and more difficult to control as you seem to have less and less patience with her. You aren't sleeping well, but you attribute this to getting up a lot with the baby, who is not yet sleeping through the night. You feel tired all the time, but never really relaxed. Lately, you have trouble concentrating. For example, if you and your husband rent a video on a weekend evening, you find your attention wandering a lot.

3. Why are you being interviewed?

You were referred by your son's pediatrician, because of an incident that took place in his office a week ago. Your son had a regular check-up scheduled, and you had taken him to the doctor's office for this. You also had your daughter with you, because the appointment was in the morning and your husband was at work. In the waiting room, your daughter wanted to climb on the chairs and got increasingly defiant and noisy every time you told her "no" or lifted her down again. Meanwhile, your son, who hadn't slept well the night before, began to fuss. By the time you got into the examining room, your daughter was screaming, your son was crying, and you were at the end of your rope. The nurse said something sympathetic, and you burst into tears. By the time the doctor entered the room, you were sobbing, your children were even more upset, and you were unable to calm them down because you couldn't stop crying yourself. The doctor expressed concern about the possibility of post-partum depression and advised you to consult your own physician for possible antidepressant medication. You are very reluctant to do this because you want to continue breast-feeding, and besides, you think you were just stressed out by the situation, not really clinically depressed. You don't have any prior history of depression and don't remember hearing of anyone in your extended family that had a history of depression. However, after getting home and talking things over with your husband that night, you finally agreed that maybe you could use some supportive psychotherapy to learn how to lower your stress level. So you agreed to start with psychotherapy and only resort to medication if therapy doesn't help.

4. How do you feel?

When asked about your mood, you say that you are just so tired all the time that you don't really feel much of anything. In fact, sometimes you feel guilty about *not* feeling things you think you should feel. For example, when your daughter said something really cute the other day, you didn't enjoy it. You felt as if you were observing it from a distance instead of experiencing it as it happened. You may tear up in the interview as you tell the interviewer that you fear you are missing out on the most precious moments of your children's development because of this apparent inability to feel joy or pleasure. You are aware of feeling sad that you are "missing out" on these moments, but you don't understand why you find yourself crying so often when you think you should be happy. You also feel worried that you are not being a good mother because of your moodiness and irritability. You love your children and think they deserve a "happy, loving mother" and this is certainly not how you would describe yourself at the moment.

You remember feeling tired and lacking energy when your daughter was born, but you were able to take naps when she slept. She was very predictable, in terms of her sleeping and eating schedule, and generally in a pleasant mood. You felt pretty good about your mothering because she seemed so content, and it wasn't long before you regained your energy and felt you were handling things pretty well. Having two children is a completely different ball game.

Your son is harder to soothe and less predictable than his sister was in terms of eating and sleeping. He often wakes crying during the night and can't be calmed by anything except walking him around the house. He doesn't nap on a regular schedule and so even though your daughter still takes a regular afternoon nap, you can't ever seem to catch up on your sleep. In addition to his being more difficult to manage than your daughter was, it seems as if she has been harder to handle since he was born. She was very close to being potty-trained before his birth, but has gone back to diapers since he arrived. She also seems more demanding of your attention and more resistant to your efforts to correct her. Not only do you feel inadequate to manage your son, you feel you have lost the easy, comfortable relationship you had with your daughter before he arrived.

5. How do you think?

You do not exhibit any evidence of delusions or hallucinations. Your thoughts center on how to be a better mother and why things have turned out this way. You chose to stay home with your children and have really made a commitment to being a full-time mother. Although you enjoyed working as a newspaper editor, you were excited when you became pregnant and glad to give up the stress of deadlines and pressure at work in order to be home starting a family. You and your husband had really talked about this a lot and you thought you knew what you wanted. You find it confusing to reconcile your expectations with the reality of how unhappy you are now. Sometimes you ask yourself if you ought to go back to work, because if that meant you were happier, it would be better for your children, too. But you can't imagine being away from them full time, and you really don't want someone else caring for them. You have also thought about trying to do some freelance writing just to take a break from motherhood once in a while. But your fatigue and difficulties concentrating make that seem impossible. Besides, what you find you miss most of all about working is contact with other adults, and writing at home wouldn't satisfy that need. Your mind feels like a rat in a maze, running around and around and ending up at the same dead ends over and over again with no way out.

6. What do you like about yourself?

You like your ability to communicate and use words well, although lately you feel as though this part of your life has atrophied from disuse. You like your commitment to full-time mothering, but don't feel you are carrying this out as well as you had hoped to. You are proud of your educational accomplishments and your previous successes at work. You also feel you and your husband have a pretty solid relationship and are glad that you were married several years before having children. In fact, when the interviewer inquires about what you like about yourself, you say that the only thing you don't like about yourself is that you aren't as happy as you think you should be, now that you have everything you ever thought you wanted. You say, "If I could just make my feelings on the inside match all the good things I have on the outside, I wouldn't be here talking to you!"

7. How have you been doing at work?

You haven't worked since Sarah was born, but if the interviewer asks about your work history, you say that you felt you were good at your job. You enjoyed the fact that every day seemed to pose new challenges, and you found the pressure of deadlines really kept you energized. You got lots of positive feedback. You miss those aspects of the job, although in your current state you find it hard to imagine how you ever had the energy to keep up that pace. You do expect to work again someday, when your children are in school, but you may look for part-time employment or do freelance writing in order to fit the work hours around their school schedule and be home when they are home.

8. How have you been doing in school?

This question is not applicable to this client.

9. How is your health?

Your health has basically been good, and you are not currently under treatment by a doctor for anything. However, you are tired all the time. You think you might feel better if you could exercise regularly, but you haven't found a way to do this with the two children. You admit that your eating habits are not great. In fact, you haven't been able to make much progress toward losing your pregnancy weight gain. It is hard to find time to plan meals or cook good food, and you often resort to whatever you can grab quickly from the cupboard or refrigerator. Because your husband is rarely home in time for dinner anyway, it just seems easier to fix something for your daughter and not plan a full meal. One of the few "nice" things you can do for yourself on short notice is grab something sweet to eat, and you find yourself doing this more and more often lately. You know you should eat more carefully in order to support proper nutrition for yourself and your son, but working on this just seems like one more thing you don't have the energy for right now.

10. How do you relate to others?

You are the oldest of three children in your family of origin, and the only daughter. Your relationship with your mother has always been a close one, but she lives in another state and you do not see her often. You try to talk on the phone several times a week, but it is hard to find a time when you will not be interrupted by your children. You have often wondered how she managed to raise three children who were close in age when you are having trouble raising two. She was a stay-at-home mom, and you have never heard her complain about this choice. Both your parents supported your educational and career choices, but you know your mother was particularly pleased when you got pregnant and decided to stay home with your children. She has talked about moving closer to where you are when your father retires from his job as a bank manager, but your father loves his work and you don't see this happening any time soon. Your two younger brothers are unmarried. One is in the air force, and the other is in graduate school. You enjoy keeping in touch with them and your family generally gets together for the holidays, but you don't see your brothers as resources right now as neither of them is married or raising children and you don't think they can understand what you are going through.

You describe your relationship with your husband as solid and committed. You share the same values about family and children. You met in graduate school and were married about four years before Sarah was born, so you feel you know each other well. If pressed by the interviewer to describe your current relationship, you may hesitate and then reluctantly admit that you do not feel as close to your husband as you did before the children were born. His job keeps him away long hours, and you feel as though he really can't imagine what it's like for you to be home all that time with the children. Although he tries to listen when you bring up your feelings, he usually either says he doesn't understand why you aren't happy since this was what you said you wanted, or tries to come up with solutions that you really don't find helpful, like saying that if you want to go back to work, you should just find a good babysitter and do it. He is the kind of person who takes action to solve problems without a lot of agonizing over it or changing his mind. You, on the other hand, frequently consider everything from multiple perspectives for a long time before you are ready to make a decision or take action. You wish he would just listen and let you do this out loud with him, but you can tell that he gets impatient when the discussion continues for any length of time without reaching a conclusion.

You had a number of friends with whom you socialized when you worked at the newspaper, but you have less contact with them now. It seems like such a lot of work to line up babysitters, and none of your friends have kids close in age to yours, so getting together for activities that include the children seems like an imposition on your friends. You and your husband used to go out regularly before Sarah was born, and after she was a year old, you began to do that again because you felt more comfortable leaving her with a sitter once she was weaned. But now you are breast-feeding your son and it seems harder to work out the logistics to arrange a date than to just stay at home. Your husband is willing to stay home and watch a video, but often you are distracted by your son waking up, or you are so tired that you can't concentrate on the movie anyway. Once last week, you actually fell asleep watching a movie with him, and he was irritated with you because he had come home earlier than usual so you could spend time together.

11. How do you view your life?

You say that your life now has everything in it that you thought you always wanted: an interesting career that you can return to eventually, beautiful children, a loving husband, a comfortable home, and so on. You "should" feel good about all of it, but you have to admit you don't. This puzzles you, and you feel you need to hurry up and find a solution, a way of getting your feelings on the inside to match what you have on the outside, so you can be a good mother and begin enjoying your life again.

EXERCISES FOR THE INTERVIEWER

Exercise 1: Develop a diagnosis for Brenda

A. What criteria does Brenda meet for a diagnosis of Major Depressive Disorder (Postpartum Onset Specifier) on Axis I?

_____

_____

_____

_____

Name two other Axis I diagnoses you might want to rule out for Brenda, and indicate what additional information might be needed to differentiate between Major Depressive Disorder and these diagnoses.

_____

_____

_____

_____

Does Brenda meet all the criteria for an Axis I disorder, should the diagnosis be deferred, or is a diagnosis not needed?

_____

_____

_____

_____

B. What criteria does Brenda meet for an Axis II diagnosis (Personality Disorders and Mental Retardation)? Should a diagnosis be deferred, or is a diagnosis not needed? Explain and be as specific as possible.

_____

_____

_____

_____

C. Is there anything you might report for Brenda on Axis III (General Medical Conditions that are potentially relevant to the client's mental disorder)?

_____

_____

_____

_____

D. List all relevant categories of psychosocial and environmental stressors for Brenda and specify examples of each one on Axis IV. Indicate if each stressor is mild, moderate, or severe.

_____

_____

_____

E. What is your global assessment of Brenda's functioning for Axis V (current, highest in past year)?

_____

_____

F. Double-check your diagnostic choices starting at Axis V and proceeding backward through Axis I to determine if you may have overestimated or underestimated the impact of the situational, biological, or individual psychological factors on Brenda's current functioning. Should you change anything? Be specific in describing why or why not.

_____

_____

_____

G. Review your diagnostic choices again from Brenda's point of view. Do your choices support the discussions you have had with her? Would she be disturbed by your choices? Be specific in discussing why or why not.

_____

_____

_____

Exercise 2: Practice deepening the interview with Brenda

A. Brenda feels overwhelmed by both the external stressors in her life and the internal emotional upheaval she is currently experiencing. However, she thinks she should be happy with her life and doesn't perceive her feelings as valid. Use summarizing statements to help Brenda feel you listened to her, to highlight a theme, to serve as a transition, or to decrease her emotional intensity. An example has been provided that highlights a theme.

Brenda: My mind is like a rat in a maze. I keep looking for answers, for a way to get myself together, but I keep getting detoured. It's not just one thing. Like maybe I could handle Steven crying if Sarah would behave, or I could be more patient with Sarah if Steven weren't fussy, or I could figure out what to do if I could just get some sleep. It might help if Bob were around more. But we depend on his income now that I'm not working, and if he were working less I'd probably have to go back to work and that seems impossible in my current state.

Theme: There are so many needs.

You keep thinking if you could just come up with a solution, it should all fall into place, but

there are so many variables to consider: Steven's needs, Sarah's needs, your need for sleep,

Bob's work schedule. It's not a simple problem with a simple solution.

Develop a different summarizing comment to help reduce Brenda's level of emotional arousal so that she will be able to think effectively about her current situation. Assume that she showed signs of extremely high emotional arousal in the tone of voice she used in relating the previous information, in her agitated nonverbal gestures, and in her autonomic signs (fast breathing, sweating).

_____

_____

_____

Brenda: My mind is just mush and I can't think clearly anymore. I miss the stimulation of work and grown-up conversation. Sesame Street just doesn't do it for me. Sometimes I think I need to find ways to have more adult contact, but so many things get in the way. Getting a sitter for two little kids is hard—I can't even manage them myself, so how can I expect someone else to do it? And my friends from work just can't relate to me as a full-time mom with mush for brains—I mean, just look at me! I never used to go out in public looking like this. Even if I try to make a phone call, the kids interrupt me and it's hard enough to concentrate without trying to do two things at once. It makes me feel tired even to think about making the effort to call someone.

_____

_____

_____

_____

_____

B. Brenda experiences a great deal of conflict between what she feels and what she wants to feel or thinks she should feel. Reflect what Brenda is saying in a way that captures both sides of the conflict she is experiencing. An example is provided.

Brenda: I have everything I ever wanted: an interesting career that I can go back to eventually, beautiful children, a loving husband, the freedom to stay home with my kids while they're small, a great home. I should be so happy, but I'm miserable.

Your feelings on the inside don't match the picture that you see on the outside.

Brenda: I have a great husband and we have a solid relationship. We have the same values and we respect each other's opinions when we make decisions for our family. But lately I just don't feel close to him. It's as if we live in two separate worlds, and I really don't think he gets how much my life has changed since the kids. He tries to make suggestions and be helpful, but to him it always seems simple and obvious—like "just get a sitter and go back to work if you're not happy"—and I don't know how to make him see that it's so much more complicated than that.

_____

_____

_____

_____

_____

Brenda: I'm embarrassed to cry like this. I told myself I wouldn't cry today, and here I am blubbering like a big baby. That's what happened in the doctor's office, which is why I think he thought I needed help. I'm really a pretty together person, with a good head on my shoulders, and a good life, but you'd never know it to look at me now.

_____

_____

_____

_____

_____

Exercise 3: Thought questions related to Brenda

A. Consider who you are as an interviewer and write down what you think might be most difficult about establishing rapport with Brenda based on your age, ethnicity, gender, socio-economic status, sexual orientation, religion, physical characteristics, and personality style. What specifically might happen?

_____

_____

_____

_____

_____

B. Is there anything you could do to enhance your ability to establish an effective working relationship with Brenda? What specifically might you do?

_____

_____

_____

C. One of the challenges an interviewer faces with a client like Brenda is deciding how much of what she is experiencing can be considered normal given her current circumstances and how much it reflects a disorder such as depression. In what ways is Brenda's experience normal for a mother of young children and in what ways does it reflect depression?

_____

_____

_____

_____

_____

_____

D. What information would you need to collect to make a choice between these two possi-bilities. Be specific in identifying what factors you would need to weigh.

_____

_____

_____

_____

_____

E. In what ways do you think Bob's and Brenda's ideas about gender roles may be contrib-uting to the difficulties Brenda and her children are experiencing?

_____

_____

_____

_____

_____

F. How might your own gender role socialization and ideas about gender roles influence your ability to establish rapport with Brenda (and/or Bob, if he later decides to participate in her treatment)?

_____

_____

_____

_____

_____

_____

G. The pediatrician recommended that Brenda consider antidepressant medication. Brenda is reluctant to do so because she is breast-feeding her son. Do you think Brenda should be referred for medication? Discuss specifically why or why not, and what you might say to Brenda about this issue.

_____

_____

_____

_____

_____

Case of Aaron

1. What are your basic statistics?

Your name is Aaron and you are a twenty-five-year-old, African-American male. You are single and currently live with your mother in a large urban city. You have no siblings and haven't had contact with your father since you were very young. You are a high school graduate receiving disability benefits due to your history of psychological problems. You are being interviewed within an inpatient setting. You are requesting a voluntary admission.

2. How do you behave in the interview?

You are of average intelligence and you understand the questions asked of you if they are concrete and specific. You become very confused about what to say in response to abstract questions. For example, if asked what you like to do, you become confused. If asked what music you like to listen to, you easily list out titles of your favorite songs. You are very passive and never initiate conversation during the interview but you attempt to answer any questions from the interviewer. You always speak slowly, and your responses are vague and tangential to the question you are answering. You don't like to look people in the eye because it makes you feel uncomfortable. You prefer to look down in your lap or at the ground when you are talking. You don't think much about yourself and how you live. You are poorly groomed and you don't bathe often. As a result, your skin is itchy and you frequently scratch yourself. If asked why you are scratching, you are vague and say things like, "Everyone scratches, you have to scratch."

If the interviewer asks you about your voices in a way you consider disrespectful, you get angry about being questioned. However, you calm down quickly if the interviewer makes any attempt to soothe you. If asked, you admit to hearing voices during the interview. Your voices tell you that you have to protect yourself from evil people and that maybe the interviewer is evil. You are very unclear about whether you will need to behave violently to protect yourself. However, if the interviewer makes empathetic or supportive statements, you respond positively by saying things like, "You're nice like my mom."

If asked, you admit to using cocaine and marijuana on a daily basis. You also drink beer but not as frequently. The last time you had a drink was two days ago. You do not recall how much you drank. You deny any feelings of depression or any thoughts of suicide if the interviewer asks about these issues. You admit to feeling anxious when you are outside of your home because people spy on you. You admit to having anxiety attacks when you are outside, and you respond to these by running home and hiding in your room. You then listen to music and the anxiety goes away. You deny you ever have violent thoughts but admit that your voices do suggest a lot of violent things.

3. Why are you being interviewed?

Your mother suggested that you make an appointment for this interview, and you brought yourself down to your local community hospital to request admission out of respect for her wishes. If the interviewer asks you what you hope to gain from the appointment, you say that you want to please your mother. If asked why your mom wanted you to come, you say that your mom is afraid of you. She became afraid of you about two weeks ago when you told her you had thoughts of killing her because the voices felt she had become evil.

If asked, you admit that you have sought help on many past occasions. You remember that your past diagnoses were of schizophrenia, paranoid schizophrenia, and antisocial personality disorder; these labels don't mean anything to you.

4. How do you feel?

You never spontaneously mention having feelings. You sound emotionally blunted during the interview process, but you admit to having feelings if asked specifically about them. For example, if asked how you feel when you are around other people, say you often feel first anxious and then scared even if you have known the people for quite a long time. These bad feelings go away as long as you get away from people. You do not feel anxious when you are alone. You feel most relaxed when you are home alone in your room. You spend most of your time each day alone. You don't feel lonely; the voices always provide you with any companionship or reassurance that you need. You may fidget a lot when you say this. If the interviewer notices this and asks if you are anxious, you say no unless the interviewer has been very supportive.

If asked, deny any depression or suicidal ideation. You don't ever remember feeling sad and discontented with your life. You also deny any symptoms of mania. If asked about anger, say you do feel very angry now, but you aren't sure where the anger is coming from. If asked, admit that you are currently hearing voices that are telling you that your mother is out to get you. Openly say that the voices used to like your mother but now they don't, and they are sure that in some way, your mother is going to harm you. You don't have any specific ideas about how she would harm you. If asked, you deny that your mother has ever abused you, and you indicate that she has always taken good care of you in the past. You love your mother and you are sure she loves you. If asked further questions, you express ambivalence about whether the voices are right and your mother has become evil or whether the voices are wrong and you should argue with them. On the one hand, you indicate that your voices have always been your friends and they have always given you good advice in the past. These voices now say you have to physically assault your mother in order to protect yourself. On the other hand, you haven't seen any evidence that your mom has become evil. She is still leaving you in peace in your room. She is still making your favorite foods and noticing if you look healthy or sick. You should express these ideas in a blunted voice and never make it clear whether you are an imminent risk to your mother or not.

5. How do you think?

You should show signs of loose association, tangential thinking, and thought blocking when you respond to questions. You frequently ask questions about the questions the interviewer is asking you. You ask these questions in a suspicious manner. Look intently at the interviewer when your questions are answered. Then, while still seeming guarded, answer the questions honestly. If you feel too pushed by the interviewer, experience thought blocking.

Your thinking has changed recently because the messages of your voices have changed. Instead of being helpful messages, they are disturbing. They are calling your mother a devil and telling you that you must hurt her before she hurts you. If asked, admit that you have had violent thoughts about your mother. You have thought about how you could beat her up so that she would be too hurt to do anything to you. Sound very conflicted as you describe this, as you are very ambivalent. You have a strong urge to listen to the voices but an equally strong sense that it would be very wrong to hurt your mother or anybody else. You are interested in the interviewer's opinion about what you should do. You think everyone has voices like you do.

If asked, admit to some paranoid ideas about the people in your neighborhood. Mention that when you go out, you feel as if people are watching you from behind the curtains of their windows. Say that you often rush down the street because you feel that, otherwise, people will follow you and try to do you harm. You don't have any specific ideas about why they would harm you or follow you. If directly asked, look down but admit that you wonder if the interviewer will help you with your mother or be out to get you. Your initial reaction to some of the interviewer's questions is that the interviewer is hostile toward you; however, be reassured by anything the interviewer says to indicate you are safe in the interview situation.

6. What do you like about yourself?

You get confused if asked what you like about yourself. You stare off into space and are quiet. If gently probed by the interviewer, you say you like your mother and you like your music.

7. How have you been doing at work?

You are currently unemployed and receiving social security disability benefits. Your prior work experience was in the construction industry. You never did very well at work because the other men on the job would always be out to get you. Sometimes, you had to fight with them to get them to stop staring at you. Once, you beat a man so badly that you were sent to jail for a year. This was a bad time for you because you couldn't get away from people. You couldn't get any cocaine or beer when you were in jail, and so you had nothing familiar to help you with the stress. You were forced to take pills by the guards for the whole year you were in jail. The voices were so angry that you were taking pills that they abandoned you. They forgave you once you went home and threw the pills away. If you are asked what you mean by "forgave you," you say that they started advising you again about your life. After this prison experience, your mother submitted forms about you and you had to take a test, but since then, you have received money from disability benefits and don't have to work anymore.

8. How did you do in school?

You never had trouble keeping up with work at high school and maintained a "C" average throughout. You remember being evaluated in junior high school because your teachers had some concerns about you, but you don't know what these concerns were. You remember that your mom went to a number of meetings at the school. You had asked her what these were about, and she said that the school had wondered if you had a learning problem but that your test scores were just fine; you didn't have a learning disability and you didn't need any special services. If asked, you say that school had been okay. If asked about your relationship with peers, say you had no friends. If pressed for more information, say that the other kids teased you a lot. They called you "zombie" and "weirdo." This is where the voices helped you so much. You could listen to them and not hear the other kids. These voices have always been your friends and given you comfort when you were stressed. The voices said you are a very important person and that drugs and drinking alcohol enhance your power; you have found this to be true. You had tried drugs for the first time the weekend the voices became your friends. You remember that you enjoyed the drug experience, but you don't remember any details about it. You didn't have a lot of money and might not have taken the stuff that was offered to you except the voices really encouraged you to do so. It was easy for you to continue to get drugs and alcohol from the sellers who hung out near the school and at other corners near your home; these guys also encouraged you to keep trying new stuff. The drugs really have helped you lots of times. If asked for a specific example, say that at the very end of your junior year of high school you were supposed to pick out your courses for your senior year. You were finding making these decisions very difficult. The voices reminded you that drugs had always helped, so you went out and bought some cocaine. You found that taking cocaine did increase your power and that you had no trouble deciding what courses you wanted to take. The voices praised your course decisions and encouraged you to keep using drugs. You found that high school became a lot less stressful when you came to school high. When high, nothing seemed hard anymore.

9. How is your health?

You deny having any physical complaints. You sleep an average of nine hours at a time; however, you tend to sleep during the day rather than at night. You eat the three meals a day that your mother cooks for you, but you say that the drugs make you so powerful that you often don't feel the need for food.

If asked, you state that you have been put on a number of medications in the past. You won't remember what they were, but you could describe them as pills that made you drowsy. You also indicate that the voices didn't like you when you were on the pills. The voices wouldn't talk to you. So, you would always take the pills for a few days to please your mom, but after maybe a week, you would stop taking them so the voices would forgive you.

10. How do you relate to others?

You are a quiet person who prefers to be alone. Your mom is the only person who ever understood this. She lets you stay in your room as long as you want. The only time she encourages you to leave your room is on Sundays. She always wants you to go to church with her. In the past, you didn't mind going to church too much because people didn't talk to you; they just listened to the Reverend. There was a lot of music at church, and you always liked to listen to music. After the service, mom would always take you straight back home and let you eat in your room. Recently, you have become uncomfortable at church because the Reverend keeps coming up to you to talk. You don't want to talk to him, but you don't want to be rude. You think your mom asked the Reverend to talk to you about drugs and alcohol. You think that the Reverend stares at you to try and make the voices go away. Because of this, you have recently started refusing to go to church even though it makes your mom sad. When you talk to your mom, it is mostly about things that you like to eat or if she asks, you may tell her what you listened to on the radio. Until recently, you have always felt comfortable with your mom. Now, things are spooky because you don't know what to do about her. She has been looking at your strangely in the last few weeks. The voices tell you she is planning something bad and she has to be stopped. You are worried that the voices will leave if you don't do what they tell you to.

You don't have many memories of your dad. You remember that he used to hit and kick your mom a lot. This would make your mom cry. You would hide under your bed when the fighting started. The next time you saw your mom, she would be covered with bruises and she would have trouble taking care of you for a while. You did your best to stay away from your dad.

You are suspicious of your neighbors. You want them to stop staring at you and leave you alone. Your mother has told you not to worry about the neighbors, but the voices disagree with her. The voices think the neighbors are jealous of your power. The drug dealers are the only neighbors you feel comfortable with. They don't try to talk to you at all. When you approach, you only have to hand them money to get the drugs you want.

11. How do you view your life?

You are confused and discontented right now. You feel torn between your mom and your voices. Whenever you had a problem in the past, it was the voices that helped you. But now, the voices are actually causing problems for you.

EXERCISES FOR THE INTERVIEWER

Exercise 1: Develop a diagnosis for Aaron

A. What criteria does Aaron meet for a diagnosis of Schizophrenia and/or Substance-Related Disorders?

_____

_____

_____

_____

Name at least two other Axis I diagnoses that you might want to rule out for Aaron and indicate what additional information might be needed to differentiate between the diagnostic choices for him.

_____

_____

_____

_____

Does Aaron meet all the criteria for an Axis I disorder? Should the diagnosis be deferred, or is a diagnosis not needed?

_____

_____

_____

_____

B. What criteria does Aaron meet for an Axis II diagnosis (Personality Disorders and Mental Retardation)? Should a diagnosis be deferred, or is a diagnosis not needed? Explain, being as specific as possible.

_____

_____

_____

_____

C. Is there anything you might report for Aaron on Axis III (General Medical Conditions that are potentially relevant to the client's mental disorder)?

_____

_____

_____

D. List all specific psychosocial and environmental problems that are influencing Aaron at this time for Axis IV. Indicate if each stressor is mild, moderate, or severe.

_____

_____

_____

E. What is your global assessment of Aaron's functioning for Axis V (current and highest in past year)?

_____

_____

_____

_____

F. Double-check your diagnostic choices starting at Axis V and proceeding backward through Axis I to determine if you may have overestimated or underestimated the impact of the situational, biological, or individual psychological factors on Aaron's current functioning. Should you change anything? Be specific in describing why or why not.

_____

_____

_____

_____

G. Review your diagnostic choices again from Aaron's point of view. Do your choices support the discussions you have had with him? Would he be disturbed by your choices? Be specific in discussing why or why not.

_____

_____

_____

_____

Exercise 2: Practice deepening the interview with Aaron

A. How might your nonverbal attending behavior unintentionally change as Aaron begins to tell you of his voices, and how might he react to this? Behaviors to consider include eye contact, orientation of body, posture, facial expression, and autonomic behavior.

_____

_____

_____

_____

What might you need to do, in terms of nonverbal attending behavior, to insure that Aaron feels listened to and respected even if his experiences are unusual or problematic?

_____

_____

_____

_____

B. Write a series of open-ended and closed questions to assess Aaron's voices using the following prompts as a guide. Include questions that might help to clarify whether hearing the voices is dependent or independent of alcohol and/or drug use. An example is provided of one open-ended question and one closed question in response to the first prompt.

Prompt 1: Perceived source of voices

When you hear the voices, where do they seem to be coming from? Do the voices come after
you drink?

Prompt 2: Quality/characteristics of the voices (intensity, duration, clarity)

_____

_____

Prompt 3: Frequency of voices

_____

_____

Prompt 4: Aaron's reactions to the voices

_____

_____

Prompt 5: Predictability of voices

_____

_____

Prompt 6: Content of voices (directives, questions, level of dangerousness)

_____

_____

Prompt 7: Level of control Aaron has over the voices

_____

_____

C. Aaron is confused and upset about his current relationship with his voices. After he expresses his thoughts to you, write two types of comments. Have the first be a simple, reflective listening comment and the second be a more complex empathetic comment to either validate his experience or let him know you understand what he is experiencing. Use information from Aaron's profile to guide you in developing your empathetic comments. Be careful not to support the validity of his voices in your statements. An example is provided.

Aaron: They say I have to hurt my mom but I don't want to.

1. *You don't want to hurt her (reflective listening).*

2. *The voices tell you to hurt your mom but you don't want to. I can understand*
   your feelings. I wouldn't want to harm my mom either (empathetic comment).

Aaron: They will leave me if I make them mad and then I will be all alone.

1. _____

   _____

2. _____

   _____

Aaron: If I hit her she will cry, but my voices say she is evil.

1. _____

   _____

2. _____

   _____

Exercise 3: Thought questions related to Aaron

A. Consider who you are as an interviewer and write down what you think might be most difficult about establishing rapport with Aaron based on your age, ethnicity, gender, socioeconomic status, sexual orientation, religion, physical characteristics, age, and personality style. What specifically might happen?

_____

_____

_____

_____

B. Is there anything you could do to enhance your ability to establish an effective working relationship with Aaron? Be specific and detailed in describing your ideas.

_____

_____

_____

_____

C. What might you say if Aaron asks you if you think he is crazy?

_____

_____

_____

_____

D. What might you say if Aaron asks you if you hear or see his voices?

_____

_____

_____

_____

E. What might you say to Aaron if he asks you if you think drugs are good for him? Remember that he stopped going to church because he suspected his Reverend would condemn his drug use.

_____

_____

_____

_____

Case of Mary

1. What are your basic statistics?

Your name is Mary and you are a fifty-eight-year-old, European-American woman. Your husband died in a car accident about one year ago coming home from work during a bad storm. You had been married for thirty-two years. You and your husband had three children. They are now all married. Two of your children, Beverly and Jason, live in distant cities but Cynthia lives with her family about twenty minutes from you. You are the manager of a midsized department store and live alone in an apartment near the store. You have come for help to a practitioner who is in private practice.

2. How do you behave in the interview?

You are well groomed, intelligent, verbal, highly analytical, and introspective. You can easily explore your thoughts, but you struggle more in considering your feelings as you tend to function very much as a thinker. You respond openly and articulately to all general questions about your life. You feel comfortable with eye contact and don't hesitate to question the interviewer if you don't understand what you are being asked to do. You ask questions, not in a challenging manner, but rather to gain clarification so that you can respond appropriately. You very much want to behave appropriately in all circumstances, and you get uncomfortable when you don't know what people want from you.

When asked about the symptoms that brought you in for treatment, you are hesitant and respond tentatively. You begin responding without hesitation to any questions that are asked of you, but then pause and turn inward as you struggle to respond clearly. Your ideas flow logically, and there are no signs of cognitive confusion, unusual thoughts, or delusional thinking despite the fact that you feel unsure how to respond.

If asked mental status screening questions, you admit to some depression and anxiety but you deny any suicidal ideation. If pressed on the suicide issue, you say honestly that you consider suicide an illogical course of action. You deny any use of illegal substances and admit only to highly infrequent uses of alcohol. You drink one glass of wine at occasions such as weddings and anniversaries. If asked further questions about alcohol, you say you don't approve of people who drink too much.

3. Why are you being interviewed?

You referred yourself for treatment at the insistence of your daughter Cynthia. She came to your apartment last week without prior warning. She found you in a dirty bathrobe staring off into space. As you are usually a very vital person, who is always impeccably groomed, your daughter was seriously disturbed by this situation. Your daughter sat next to you and refused to leave until you made the phone call requesting this appointment. You are annoyed that Cynthia is interfering in your life, and you feel that her actions were condescending and unnecessary. On the other hand, you do admit that you have been unusually down recently and that it has affected your work. You have been feeling generally unfocused for the last few months. You are struggling to make simple decisions such as what to wear to work. You are having difficulty making schedules for yourself. You have lost your appetite and have been having trouble sleeping. It may take you more than an hour for you to finally fall asleep and then you wake up at 4:00 a.m. and are unable to go back to sleep. These sleep difficulties began right after your husband's accident. At that time, you were having episodic difficulties going to sleep, but most of the time you did not have any difficulties. In the last three weeks, you have had problems every single night and have become very sleep deprived.

If asked what you think you will get from therapy, say you expect that you will get help logically evaluating what has gone wrong and what you need to do differently. You have not been in treatment before and if asked how you are currently feeling, state you are embarrassed to be here.

4. How do you feel?

You indicate that you have felt very anxious in the last three weeks because you did not go to church on the anniversary of your husband's death. It was unusual that you did not attend because you have always attended church regularly, and your Protestant faith has been an important source of guidance in your life. The service you missed was special because it was in honor of your late husband and all of your children had come from out of town to attend it. They went to church ahead of you to help with the arrangements. They waited three hours for you to show up, but you never did. You spent most of this time at your local hospital, but you didn't tell them this. They made frequent calls to your house and left phone messages that you intentionally ignored once you got home from the hospital. When they came back to your house, you lied to them and said that your car broke down on the way to the church and you had to be towed to a garage. If asked about this, you twist your hands and say you feel very guilty for lying to them and admit that you told your children that you had not brought the church phone number with you so it was impossible for you to call them from the garage to tell them what had happened.

In fact, half an hour before you were supposed to leave for church, you felt an overwhelming sense of doom. You took a walk to try and calm yourself down. This has been a standard practice of yours for years, and it usually has been quite effective in calming yourself down when you are upset. On this instance, however, it did not work. Rather, halfway around the park, your heart began to hammer so loudly you were sure others could hear it. You felt like you could barely breathe and you broke out into a sweat. A neighbor, who was out jogging, noticed your difficulties and drove you to the emergency room afraid that you were having a heart attack. You had a complete medical screen and all the tests came back negative. The doctor told you that you had probably had a panic attack. Rather than being relieved to hear this, you felt tremendously embarrassed to have gone to the emergency room for no good reason. You apologized repeatedly to the doctor for wasting his time.

You have told no one, including your neighbor, about the results of your evaluation. If probed about this, you express a lot of anger toward yourself for what you consider "your foolishness." You don't know what came over you. You don't deny that it was an anxiety attack, but its cause is a mystery to you. If the interviewer helps you, you are then able to reflect on this experience and slowly come to the conclusion that the attack was related to your painful memories of your husband's death. If asked how you adjusted to his death, you say that you were very distressed at first but that you were back at work after a week and doing everything you were supposed to do. You feel that you have adjusted well to the loss, given your circumstances. You believe your faith guides you to be in control of your emotions and accept God's will and be stoic about your loss.

If asked many questions about your husband, you become tearful and overwhelmed by emotional pain. You respond to empathetic remarks from the interviewer by revealing more details about your husband's accident and how it affected you. The accident occurred when your husband was rushing home, during bad weather, to be present at the baptism of a grandchild. You didn't do anything to encourage him to drive in bad weather but feel that he knew how much you wanted him to be home and that this probably led him to his driving too aggressively. You admit to having suffered intense loneliness and misery since his death. Whereas you have continued to work and function well as a manager, your personal life has become empty. As the anniversary of the death has approached, your feeling of being lost has deepened. You have been able to get to work, but you spend a lot of time sitting at your desk and feeling like you are in a fog. When you are at home, you have almost completely stopped doing housework because you feel there is no point anymore in caring for the house now that he and your children are gone.

5. How do you think?

If asked about your thoughts, you say that in the past you have prided yourself on your logic and your ability to solve problems. Everyone in your family, including your husband, always depended on what they call your common sense and good judgment. You actively analyze any problem and always come up with a highly organized plan of action to solve it.

At this time, however, you really can't think. You are having trouble figuring out how to get "back on track." This makes you angry because you feel that you should be able to handle this current situation logically. You should have been able to calm yourself down and get to the church. You should have stood by your children. You let everyone down by not showing up. You see your anxiety attack as completely irrational. If asked why you think you had the attack that day, you get flustered and indicate that you don't understand why you just can't get on with your life as it has been so long since your husband died.

You are a firm believer in taking action to solve all problems. So, if asked what you want from therapy, you say that coming in for this session is a good idea because you didn't make it to the church, and this is a problem that should be looked into and fixed.

6. What do you like about yourself?

You like how dependable you are and how easily you can shift focus from one task to another and get everything done well. You also think it is good that other people come to you when they need help. If asked why this is something you like about yourself, say you like knowing that you are someone everyone can depend on.

7. How have you been doing at work?

You worked for years in low status jobs to work your way up to being a manager. You are very proud of the skills you have developed, and you enjoy the opportunity to push yourself and see just how well you can make your store function. You also believe that working hard and being successful means you are living a well-spent life. Thus, you are never satisfied with your performance as a manager. You always feel that there is something to be discovered that can make things better. You are very proud that each year you have received a high merit bonus because the owner of the store appreciates your work. You say that the store is doing well, but you are still sure things could go even better.

8. How have you been doing in school?

This question is not applicable to this client.

9. How is your health?

You are in good health. Your recent screen at the emergency room showed your heart and lung functions to be excellent. You have begun to show some signs of osteoarthritis which was troubling for a while, but you are now on a twice daily medication that keeps your discomfort under control. You don't have any troubling side effects from the medication. The emergency room physician gave you a prescription for Xanax that you had filled but have not taken.

You get a full physical every two years as dictated by company policy. You don't really feel it is necessary, but you can see the logic behind the policy. You haven't decided what you will say the next time you see the internist because this doctor will have gotten a report from the emergency room and the whole episode is still very embarrassing for you to think about.

10. How do you relate to others?

Everyone in your personal and professional life sees you as a resource. You have always been dependable, reliable, and helpful. Your children learned good skills from you and usually solve their problems themselves. However, they have confidence that, when they need you, you will always be there. Each of your three children has told you how shocked they were when you didn't come to the church. They were terrified you had been in an accident like their father.

You have always had a very calm and friendly manner of relating to people at work that has made your employees have confidence in your decisions. You have shown concern for your employees' lives without being intrusive. This has led many of them to confide their life problems to you. You see them as your responsibility and feel that happy home lives make happy and productive employees. You do not express any direct resentment that so many people are leaning on you for their social support. However, if asked, you express some feelings of being overwhelmed with trying to work through your husband's death while so many people were making demands on you. Your employees did try to help you by sending flowers and food. But, you feel it is inappropriate for a manager to lean on her employees. You have put up a good front for them so that they believe you have adjusted well to the loss.

You and your husband used to socialize regularly with several other couples. Typically you played card games together and had dinner parties. You avoid these couples now. You feel out of place as the only single in the group. Immediately after the death, the wives called you regularly to chat and dropped by with food. However, you never called them, and their calls slowed up and then finally stopped. You feel that this phase of your life is over.

11. How do you view your life?

You are currently very motivated to change because you are quite puzzled by your current difficulties. You "shouldn't" be feeling down or anxious as "nothing" is really wrong at this time. You are willing to follow all the directives of the interviewer. You view your work as being the highlight of your life at this time. You believe that you are at the time of life when intimate relationships are best left for younger people. Thus, you have no plans to reach out to form any new relationships with a man.

EXERCISES FOR THE INTERVIEWER

Exercise 1: Develop a diagnosis for Mary

A. What criteria does Mary meet for an Axis I diagnosis of Major Depressive Disorder and/or Bereavement?

_____

_____

_____

_____

Name two other Axis I diagnoses that you might want to rule out for Mary and indicate what additional information might be needed to differentiate between the diagnostic choices for her.

_____

_____

_____

_____

Does Mary meet all the criteria for an Axis I disorder? Should the diagnosis be deferred, or is a diagnosis not needed?

_____

_____

_____

_____

B. What criteria does Mary meet for an Axis II diagnosis (Personality Disorders and Mental Retardation)? Should a diagnosis be deferred, or is a diagnosis not needed? Explain and be as specific as possible.

_____

_____

_____

_____

C. Is there anything you might report for Mary on Axis III (General Medical Conditions that are potentially relevant to the client's mental disorder)?

_____

_____

_____

_____

D. List all specific psychosocial and environmental stressors that are influencing Mary at this time for Axis IV. Indicate if each stressor is mild, moderate, or severe.

_____

_____

_____

_____

E. What is your global assessment of Mary on Axis V (current and highest in past year)?

_____

_____

_____

_____

F. Double-check your diagnostic choices starting at Axis V and proceeding backward through Axis I to determine if you may have overestimated or underestimated the impact of the situational, biological, or individual psychological factors on Mary's current functioning. Should you change anything? Be specific in describing why or why not.

_____

_____

_____

_____

G. Review your diagnostic choices again from Mary's point of view. Do your choices support the discussions you have had with her? Would she be disturbed by your choices? Be specific in discussing why or why not.

_____

_____

_____

Exercise 2: Practice deepening interview with Mary

A. What might you do, nonverbally, as you listen to Mary to let her know that you are attending closely to what she is experiencing? Behaviors to consider include eye contact, orientation of your body, posture, facial expression, and autonomic behavior.

_____

_____

_____

B. Mary tends to make comments that are too general for you to understand her situation. In response to the following comments from her, write an open-ended, follow-up question to probe more deeply into her experience.

Mary: Things are better than they were the first year after my husband died.

_____

_____

Mary: My daughter was surprised by how I looked and by the state of my apartment.

_____

_____

Mary: My health has been okay I guess.

_____

_____

Mary: My employees trust me.

_____

_____

C. Mary has many feelings bottled up inside of her that need to be expressed and understood. In response to her remarks, write two types of comments. Have the first be a simple, reflective listening comment and the second be a more complex, empathetic comment to either validate her experience or let her know you understand what she is experiencing. If Mary is expressing more than one feeling, or is ambivalent about a situation, make sure you make comments that take this into account. Use information from Mary's profile to guide you. An example is provided.

Mary: Why does my daughter interfere so much in my life? I am so tired of her condescending attitude.

1. *You find her behavior condescending (reflective listening).*
2. *You are an adult and I can understand why you wouldn't appreciate your daughter telling you what to do. It feels disrespectful (empathetic comment).*

Mary: I don't want to be here in therapy asking for help. I am a strong person.

1. _____
2. _____

_____

Mary: I reach out to my employees when they are in distress and so they really trust me. I am proud of that, but sometimes it is too much.

1. _____
2. _____

_____

D. Assume that Mary has hinted about suicidal ideation. Develop a series of open-ended and closed questions to assess her risk for suicide using each of the following prompts as a guide. An example is provided of one open-ended question and two closed questions for prompt 1.

Prompt 1: Level/amount of current psychological pain

How would you describe your feelings of pain over your husband's death? Have you ever felt so

bad that you didn't feel you could go on? On a scale of 1 to 10, how would you rate your pain

right now?

Prompt 2: Level/amount of current life stress

_____

_____

_____

Prompt 3: Existence of suicide plan

_____

_____

_____

Prompt 4: Ability to carry out suicidal plan

_____

_____

_____

Prompt 5: Use of substances that increase impulsivity

_____

_____

_____

Prompt 6: Reasons for wanting to die

_____

_____

_____

Prompt 7: Reasons for living and quality of current support system (family, friends, work, religion)

_____

_____

_____

Prompt 8: Past attempts

_____

_____

_____

Prompt 9: Friends or relatives who have attempted suicide

_____

_____

_____

Exercise 3: Thought questions related to Mary

A. Consider who you are as an interviewer and write down what you think might be most difficult for you in establishing rapport with Mary based on your age, ethnicity, gender, socioeconomic status, sexual orientation, religion, physical characteristics, age, and personality style. What specifically might happen?

_____

_____

_____

_____

_____

B. Is there anything you could do to enhance your ability to establish an effective working relationship with Mary? Be specific and detailed in describing your ideas.

_____

_____

_____

_____

_____

C. Assume that Mary lost a lesbian partner instead of a husband. How might this change your reaction to her?

_____

_____

_____

_____

_____

D. What will you say to Mary if you believe she is at serious risk for suicide?

_____

_____

_____

_____

_____

E. How might Mary's Protestant work ethic and cultural desire to always control her emotions be influencing her ability to grieve for her husband?

_____

_____

_____

_____

Case of Mark

1. What are your basic statistics?

Your name is Mark and you are an eighteen-year-old European-American male. You are a freshman in college, majoring in business. You currently live in a dorm with a roommate you knew from high school. The two of you have discussed getting an apartment off campus next year. Your parents live in a town about an hour's drive from here. Your father works as a car salesman, and your mother works as a bank clerk. You have two older brothers. One is married and lives in another state. The other is a senior in the same college you attend. You also have a younger sister, age fifteen, who lives at home. You are being interviewed at your college's counseling center.

2. How do you behave in the interview?

You are casually but neatly dressed and well groomed. You sit leaning forward in your chair, with your elbows resting on your knees. You make good eye contact with the interviewer and want to be perceived as friendly, open, and cooperative. You are intelligent, but not very introspective. You answer factual questions about your family, major, living situation, and future plans fairly easily, but hesitate when asked questions about your feelings or inner experience.

When asked about what brought you to the interview, you describe your problem as if it was something external to you, a puzzling anomaly, something that happens to other people and which you should be able to figure out and resolve quickly. You drum your fingers on your knees, jiggle your legs, or otherwise exhibit physically your impatience to "get this over with." You are used to dealing with challenges in a straightforward, concrete way, and you like thinking of yourself as independent and self-sufficient. Your attitude toward the interviewer is one of ambivalence: You need help to "put this thing behind you," but you are embarrassed to be asking for help at all and worried that the interviewer may perceive you as weak, vulnerable, or inadequate in some way.

If asked mental status questions, your discomfort increases, because you are afraid that a "wrong answer" may cause the interviewer to form a negative impression of you. If asked about unusual thoughts or suicidal ideation, for example, you deny these adamantly, insisting that you are "not crazy." You admit to some sleep difficulties, which you attribute to nightmares you have been having. You also admit to some irritability and difficulty concentrating at times. You say that this is probably due to not sleeping well, but admit that this is a change for you because you were always a pretty happy, easygoing person before. You deny being depressed or anxious, although you admit that you worry about things more than you did in high school. For example, you call home to check on your younger sister because you often find yourself thinking that "something bad might happen to her," although you are not sure why this worries you. If asked about drugs and alcohol, you deny any problems in this area. If pressed, you admit that you had a "pretty active" social life in high school, which included a good bit of drinking and partying. Although you tried the party scene when you first came to college, somehow it didn't seem as much fun as it used to be. In fact, you find that you feel "uptight" instead of relaxed in these situations, which seems strange to you. You admit that you have a drink "once in a while" to relax, especially when you have trouble sleeping, but deny drinking to get drunk or to the point where it interferes with classes or studying.

3. Why are you being interviewed?

You are here because you are having trouble "getting over" an incident that took place last summer, shortly after graduation from high school. You were asked to participate as a groomsman in the wedding of a good friend. The Friday night before the wedding, you and several of your friends who were also in the wedding, including the groom, were driving to a restaurant for an impromptu bachelor party. A drunk driver hit your car head-on. The two friends in the front seat (one of whom was the groom-to-be) were killed. You and the two in the back seat were taken to the hospital. You woke up in the hospital with no memory of what had happened and had to find out from your parents that you had lost two friends and might lose another. You recovered and were discharged from the hospital a week later, but one of your two friends is still in a coma and the other lost an arm.

You explain that you spent a lot of time shortly after the accident replaying the events of that evening and wondering if you could have done anything to prevent the accident. There was some discussion about whether to go out that night at all, and you pushed for the outing because you argued that it was your last chance to go out and have a good time together as a bunch of single guys. Although no one is blaming you for this, you did spend a lot of time imagining how things might have been different if you hadn't pushed for the outing. You also remember wondering why you ended up with the safest seat in the car, the middle of the back seat.

You would like to be able to put this event behind you, but you continue to have nightmares about it. In these dreams, it is as if you are reliving the event, and you know what is going to happen but are unable to prevent it. You wake up sweating and with your heart pounding, and it sometimes takes an hour or two to go back to sleep. You secretly wonder if this is normal, and you're hoping that the interviewer will be able to reassure you about this. You hesitate to express this directly because it means admitting that you are worried about it, and you don't want to appear that vulnerable.

4. How do you feel?

You feel guilty about the fact that you survived the accident in better shape than any of your friends. You also feel guilty about having encouraged them to go out that evening, even though no one is blaming you for this. You also feel worried about whether you will ever get your old "happy-go-lucky" self back again. You don't enjoy life the way you did in high school, and you find you worry a lot more about bad things happening to people you care about. In high school, you felt invincible and never understood your parents getting on your back about the times you defied curfews or neglected to tell them where you were or when you would be home. You thought they were just overprotective. Now you find you worry about your younger sister in the same way. You feel compelled to call home and find out where she is and whether your parents are supervising her comings and goings closely enough. These feelings seem to peak on Friday and Saturday nights, and you don't feel reassured unless you call on Sunday and find out that she is home and nothing bad has happened to her. This seems silly to you, but you can't seem to shake it. Even your roommate has noticed and complained that you seem really edgy on weekends. You generally get along well, but you have snapped at him about something minor almost every weekend. He used to try to get you to go out and party with him to "de-stress," but now he just avoids you when you are irritable.

5. How do you think?

You are more of a "doer" than a "thinker." You like your business classes because they present you with problems you can solve in a straightforward fashion. You have always been able to size up a situation, determine a strategy for achieving the goal, and carry it out. You played a lot of sports in high school, and this approach worked well in that arena. You got by with B's and C's in high school because you were good at figuring out how to do just enough to get by, so you could put your energy into the extracurricular activities and socializing you preferred. You're actually doing better in college than you did in high school because you can visualize the concrete goal of getting a job with a large firm and being able to travel and live in different parts of the country after graduation. Unfortunately, the problem of your nightmares and anxious and irritable feelings is not something that responds to your usual style of problem solving. You don't know what to do about feelings that come over you without a clearly defined cause or solution. After all, you can't go back and change the past. You'd like to move on and leave the past behind you, but the past seems determined to haunt you. Although you do well during the weekdays as long as you concentrate on your classes, you don't know how to deal with nightmares that attack you when you are sleeping or feelings that seem silly but can't be shaken when the weekend rolls around again. It does not seem logical to you that these nightmares and feelings still persist, and you don't have any idea how to get a handle on them.

You are hoping that the interviewer will take a role similar to that of your coaches in high school, giving you tips on how to be stronger and pointing you toward the skills you need to solve your current problem. You are afraid the interviewer will be more like a doctor, focusing on what's wrong with you, giving you some scary diagnosis, or telling you that you need medication.

6. What do you like about yourself?

You like your ability to get along with others and make a good impression on people. You have always liked your ability to solve problems and meet challenges head on, although you are stumped when it comes to deciding how to solve the current challenge of your troubling feelings. You like your athletic ability, although you haven't been as active lately and haven't felt the same enjoyment either participating or observing sports as you did in high school.

7. How have you been doing at work?

This question is not relevant for this client.

8. How have you been doing in school?

You have been getting A's and B's in your classes. Your grades in your business classes tend to be A's, whereas some of your general requirements courses are B's. You find it is easier to concentrate in the business classes, which seem more practical and challenge you with solvable problems. In some of your general classes, you find it harder to concentrate. However, you have been able to keep up with the work so far, and you are satisfied with your grades. Your least favorite class is your introductory class in psychology. You have been studying psychological disorders lately, and you have been uncomfortable with this because you secretly fear finding out that there is something really wrong with you. You do not share this with the interviewer unless he or she makes you feel really comfortable, but instead say that you just don't find it relevant to what you want to do in life.

9. How is your health?

You are in good health. You didn't have any lasting effects from the accident last summer and have always been fairly active and physically fit. You don't have any complaints about appetite, although you have admitted not sleeping well because of the nightmares. You are not under the care of a physician for anything currently, and you are not taking any medications. You have wondered about the way your heart races when you wake from one of your nightmares, but have not consulted a physician about this.

10. How do you relate to others?

You have always had a lot of friends and gotten along well with others. You were active in sports in high school and popular with your classmates. It was an easy decision to choose your roommate, who was one of your buddies in high school (but not a member of the wedding party in the accident last summer). You get along well, except for the times when you are feeling edgy and every little thing he does seems to annoy you. For example, last weekend he came in drunk at 3:00 a.m. and tripped over a chair in the dark. The noise woke you up and you got really mad and chewed him out. You realized in retrospect that your reaction was really out of proportion, because you hadn't been in bed that long yourself and he wasn't deliberately trying to disturb you. But you just kind of "blew up." You apologized the next day, and things are okay again between you, but that's when he pointed out that you have been really irritable lately and he has been avoiding you more, especially on weekends.

You have made some new friends at college and have dated a few girls, but none of these relationships have developed into the kind of closeness you enjoyed with your high school friends. You say that you figure this just takes time, but you have noticed that you seem to be a little detached in these relationships and you admit, if pressed by the interviewer, that you don't know if you really want to be that close to anyone in the near future. It's just too weird to be that close to someone and have them suddenly gone from your life. You never thought about that before, but now it seems each time you meet a new person, you have this little question in your mind about how long this person will be in your life and whether it's really worth going to the trouble of getting to know them.

You and your roommate sometimes travel home together for the weekend; he has a car and you contribute to gas money, so it works out for both of you. However, whereas he seems eager to use the time at home to get together with many of your old friends and have a good time, you find you are less interested in seeing your friends and more likely to stay home with your family or spend the weekend catching up on sleep. You haven't really thought about why this is so, but if the interviewer probes, you acknowledge that most of the places and people you would see if you went out on your weekends home are places and people who remind you of the friends who were in the car with you. You don't really want to get into conversations with your friends about the accident, and the idea of going places and doing things you used to do with your friends who were in the accident now makes you feel uncomfortable. The first few times you went home, you did try making contact with the friend who lost an arm, but the interaction was so awkward and you had so little to say to each other that you haven't tried to contact him since then. You acknowledge that this seems strange to you—that you could be such good friends before and feel so disconnected from each other now. You have not gone to visit the friend who is in a coma because you don't want to go back to the hospital and be reminded of what is was like to wake up there after the accident. You do not directly connect these changes in your relationships to the accident, but you say that you guess you just don't have much in common with your old friends since you started college.

You describe your relationship with your parents as good. You love and respect your parents and have more sympathy now for what you used to consider their "overprotectiveness."

In fact, your younger sister complains that you have become another parent because of the way you "give her the third degree" about her friends, activities, and decisions when you are at home.

11. How do you view your life?

In general, you feel your life is pretty good. You have a career path mapped out, and you are enjoying your classes. You have a supportive family and have always had a lot of friends, even if you feel a little disconnected from them at the moment. You often find yourself thinking that if only you could go back and erase last summer, everything would be great. But you can't, and you wonder if you will ever be able to put it behind you and recover your previous carefree attitude toward life.

EXERCISES FOR THE INTERVIEWER

Exercise 1: Develop a diagnosis for Mark

      A. What criteria does Mark meet for Posttraumatic Stress Disorder on Axis I?

_____

_____

_____

_____

    Name two other Axis I diagnoses that you might want to rule out for Mark, and indicate what additional information might be needed to differentiate between Posttraumatic Stress Disorder and each of these diagnoses.

_____

_____

_____

_____

    Does Mark meet all the requirements for an Axis I disorder? Should the diagnosis be deferred, or is a diagnosis not needed?

_____

_____

_____

_____

      B. Does Mark meet the criteria for an Axis II disorder (Personality Disorders and Mental Retardation), should a diagnosis be deferred, or is a diagnosis not needed? Explain and be as specific as possible.

_____

_____

_____

_____

      C. Is there anything you might report for Mark on Axis III (General Medical Conditions that are potentially relevant to a client's mental disorder)?

_____

_____

_____

_____

      D. List all relevant categories of psychosocial and environmental stressors for Mark and specify examples of each one on Axis IV. Indicate if each stressor is mild, moderate, or severe.

_____

_____

_____

_____

E. What is your global assessment of Mark's functioning for Axis V (current, highest in past year)?

_____

_____

_____

_____

F. Double-check your diagnostic choices starting at Axis V and proceeding backward through Axis I to determine if you may have overestimated or underestimated the impact of the situational, biological, or individual psychological factors on Mark's current functioning. Should you change anything? Be specific in describing why or why not.

_____

_____

_____

_____

G. Review your diagnostic choices again from Mark's point of view. Do your choices support the discussions you have had with him? Would he be disturbed by your choices? Be specific in discussing why or why not.

_____

_____

_____

_____

Exercise 2: Practice deepening the interview with Mark

A. Mark has trouble putting his feelings into words, partly because he is experiencing emotions that are unfamiliar to him, and partly because his usual style of coping is action rather than introspection. Help Mark get in touch with his emotional experience by making two types of responses to his comments. Make the first comment a simple, reflective listening comment, and make the second a more complex, empathetic comment that goes beyond the surface of what Mark has shared to invite him to explore the deeper emotions of which he may not be entirely aware. Use information from Mark's profile to guide you in developing these comments. An example is provided.

Mark: I'm not sure why, but I'm always calling home to check up on my younger sister, and worrying that something bad might happen to her. I never used to think about stuff like this. It's weird.

1. *You worry about your sister more than you used to and you're not sure why (reflective listening).*

2. *It's as if there is this new vulnerability, this new awareness that really bad stuff can happen to the people you love, and you might not be able to prevent it (empathetic comment).*

Mark: I was the one who pushed for the guys to go out that night, to have one last good time together as a bunch of single guys. Sometimes I wish I could go back and change that. It doesn't seem right that I pushed for us to go out and then I got the safest seat in the car.

1. _____

_____

2. _____

_____

Mark: I always was pretty good at tackling problems head-on, and I always seemed to know how to get a handle on stuff that happened in my life. But how do you get a handle on nightmares that attack you when you're sleeping? I can deal with anything when I'm awake, but I don't know how to stop the nightmares.

1. _____

_____

2. _____

_____

Mark: I didn't know what to say when I visited my friend in the hospital; the one who lost an arm. There he was, with just a bandage and a stump, and it was so obvious, but I didn't want to comment on it. But he didn't comment on it, either, and yet it was like that was all either of us could think about, but we were trying so hard not to talk about it that there was nothing else to say. I haven't been back since.

1. _____

_____

2. _____

_____

B. Mark has a hard time talking about the accident and typically changes the subject when you try to draw him out about what happened. Write a redirecting comment that supports Mark emotionally but encourages him to face the subject he is avoiding. An example is provided.

Interviewer: Tell me what you remember about that night and the accident.

Mark: I didn't remember much about it at first. I guess that's pretty normal, from what the doctors said. It's some kind of amnesia or something, isn't it?

You didn't remember much at first, but tell me what you do remember. It will help me to understand what you are going through now.

Interviewer: You lost two really good friends in the accident. Tell me about your friends, what they were like, what you miss about them.

Mark: I had a lot of friends in high school. We always had a good time. It's different in college. I haven't really made those kinds of connections here. But I'm busy keeping up with classes, so it's kind of good that I don't have a lot of friends.

_____

_____

_____

_____

Interviewer: You got the safest seat in the car, and you came out of the accident with the least injuries. How does that make you feel?

Mark: I never thought about where I sat before. I never even knew that it made any difference, safety-wise. But now, when I take my younger sister anywhere, I make her sit in the middle of the back seat. She complains, but there's no way I'm taking any chances with her.

_____

_____

_____

_____

Exercise 3: Thought questions related to Mark

A. Consider who you are as an interviewer and write down what you think might be most difficult about establishing rapport with Mark based on your age, ethnicity, gender, socioeconomic status, sexual orientation, religion, physical characteristics, and personality style. What specifically might happen?

_____

_____

_____

_____

_____

B. Is there anything you could do to enhance your ability to establish an effective working relationship with Mark? What specifically might you do?

_____

_____

_____

C. Interviewing clients who have been through horrific experiences can arouse strong emotions in the interviewer. These emotions can range from fascinated curiosity and a desire to probe for every detail, to anxious avoidance and colluding with the client in keeping the discussion superficial and nonemotional. If the client becomes upset and overwhelmed by emotion in the interview, the interviewer may feel responsible for upsetting the client and may feel compelled to provide reassurance or minimize the client's emotions. Consider what internal emotions might be aroused in you as Mark reveals the details of the accident and/or becomes upset and overwhelmed by traumatic memories in the session. Describe the emotions you might feel, and discuss how these emotions might affect your behavior toward Mark in the interview. Be specific in describing what might happen and the possible impact on Mark and on the interview process.

_____

_____

_____

_____

_____

_____

_____

_____

_____

D. Assume that your own personal reaction of shock to hearing about the car accident has had a negative impact on Mark. What might you do and say to return the session to a therapeutic atmosphere?

_____

_____

_____

_____

Case of Sarah

1. What are your basic statistics?

Your name is Sarah and you are a 70-year-old, European-American female. You live with your husband, Robert, who is 74 years old and has been diagnosed with Alzheimer's disease. You still live in your family home, where you raised your four children. Your children are Robert, junior (age 50), Daniel (age 49), Mary (age 46) and Janet (age 44). All of your children are married, with families of their own, and live some distance away from you. Janet is the nearest one. She lives in a city about two hours' drive from you, but she works full-time as an elementary school nurse and you do not see her often. Your children keep in touch with you by telephone and visit during the holidays, but are not available to assist you with the daily tasks of caring for the family home, managing doctors' appointments, and so on. You are being seen in a community mental health center at the urging of your daughter, Janet, who is concerned that you seem increasingly overwhelmed by the task of caring for Robert and may need help deciding how to handle the current situation and plan for the future. Janet took a personal day from her job to stay with her father so you could come to this appointment.

2. How do you behave in the interview?

You are neatly dressed and your hygiene is good. You move somewhat stiffly due to arthritic joints. You sit quietly in your chair and answer all the interviewer's questions politely and cooperatively. You are intelligent but preoccupied, and may ask the interviewer to repeat questions from time to time, apologizing for "having a lot on my mind." Your primary focus is on how to manage your responsibility to care for your husband, and you will find questions about your emotional state or well-being uncomfortable, as you are not used to thinking about your own welfare. If asked questions that require you to be somewhat introspective, you take your time, as if searching for an answer, and then respond either by telling the interviewer what your daughter has said on the subject or by returning the discussion to the problem of how to take care of your husband.

When asked about the problems you are experiencing in caring for your husband and maintaining the family home, you appear sad and may even cry a little. You make it clear that you see these problems as your responsibility to solve, that you are not interested in any solutions involving placing your husband in a nursing home or giving up his care to others. Although you acknowledge that you are having a hard time, you insist that marriage is for you a lifetime commitment, and that you take your vows seriously to "love and to cherish in sickness and in health until death us do part." You appreciate your daughter's concern and would not mind accepting help from her or from your other children if they lived near by. However, you do not expect them to give up their lives in order to help you, and you are determined to manage on your own.

You do not have any difficulty with mental status questions, although you may take some time to answer questions involving memory or concentration and may ask to have questions repeated. You adamantly deny suicidal ideation, saying that this is against your religion. Besides, people who commit suicide are "quitters" and you are not a quitter. You admit feeling sad and worried much of the time and sleeping poorly, but you attribute your poor sleep to your efforts to monitor your husband at night in case he tries to get out of bed or needs help getting to the bathroom.

3. Why are you being interviewed?

Your children are concerned about your ability to continue caring for your husband and for the family home as his condition continues to deteriorate. They have been urging you to consider placing him in a nearby nursing home with specialized care for Alzheimer's patients. You have steadfastly refused to do so, saying that he would be even more confused than he is now, and that you still believe you are able to care for him adequately in the familiar surroundings of the family home. However, there have been a few incidents recently which really alarmed your children. For example, you had to call an ambulance in the middle of the night because Robert tried to get out of bed, fell, and you were physically unable to get him up off the floor and back into bed. Also, one day when you came back from a quick trip to the grocery store, you found Robert trying to vacuum the dandelion heads off the lawn with the vacuum cleaner. He has also occasionally turned on a burner on the stove and then forgotten to turn it off. These incidents have led to increased pressure from your children to do something to get help for yourself and for Robert. You finally agreed to Janet's compromise offer that you at least make an appointment at the community mental health center to see if you could get some support, help with problem solving, and access to resources that might be available in the community.

Neither you nor Robert has any prior mental health treatment history, and you are not aware of any history of mental health treatment in any of your extended family. Robert has an older brother who died several years ago and also suffered from Alzheimer's disease. You have an older sister who lives with her husband in a retirement community in Florida and a younger brother who recently retired from his job as an insurance salesman and plans to move with his wife to Florida as well.

You are hoping the interviewer will not side with your children and tell you to place your husband in a nursing home. You are also hoping that participating in this interview will reassure your children that you are doing all you can and that they do not need to worry about you. You don't mind the idea of talking to someone because it might be a relief to share your concerns, but you do not want to be told what to do. You are skeptical that the interviewer will be able to help you find a way to keep your husband at home while reassuring your children that you can manage, but the truth is that the recent incidents at home have scared you, too, and you are willing to take a chance that talking to someone outside the situation might help you to come up with a solution you may have overlooked.

4. How do you feel?

You feel worried all the time about Robert and afraid that something will happen that you will be unable to anticipate, prevent, or handle. When he fell during the night, you experienced a sense of hopelessness and failure for the first time. You did not want to call an ambulance, but you could not leave him lying on the floor and you had tried repeatedly to get him up without success. You felt angry at him for trying to get out of bed without calling you for help, but at the same time you felt guilty about feeling angry. Even when the days pass without a major incident, you feel sad much of the time. It is difficult to be around Robert when he doesn't always recognize you. Sometimes he thinks you are his mother or one of your daughters. It is as if the man who used to be your husband is gone and yet not gone. Most of the time, this mixture of guilt, sadness, anger, and failure seems to sum up your emotional experience. Yet there are moments when you still get glimpses of the old Robert. For example, the other night you had put on an old album of love songs the two of you used to enjoy, and he held your hand and smiled at you the way he used to, and you were sure he knew who you were. At those moments, you feel hopeful again, and it seems worth the effort to keep caring for him in your home, as long as he can occasionally be "himself" with you again. You find it unbearable to imagine him in a home where nothing is familiar and even those moments will be lost.

How much of these feelings you share with the interviewer depends on how comfortable he or she makes you feel. If the interviewer is very young, you doubt that he or she can understand your experience, and you may be less willing to open up in the interview. You may ask questions to reassure yourself about the interviewer's ability to understand, for example, asking if the interviewer has had a family member with Alzheimer's or has ever worked with Alzheimer's patients before. If the interviewer responds supportively and seems able to empathize with your experience, you may share more of your feelings than if he or she seems judgmental or impatient to get on with problem solving.

5. How do you think?

Your thinking is clear and your thoughts are well organized. Your thoughts are focused on your desire to care for your husband in your own home and your fear that others (your children, the interviewer, your husband's physician) or circumstances (e.g., your husband's fall the other night) will interfere with your ability to make this choice. You believe that it is your responsibility as a good wife to care for your husband yourself until he dies, and you are worried that you will be physically unable to do so. You also recognize that you are increasingly unable to keep up with housecleaning and yard work, but you believe you can manage these tasks by hiring someone occasionally to help out. You are more willing to hire someone to do these things than you are to get help with the actual care of your husband. For example, you now have to help him get bathed and dressed because he cannot or will not do these things himself. Although this is enormously difficult for you physically, you dislike the thought of having anyone else invading his privacy to do these things for him.

You appreciate your children's concern, but feel that they should be focusing on their own families and not be burdened by trying to take care of you or their father. Although it is a relief whenever Janet can spare a day to come and help you clean or stay with Robert so you can do errands, you would never think of asking her to do this, and you feel ashamed of the relief you feel when you can get out of the house and away from Robert for a few hours. If your children lived nearer to you, you would be more willing to accept their help, and you sometimes secretly imagine how nice it would be to have them more available, but you would never think of expressing this to them for fear they might feel guilty about living so far away.

6. What do you like about yourself?

You are proud of your children and their families, and feel that you and Robert did a good job of raising them. You like the fact that you are hardworking and loyal, and you think of yourself as a responsible person and devoted wife. You consider yourself to be pretty good at needlework and baking. You once won a prize at the county fair for your apple pie, and your children always request your home baked pies when they visit at the holidays. You also enjoyed regular church attendance and were an active member of the women's group at your church for many years. However, as Robert's need for supervision has increased and he is no longer able to sit through a church service, you have gradually given up these activities, and do not know if you will ever have the time or energy for them again.

7. How have you been doing at work?

This question is not relevant for this client.

8. How have you been doing in school?

This question is not relevant for this client.

9. How is your health?

You say that you are in reasonably good health. Your arthritis bothers you a bit, but is not incapacitating. You have always been active and enjoyed walking from your home to church and the grocery store, although you have gradually become less active as you have become more involved in Robert's care. You admit that you have been feeling very tired lately, but you think this is because you don't sleep well at night due to listening for Robert to stir or call out to you. You also admit, if asked, that you are not eating very well. It is hard to motivate yourself to cook a good meal just for yourself, and Robert doesn't seem to care what you prepare for him. Sometimes you are just too tired after feeding him and caring for him to bother with anything other than a can of soup or some applesauce. If asked if you have lost any weight, you say no, but then say that you actually haven't weighed yourself lately and may have lost weight, since some of your clothes seem a bit looser recently.

10. How do you relate to others?

You and Robert always had an active social life before he became ill. You were active in your church and had friends your own age with whom you would go to dinner or attend plays or concerts at the university in town. You both volunteered for the Red Cross as well, and Robert used to play golf with some of his retired friends. Your women's group at the church always has a number of projects going on to raise money for charity, and you loved participating in these. You were also an active volunteer in the church kitchen, helping with preparation and clean-up for numerous church events, wedding receptions, and funeral dinners throughout the year. Before Robert's illness, you also made several trips together each year to visit your children and grandchildren, and both of you enjoyed seeing new places and having new experiences on these trips. You have given up most of these social activities, however, and have become increasingly isolated due to the demands of caring for Robert. If asked about these activities, you say that it's not only Robert who has changed, but you also have changed, and are not the "people person" you used to be. You miss these interactions with other people, but feel that Robert is and must be your priority.

You describe your relationship with your children and grandchildren as good, but admit that you do not have as much contact with them as you would like. You are closest to Janet, just because she lives nearest to you. But even your relationship with Janet has changed, as you have become increasingly reluctant to be away from Robert and cannot spend a Saturday shopping and having lunch with her as you once did. Your relationship with Robert has also changed, of course. The two of you always discussed every decision with each other. Now you make all the decisions for both of you. You say that you feel more like a mother than a wife most of the time. Even though you understand why he does not always recognize you or show affection to you, it still hurts when he is irritable or antagonistic toward you, or thinks that you are someone else.

11. How do you view your life?

You view your life as being rather bleak at the present time. You know that Robert will never really be well again, even though you hope for more of those moments when he seems to be himself again. In a way, you feel as though your entire life has come to consist of waiting for Robert to die and trying the best way you can to honor your commitment to love and care for him until that happens. You no longer look forward to the future, as you once did when you and Robert used to dream of moving to Florida to be near your siblings or moving closer to some of your children and grandchildren. You cannot even allow yourself to think hopefully about a future after Robert dies, because this makes you feel guilty and because you have no way of knowing how long his illness will last or what your state of health will be when he is gone. Without a future to anticipate, and in the midst of a present with little enjoyment or relief, you have only one goal: to give your husband the best possible care for as long as you are able to do so.

EXERCISES FOR THE INTERVIEWER

Exercise 1: Develop a diagnosis for Sarah

A. What criteria does Sarah meet for an Axis I diagnosis of Adjustment Disorder (with Depressed Mood, with Anxious Mood, or with Mixed Anxiety and Depressed Mood)?

_____

_____

_____

_____

Name two other Axis I diagnoses that you might want to rule out for Sarah, and indicate what additional information might be needed to differentiate between an Adjustment Disorder and each of these diagnoses.

_____

_____

_____

_____

Does Sarah meet all the requirements for an Axis I disorder? Should the diagnosis be deferred, or is a diagnosis not needed?

_____

_____

_____

B. What criteria does Sarah meet for an Axis II diagnosis (Personality Disorders and Mental Retardation)? Should a diagnosis be deferred, or is a diagnosis not needed? Explain and be as specific as possible.

_____

_____

_____

_____

C. Is there anything you might report for Sarah on Axis III (General Medical Conditions that are potentially relevant to a client's mental disorder)?

_____

_____

_____

D. List all relevant categories of psychosocial and environmental stressors for Sarah and specify examples of each one on Axis IV. Indicate if each stressor is mild, moderate, or severe.

_____

_____

E. What is your global assessment of Sarah's functioning for Axis V (current, highest in past year)?

_____

_____

F. Double-check your diagnostic choices starting at Axis V and proceeding backward through Axis I to determine if you may have overestimated or underestimated the impact of the situational, biological, or individual psychological factors on Sarah's current functioning. Should you change anything? Be specific in describing why or why not.

_____

_____

_____

G. Review your diagnostic choices again from Sarah's point of view. Do your choices support the discussions you have had with her? Would she be disturbed by your choices? Be specific in discussing why or why not.

_____

_____

_____

Exercise 2: Practice deepening interview with Sarah

A. Sarah is used to focusing on the needs of others and finds it difficult to talk about her own needs and emotions. When asked about her current difficulties, she frequently answers by referring to something her daughter has said, or something her husband needs, instead of talking about her own emotional experience. For each of the following exchanges, generate a redirecting comment that will sensitively encourage Sarah to focus on her own needs and emotions. Use information from Sarah's profile to guide you. An example has been provided of using redirection to change the focus of the client's attention.

Interviewer: What is it like for you when you are so tired and yet you can't let yourself fall asleep for fear Robert will try to get up or need your help in the night?

Sarah: My daughter thinks we should hire someone to be there at night in case Robert tries to get up, but I don't think he'd really be comfortable with a stranger showing up by his bed at night, and I don't want him to be frightened.

You aren't comfortable with anyone else tending to Robert at night because you know you can reassure him better than any stranger would be able to, but having your sleep interrupted every night is taking a toll on you. Can you tell me more about how the lack of sleep is affecting you?

Interviewer: How did you feel when Janet took the day off to come and stay with her father so you could get to this appointment today?

Sarah: My children have lives of their own, and I don't expect them to be at my beck and call. Janet works full-time and has children of her own, and she is needed there. I wish she just didn't worry so much about me.

_____

_____

_____

_____

Interviewer: How has it affected you to give up attending church and participating in the women's group there?

Sarah: Robert used to love going to church so much. But he just can't seem to sit still through an entire church service anymore. I can't see dragging him there just to have to make a scene and leave in the middle of the service, and besides, if he isn't getting anything out of it, what's the point of going?

_____

_____

_____

_____

B. Sarah does not volunteer verbal information about her feelings. She is accustomed to focusing on other people's needs and doing what she must to meet those needs, rather than focusing on her own emotional experience. Help Sarah identify and explore her feelings by sensitively commenting on her nonverbal cues in the interview. An example is provided.

Sarah has been talking about the night Robert fell and she was unable to get him up off the floor and back into bed. As she talks, she clenches and unclenches her hands and her voice quivers. She looks as if she is about to cry.

I see you sitting there clenching and unclenching your fists, and I hear the quiver in

your voice, and I can't help wondering if you must have felt so helpless, so powerless to take

care of Robert in that situation, no matter how much you wanted to help him.

Sarah has been talking about how much she enjoyed the activities of the women's group at church before she gave up her participation to care for Robert's increasing needs at home. She is smiling and talking in an animated tone of voice, as she describes the fun of quilting and baking with these women and the laughter and camaraderie they shared.

_____

_____

_____

Sarah has been describing the day she came home and found Robert trying to vacuum the heads off of the dandelions in the back yard. Her tone of voice is harsh, and she pounds her clenched fist on the arm of the chair as she describes Robert's inability to recognize the dangers of this behavior and keep himself safe without constant supervision.

_____

_____

_____

Sarah has been talking about her children pressuring her to place Robert in a nursing home. She says she and Robert always made every major decision together and she wishes she could consult with him now, but he is the one person who cannot help her make this decision, even though the decision is about him. As she says this, her voice drops and trails away into almost a whisper, she wrings her hands together in her lap, and her eyes dart back and forth from looking in her lap to looking at the door.

_____

_____

_____

Exercise 3: Thought questions related to Sarah

A. Consider who you are as an interviewer and write down what you think might be most difficult about establishing rapport with Sarah based on your age, ethnicity, gender, socioeconomic status, sexual orientation, religion, physical characteristics, and personality style. What specifically might happen?

_____

_____

_____

_____

_____

B. Is there anything you could do to enhance your ability to establish an effective working relationship with Sarah? What specifically might you do?

_____

_____

_____

C. Sarah is likely to have doubts about the interviewer's ability to understand her situation, particularly if the interviewer is much younger than she is, or unmarried. She is likely to ask questions to determine if the interviewer is competent to help her. For example, she may ask if you are married, if you have had a family member with Alzheimer's, or have ever worked with Alzheimer's patients, or have any training in this area. Questions such as these press for self-disclosure on the part of the interviewer. Discuss your views on the appropriateness of self-disclosure in this interview situation, and describe how you might respond to such questions from Sarah. Be specific.

_____

_____

_____

_____

_____

_____

_____

D. Sarah is in conflict with her children about her decision to care for her husband at home. What is your opinion of her decision? Would you share this opinion with her? Be specific as to why you would or why you would not.

_____

_____

_____

_____

E. What do you know about Alzheimer's disease? How relevant is your knowledge or lack of knowledge of this disease to providing effective treatment to Sarah?

_____

_____

_____

_____

Case of David

1. What are your basic statistics?

Your name is David and you are a thirty-four-year-old, European-American male. You are a high school graduate. You were divorced by your wife several years ago. You are now living with Susanna, age twenty-seven. You dated her for about one month before you asked her to move in with you. You and Susanna have now been together for about two years. You have been working since you graduated, as a salesman at an automobile company. You live in a condo that you own in the downtown area of a small, northeastern U.S. city. You drive a sports car that you are leasing from your employer. You are being interviewed by a practitioner in private practice.

2. How do you behave in the interview?

You are well groomed and care a great deal about your appearance. You are highly intelligent and good at creating an initially positive impression. You tend to speak quickly, but you are always logical and coherent. You ask questions of the interviewer in a friendly way, trying to keep in control of the topic of conversation. You are quick and smooth at complementing whoever you are with, and you give good eye contact when you don't feel threatened. You are not very curious about other people and don't look much beyond initial impressions based on appearance.

When the interviewer asks sensitive questions, about your relationships, job, or substance use, you quickly become defensive. You look down at the floor and rub your hands against the top of your legs when you answer these "tough" questions. If asked about this behavior, you deny you are nervous and say something like, "It's just a habit. I've always done it."

If asked mental status questions, you show no signs of cognitive confusion, hallucinations, or delusions. You deny any homicidal or suicidal ideation. If probed in a compassionate way, you reveal deep anxiety about losing your job. Being a "star salesman" is really important to you, and somehow you have recently lost this "status" position at work. If given a lot of support, you also admit to feeling sadness because Susanna is threatening to leave you. You admit to the regular use of alcohol and heroin but become defensive at any suggestion that this isn't normal for everyone.

3. Why are you being interviewed?

You referred yourself for this session because you are in danger of being fired. You have been working as a salesman at an automobile dealership since you graduated from high school. You used to be your boss' star salesman, but your performance has been deteriorating over the last year and a half. Your boss has told you to get help and get it fixed, or you are out of a job. You have been missing a lot of work in the last three months. You have also arrived at work under the influence of drugs. You are emphatic that you do not want to lose your job, but you deny that alcohol or drugs are really a problem. If asked, you are open about drinking daily after work and using heroin several times each week over the last year. While insisting that these substances are not a problem for you or causing difficulties in your life, you lose eye contact whenever you say this and shift constantly in your chair. You admit that your job is in jeopardy. You just can't admit that your use of substances is at the true root of this problem. If asked about any other troubles, you admit that your girlfriend is threatening to leave you. She is doing this because she has discovered that you were unfaithful to her while she was visiting her parents last week. You have often had brief sexual encounters with women that you would meet at bars after work. This is the first time Susanna found out. You plan to marry Susanna eventually but don't intend to give up your flings.

You have never received psychological services before and are not sure what to expect. If asked what you hope to get from the interview, you might just shrug your shoulders. Then, look down and say you don't really know what you need to do to straighten things out.

4. How do you feel?

You don't volunteer any information about how you are feeling because your feelings make you uncomfortable. You do your best to avoid considering them by changing the subject any time the interviewer tries to screen for depression, anxiety, anger, and so forth. During this avoidance, you smile and insist that you are in control with no real problems. If asked, you deny feeling anxious or depressed about your current situation, but you look down at the floor and rub your legs. Your discomfort rises the longer the focus of the conversation is your feelings. However, if the interviewer is compassionate enough, you admit to anxiety about losing your job and your relationship. You may get choked up or teary eyed. If the interviewer asks you about any suicidal ideation or intention, you reply frankly that you have never considered suicide as an option. You figure you can always find a way out of your problems. If pressed further about suicide, you say firmly that you would never do anything that stupid. You then ask for the interviewer to please move on to something else; talking about this makes you feel lousy.

5. How do you think?

You are impulsive in responding to questions, but your thoughts are very well organized and clearly expressed. You are of average intelligence and do not tend to think much before you act. You expect that people will like and respect you because you have always been good at starting relationships. You can think about precursors and consequences to your behavior if instructed to by the interviewer but you don't do this on your own. So, if asked to consider what is going on with your boss, you are able to understand his point of view and why he is considering firing you. You can consider the idea that you aren't doing your best when taking substances, but you aren't convinced you need to stop drinking and shooting up. You perceive drug and alcohol use to be very common. You know that your pattern of drinking and drug use has changed. In the past, you would have approximately two drinks before going home after work, but you never got drunk except on the weekends or at the occasional party. Now, you are getting drunk or high every day after work. However, you think you can stop whenever you want to. As proof, you say that you have not had any alcohol or heroin since confronted by your boss last week. If given guidance, you also understand Susanna's point of view and why she feels betrayed by you. You plan to keep trying to convince her that the fling you had was a one-time-only mistake because you were so lonely when she left town that you went out and got drunk and acted stupid. You are flustered that, for the first time, you are having trouble getting your boss and Susanna to forgive and forget. You know you can be a success at work, so you haven't given up hope you can resume your role as star salesman. You are less hopeful that you can save your relationship with Susanna. You show no signs of any thought disorder, mania, or loss of control. If asked, you also deny any delusional thinking or hallucinations.

6. What do you like about yourself?

You like the fact that you are good at persuading people. You like being able to change people's minds and get them on your side. You see yourself as a hard worker. You have felt like you were living the American dream. You live in a condo full of electronic gadgets, drive a fast car, and live with beautiful Susanna; this is what you deserve and what you want.

7. How have you been doing at work?

Currently, your job is in jeopardy. In the past few years, you have been the clear star of the dealership. You have had many referrals from prior clients because of your detailed knowledge of the car inventory and available options. You are very comfortable approaching new customers and were envied by other salespeople for your ability to charm difficult customers. This has been a real source of pride to you. If asked to talk more about this, you admit you have been employee of the year for as long as you can remember for selling so many vehicles.

8. How have you been doing in school?

This question is not relevant to David.

9. How is your health?

You have no health complaints. If asked, you admit that other people have been asking you if you have been sick lately. If pressed, you say that others have said you look pale and that you have been sweating a lot recently although you don't think it means anything.

10. How do you relate to others?

Your parents died in a bar fire when you were thirteen. If asked, you say you don't remember much about your parents. You do remember that your father had a reputation with women and with alcohol, and you say he was a mean drunk. You have vague memories of your mother crying a lot and your dad going off to the bars alone. You try to change the subject whenever your parents come up. If pressed, you say you are uncomfortable, don't want to talk about them, and don't consider them relevant to your current problems.

After these deaths, you were raised by your maternal aunt and uncle. You have two younger male cousins. Your uncle and aunt both worked full time to support you and your cousins. You admit that your aunt and uncle fought a lot but you don't know why. You always felt very close to your uncle. He had been "great" to you. Your uncle was a salesman at a car dealership, and he introduced you and your cousins to this business as teenagers. You were the only one to show a talent for sales. Your uncle encouraged you to come by the dealership after school to hang around. After work, your uncle would take you to bars to hang around and see how the "real salesmen" handled themselves and talked shop. Your uncle died five years ago and your aunt moved to California to be close to your cousins. Both of them moved to California five years ago to work in Los Angeles. You haven't heard much from any of them in recent years.

You met your first wife at a holiday party thrown by a mutual friend. While you had enjoyed "playing the field" for the preceding five years, you quickly developed a very serious attitude toward Cathy. You married Cathy after a six-month courtship. This marriage lasted three years. Toward the end of this marriage, you were drinking a lot and you and your wife were either avoiding each other or constantly fighting. You get very vague about what went wrong. You admit that you occasionally had sex with other women who you met after work at various bars. You say you had no serious interest in any of them. Sex with them was just a way to relax. Right before the final breakup with your wife, one of your neighbors came by to have a talk with your wife. This woman was furious that you had a one night stand with her last month and have ignored her since then. Your wife confronted you about this neighbor's story. You tried to deny it but Cathy said she was filing for divorce. You can admit that this depressed you but rationalize that it was a relief to put an end to all the fighting. For a few weeks after the divorce, you drank only occasionally. However, you quickly resumed a practice of regular drinking every weekday and heavy drinking on the weekends.

You had a series of brief affairs never lasting more than a few days. This pattern was interrupted two years ago when you met Susanna. You can't explain why you quickly developed such a serious interest in her. After an intense few weekends, you asked Susanna to move in and stopped seeing other women. At first, your drinking went down to one beer after work and maybe two an evening during the weekends. If asked, you deny that a daily drink is a problem. You insist that "everyone" does this and that you have frequently been bought drinks by your boss and coworkers after you have had a particularly "hot" sales day.

After a while, you and Susanna began to fight a lot and you began to spend more time at bars. Last month, Susanna spent a week visiting her parents and you decided to really enjoy this "vacation." You invited a friend, Peter, to go bar hopping with you. At a bar, you and Peter met Brenda and Karen, who were friends of a friend of Peter's. After about thirty minutes of drinking, you all went back to Peter's apartment. Once there, Peter suggested that everyone shoot up on some heroin. Once high, you hooked up with Karen and took her into Peter's bedroom to have sex. The two of you had at it until you both passed out. At 5:00 a.m., Peter wanted you out. You and Karen split up and went home to your own places. The moment you entered your apartment, you collapsed and went to sleep on the floor. The phone rang at 9:30 a.m. the next day. You were a mess. You had slept in your clothes and vomited in your sleep. Your head felt like it was going to explode. The car dealership was calling and screaming that you were late. At work, you were able to talk yourself out of trouble with your boss, but you had a hard time selling cars. To cheer yourself up, you called Karen and took her out again. You and Karen became heroin partners on a regular basis. Something about heroin gave you insomnia and you would be up most of the night and then have trouble getting up and concentrating at work. Your sales record deteriorated, and you were frequently in trouble with your boss. Karen doesn't know you live with Susanna.

11. How do you view your life?

You want to make changes but are very unclear about what things you need to change. If asked, you do not admit to having trouble with alcohol or drugs. You say you are in control of these substances and enjoy them, so you have no plans to stop taking them. However, you do express some confusion over how you have managed to lose your status of "prize salesman" and you would like this status back. You do not want to lose Susanna as you did your wife. You insist that Susanna is unaware of your infidelity being a long-term problem. She knows about your drinking but not about your heroin use. You know that she has become dissatisfied with you. She had threatened to walk out on you twice in the last month, but you have been able to smooth talk her out of it each time. You deny that there is any similarity between your behavior now and what led your wife to wanting a divorce.

EXERCISES FOR THE INTERVIEWER

Exercise 1: Develop a diagnosis for David

A. What criteria does David meet for a diagnosis of Substance-Related Disorders?

_____

_____

_____

_____

Name at least two other Axis I diagnoses that you might want to rule out for David and indicate what additional information might be needed to differentiate between the diagnostic choices for him.

_____

_____

_____

_____

Does David meet all the criteria for an Axis I disorder? Should a diagnosis be deferred, or is a diagnosis not needed?

_____

_____

_____

B. What criteria does David meet for an Axis II disorder (Personal Disorder and Mental Retardation)? Should a diagnosis be deferred, or is a diagnosis not needed? Explain being as specific as possible.

_____

_____

_____

_____

C. Is there anything you might report for David on Axis III (General Medical Conditions that are potentially relevant to the client's mental disorder)?

_____

_____

_____

_____

D. List all specific psychosocial and/or environmental problems that are influencing David at this time for Axis IV. Indicate if each stressor is mild, moderate, or severe.

_____

_____

_____

_____

E. What is your global assessment of David's functioning for Axis V (current and highest in past year)?

_____

_____

_____

_____

F. Double-check your diagnostic choices starting at Axis V and proceeding backward through Axis I to determine if you may have overestimated or underestimated the impact of the situational, biological, or individual psychological factors on David's current functioning. Should you change anything? Be specific in describing why or why not.

_____

_____

_____

_____

G. Review your diagnostic choices again from David's point of view. Do your choices support the discussions you have had with David? Would he be disturbed by your choices? Be specific in discussing why or why not.

_____

_____

_____

_____

Exercise 2: Practice deepening interview with David

A. David has been referred due to substance use, which needs to be assessed. Write a series of open-ended and closed questions to help you assess whether his use is low, moderate, or heavy using the following prompts. An example of two open-ended questions and one closed question is provided for prompt 1.

Prompt 1: Level of David's substance use

How would you describe your use of alcohol? What was the level of your heroin use over the last week? Exactly how much heroin did you use on Saturday?

Prompt 2: Signs of toxicity or withdrawal in David

_____

_____

Prompt 3: Function of substances in David's life (intrapersonal or interpersonal stress, habit)

_____

_____

Prompt 4: Environmental supports for usage

_____

_____

Prompt 5: Environmental supports for abstinence

_____

_____

Prompt 6: Positive impact of substance use

_____

_____

Prompt 7: Negative impact of substance use

_____

_____

B. David does not currently consider his use of substances the real problem. In response to each of the following comments from him, use supportive confrontation in an effort to get him to think more deeply about the negative consequences of his substance use. Remember to include empathy or support for David (affirmation) as well as specific information about the negative consequences of what he is doing (confrontation). Use information from the case history to help give you concrete examples of David's behavior to use in your confrontations. Use one of the following four styles: de-emphasize labeling; emphasize personal choice and responsibility; demonstrate that you have listened to his needs; or, be honest with him about his problem behaviors in terms of the likelihood they will bring him positive or negative consequences. An example is provided using style 1, which de-emphasizes labeling.

David: I am tired of people accusing me of being a drug addict.

I can hear your frustration over being called a drug addict when you don't believe you are.

However, your heroin use has been one factor preventing you from being a star salesman. You

told me that, after shooting up during the night, you had trouble concentrating well enough to

sell cars the next day.

David: My substance use is not a problem, and I can't stand all this harping about it.

_____

_____

_____

_____

David: I don't want to lose my job, but I can handle the alcohol and heroin and I don't want to stop using them.

_____

_____

_____

_____

C. David often changes the subject when you try to discuss a topic he finds uncomfortable. Use redirecting to prevent David's avoidance. Be careful to phrase your redirect in a respectful manner by starting with an element that shows you listened to David (supportive element) and then moving on to redirect him back to the topic he was trying to avoid. An example is provided.

Interviewer: What has Susanna said to you about your relationship with other women?
David: Here I am trying to stay off stuff and it's hell. When will all this pressure stop?

You are feeling under constant pressure. If you think about what Susanna has said to you, you

might feel even more pressured. On the other hand, talking about it might help.

Interviewer: What exactly did your boss say to you about your recent work?
David: I have a great record at that place. I could go anywhere and get work.

_____

_____

_____

Interviewer: What is happening with Karen now?
David: I'm committed to Susanna.

_____

_____

_____

Exercise 3: Thought questions related to David

A. Consider who you are as an interviewer, and write down what you think might be most difficult about establishing rapport with David based on your age, ethnicity, gender, socioeconomic status, sexual orientation, religion, physical characteristics, and personality style. What specifically might happen?

_____

_____

_____

_____

_____

B. Is there anything you could do to enhance your ability to establish an effective working relationship with David? Be specific and detailed in describing your ideas.

_____

_____

_____

_____

_____

C. David has a history of getting sexually involved with a woman when the stress in his life is high. If you are a woman interviewer, what might you say to David if at the end of the session, he invites you out for coffee to "discuss his case" more intimately? If you are a male interviewer, what might you say to David if, immediately after your appointment with him, you hear him ask the female receptionist out to dinner?

_____

_____

_____

_____

_____

D. What is your opinion of the role of alcohol and/or illegal substances in socializing and how might this influence your treatment of David?

_____

_____

_____

_____

_____

Case of Lisa

1. What are your basic statistics?

Your name is Lisa and you are a European-American, nontraditional first-semester freshman student at 45 years of age. You are married. Your husband is the owner of a local business. Your two older children (ages 25 and 23) have graduated from college and your youngest child (age 18) started college this semester at a different college, so you and your husband are alone in your home for the first time since you began raising a family. You got married and started raising a family soon after high school and never thought seriously about attending college until your youngest child brought home college information from high school. You never thought you were college material, but your children encouraged you to "go for it," so you did. Your husband has a college education and did not object to your going to school, but has seemed a bit resentful lately when you haven't had time to fix dinner or keep house the way you used to. You are being interviewed at your college's counseling center.

2. How do you behave in the interview?

You are casually but neatly dressed and your hygiene is good. You make good eye contact and are cooperative with the interviewer. You answer questions fully and openly, but may apologize occasionally as if uncertain that what you are sharing would really be of interest or importance to the interviewer. Your self-consciousness about "fitting in" or being judged as "out of place" or "not belonging" may come up if you are asked about relationships with other students (most of whom are younger than you are) or professors (some of whom are your own age).

When asked what brought you to seek treatment, you initially focus on the idea of counseling as an opportunity for personal growth, available to you free of charge because you are a student. If the interviewer probes further, you acknowledge that returning to school has meant a "lot of changes" in your routine and that you and your husband are still "adjusting" and you hope to get some help making that adjustment a little "smoother." Although deep down you are a little worried about whether or not you have what it takes to succeed in school after all these years, you do not readily admit this to the interviewer. If anything, you may be a little embarrassed to admit that you have these fears, especially if the interviewer looks a lot younger than you are.

If asked mental status questions, you do not exhibit any confusion, unusual thoughts, or delusional thinking. You do, however, express considerable discomfort with questions that seem to be measuring intelligence or academically related skills (e.g., serial sevens or memory questions), apologizing in advance for being "rusty" in these areas or having an "old brain that's a little out of practice" and similar comments. You deny feeling depressed or anxious, but admit some sleep difficulties, especially on nights before big exams.

If asked about drug or alcohol use, you deny more than the occasional glass of wine when eating out with your husband. You have no history of drug or alcohol use and are comfortable saying so, although you may make an awkward joke about how the interviewer probably "sees a lot of that in more typical college freshmen."

3. Why are you being interviewed?

You are taking an introductory psychology course, and your instructor happened to mention that college students are entitled to free services at the college counseling center. You had never really thought about seeking counseling or psychotherapy before, but studying psychology has made you curious about this profession, and since you are trying a lot of new things in your life right now, you thought it might be an opportunity to learn some things about yourself. You also thought it couldn't hurt to have a little help with some of the more stressful aspects of returning to college as a nontraditional student.

4. How do you feel?

Your feelings are a mixture of excitement about all the new experiences you are having and apprehension about whether or not you will be able to succeed academically. You enjoy soaking up new information and ideas from your classes and textbooks, but you feel out of place among all the "youngsters" and wonder what they think of you. If the interviewer is younger than you are, you may also wonder what he or she thinks of you. You are also a little uncomfortable about the tensions growing at home due to the role changes in your marriage.

5. How do you think?

Your thoughts are coherent and you express yourself fairly clearly. You show no evidence of hallucinations or delusions. You are, however, very concerned about how others perceive you, and this causes you to be apprehensive about the interviewer's evaluation of you. You expect others to have a hard time understanding why you would want to go back to college at this point in your life, and you really haven't thought a lot about what you will do if and when you graduate. Much of the time you don't really believe you will graduate anyway, so you don't really expect others to take you seriously. You know your husband has been confused and upset by your change in roles, and you think you are responsible for finding a way to ease his adjustment as well as your own. After all, he is nearing retirement, and you understand why he doesn't see the point of your embarking on a career at this stage in your lives together.

6. What do you like about yourself?

You are proud of your children and feel you did a good job raising them. You don't regret staying home while they were growing up and feel this is why they turned out so well. You've always been someone who took care of others, and this is the first time in your life you have chosen to do something for yourself. You are proud of this decision and proud of the fact that you have gotten good grades on several assignments recently (although you also feel some guilt and uncertainty about being "selfish").

7. How have you been doing at work?

This question is not relevant to this client.

8. How have you been doing in school?

You have gotten decent grades so far, and have a "B" average. You have been pleasantly surprised by the positive comments on some of your papers by your professors. You often have ideas or comments you would like to make in class, but typically do not speak up because you do not want to draw attention to yourself. You are apprehensive about upcoming assignments that will require you to make some sort of presentation in front of class or work in a small group with other students. You are afraid the other students will not want to work with you and that your ideas will seem "out of date" to them.

9. How is your health?

Your health is generally good. However, you have been aware lately of some peri-menopausal symptoms: hot flashes, night sweats, weight gain, and missed periods. You haven't mentioned these symptoms to your physician and may be somewhat embarrassed to discuss them with the interviewer. One of your husband's more hurtful comments recently blamed your decision to go back to school on your "hormones going haywire." You have noticed that your mood can switch from being elated and exhilarated by something you are learning in class to nervous, irritable, and "down in the dumps" as you face an upcoming exam or challenging assignment. You also notice that you seem to become irritable with your husband more than ever before, and sometimes you wonder if he is right about the "hormone" thing.

10. How do you relate to others?

You are close to your children and enjoy talking on the phone with them regularly. You also keep in touch with your parents and a sister who live about an hour's drive from your home. Your circle of friends up to now has consisted mainly of other women who were stay-at-home moms like you, and you are currently feeling some strangeness in those relationships because when you get together, you don't seem to have much in common to share with each other. You haven't had much time or opportunity to form new relationships at school, in part because it is only your first semester and you are a commuter who lives at home, but also in part because of the age difference with many of your classmates.

Your marriage has been comfortable up until now, with a fairly traditional division of roles and some shared interests and hobbies (you both enjoy camping and are active in events at your local church). That seems to be changing now, too. When you come home from class, you are tired and don't feel like cooking, especially since it is only the two of you now. You would rather get take-out or eat a sandwich and spend the evening studying, but your husband still expects a home-cooked meal. He has also expressed some resentment when you asked him to vacuum the carpets or take care of grocery shopping, both tasks you always did in the past. In summary, you feel that all your relationships are changing at the same time, and you really don't have any one person who seems to understand or relate to all aspects of your experience currently. As someone who is used to being there for others and finding much satisfaction in being needed, it is a new experience for you to feel lonely and in need of support yourself.

11. How do you view your life?

Your view of your life at the moment is that it is like riding a roller coaster: You are thrilled by the ride but holding on for dear life. Or you say that it seems like what happens to the pattern when you turn a kaleidoscope: Everything that was familiar is falling apart, and although you like the colors you see, you are wondering what the new pattern will be. You wouldn't undo the decision to go back to school, but you wish you could find a way to make the ride a little smoother and less bumpy for yourself and for your husband.

EXERCISES FOR THE INTERVIEWER

Exercise 1: Develop a diagnosis for Lisa

A. What criteria does Lisa meet for an Adjustment Disorder on Axis I and/or Phase of Life Problem?

_____

_____

_____

_____

Name two other Axis I diagnoses that you might want to rule out for Lisa and indicate what additional information might be needed to differentiate between the diagnostic choices for her.

_____

_____

_____

_____

Are there any other Axis I diagnoses that you might want to rule out for Lisa? If so, what additional information might be needed?

_____

_____

_____

_____

B. Does Lisa meet the criteria for an Axis II disorder, should a diagnosis be deferred, or is a diagnosis not needed?

_____

_____

_____

_____

C. What might you report for Lisa on Axis III (General Medical Conditions that are potentially relevant to a client's mental disorder)?

_____

_____

_____

_____

D. List all relevant categories of psychosocial and environmental stressors for Lisa and specify examples of each one on Axis IV. Indicate if each stressor is mild, moderate, or severe.

_____

_____

_____

_____

E. What is your global assessment of Lisa's functioning for Axis V (current, highest in past year)?

_____

_____

_____

_____

F. Double-check your diagnostic choices starting at Axis V and proceeding backward through Axis I to determine if you may have overestimated or underestimated the impact of the situational, biological, or individual psychological factors on Lisa's current functioning. Should you change anything? Be specific in describing why or why not.

_____

_____

_____

_____

G. Review your diagnostic choices again from Lisa's point of view. Do your choices support the discussions you have had with her? Would she be disturbed by your choices? Be specific in discussing why or why not.

_____

_____

_____

_____

Exercise 2: Practice deepening interview with Lisa

A. Lisa has made a number of comments in the interview that seem to reflect a concern about "fitting in" or being perceived as "different." She has also made a number of statements that hint at fears that she may have made a mistake in returning to school "so late in life." Finally, she has made several comments that suggest she experiences some conflict between her former role as caretaker for others and her current focus on her own self-development. Summary statements that tie several client statements or examples together can help a client feel that the interviewer is genuinely paying attention as well as help to focus the client's awareness of organizing themes that tie together a number of concerns. For each group of statements below, first identify the theme that ties these examples together, and second generate a summarizing statement that will help Lisa feel you have been paying attention to her concerns and help her become aware of these connecting themes. An example is provided.

Lisa: The students in my classes seem nice but I haven't really gotten to know any of them. Most of them live on campus and I commute. Besides, they probably would rather hang out with other students their own age." Later, she also says, "I have a lot of ideas in class but I usually save them for written assignments. I guess I don't really want to draw attention to this 'old lady' in class or for the other students to get the idea that I think I'm on a level with the professor (even if he is about my age)." Finally, she also says, "When I get together with my friends at home, we don't seem to have much in common anymore. We were all stay-at-home moms, doing a lot of the same activities with our kids in sports, and so on, but now I'm not a part of all that. Yet, I don't really think they want to hear about my classes or what I'm learning, which is what I would really like to share with someone.

What is the theme reflected in these statements?

Lisa feels "different" or "out of place" both at home and at school.

Summarizing statement:

I hear you saying that whether you're with your friends at home or with the other students in

class, you just don't feel completely connected with either group of people. It's like you

just don't really fit in anywhere.

Lisa: You're probably going to have to be patient with this old brain with these math questions. I'm a little rusty after all these years out of school." Later she says, "I've been pretty pleased with my grades so far, but I'm not sure I will be able to keep up when it comes to big exams or longer assignments. I probably could have done it when I was fresh out of high school, but that was a long time ago." Finally she says, "Most of the other students in my classes seem to have a pretty good idea of what they want to do after college. I have no idea what I'll do when I graduate—or maybe I should say *if* I graduate.

What is the theme?

_____

_____

_____

_____

_____

Summarizing statement:

_____

_____

_____

_____

_____

_____

Lisa: I feel really proud of the way my children have turned out. I don't regret staying home with them, even though it would have been nice to go to college when I was younger. I like feeling that I was able to be there for them and give them what they needed." Later she says, "My husband is a little put out when I am too tired to cook at night or when I ask him to do the grocery shopping. I can't really blame him. After all, he's getting ready to retire and here I am turning everything upside down from what he's used to." Finally she says, "I get so excited sometimes when I get a hold of some new idea in the reading or in something my professor says. Then I come home and try to tell my husband about it, and he gets this sort of glazed look. I guess I feel a little selfish putting so much energy into my classes and so little energy into my housework or my marriage.

What is the theme?

_____

_____

_____

_____

_____

Summarizing statement:

_____

_____

_____

_____

B. Lisa worries about how others perceive her. She is likely to worry about how the interviewer will perceive her, especially if you are younger than she is, have made different life choices, or hold different values than Lisa does. You can draw Lisa's attention to these feelings and invite her to explore them with you by making a content-to-process shift, in the form of questions or comments about what is happening in the current interaction. These comments should be phrased in a tentative way, as an invitation to Lisa to risk sharing more openly, rather than an accusation or judgment by the interviewer. For each of Lisa's statements below, use process comments to draw Lisa's attention to her feelings about the treatment relationship itself. An example has been provided.

Lisa: I guess I'm not very interesting to interview when it comes to drugs or alcohol. You probably see a lot more of that in "typical" college students you work with.

Process comment:
It sounds as if you might be a little worried about whether or not your concerns will be interesting to me, or whether I will even want to work with someone whose issues aren't "typical" of college students.

Lisa: I don't know how much you know about hormones or this "change of life" stuff. After all, I'm probably old enough to be your mother. You have a lot of years ahead of you before you have to worry about that.

(If you are as old or older than Lisa, change the content of the last two sentences. Assume that Lisa considers you to have progressed easily through this developmental change always knowing exactly how to handle it while she has to struggle through it highly confused.)

_____

_____

_____

_____

Lisa: It probably seems old-fashioned to most people that I decided to stay home with my kids and put off school for so long. You don't look old enough to have kids, but here you are in graduate school already!

(If you are as old or older than Lisa, change the content of this. Assume that Lisa considers that you have made very different choices to hers and consider her choices inferior.)

_____

_____

_____

_____

Exercise 3: Thought questions related to Lisa

A. Consider who you are as an interviewer, and write down what you think might be most difficult about establishing rapport with Lisa based on your age, ethnicity, gender, socioeconomic status, sexual orientation, religion, physical characteristics, and personality style. What specifically might happen?

_____

_____

_____

_____

B. Is there anything you could do to enhance your ability to establish an effective working relationship with Lisa? Be specific and detailed in describing your ideas.

_____

_____

_____

_____

C. Consider your own values and expectations about gender roles. How might your attitudes and experiences with regard to career versus family and traditional versus egalitarian roles in marriage affect your ability to empathize and establish rapport with Lisa? Also, if Lisa's husband came in with her for marital sessions, how might your attitudes and values affect your ability to establish rapport with him?

_____

_____

_____

_____

_____

_____

D. Given that Lisa seems to be reporting what could be perimenopausal symptoms, how important would it be for your evaluation to include consultation with a physician, and how might you go about suggesting this to Lisa? (She is sensitive about this topic because of her husband's tendency to say her "hormones have gone haywire.") What specific comment might you make to her about this?

_____

_____

_____

_____

E. Do you have any beliefs about the existence of general characteristics of perimenopausal or menopausal women? Be specific in articulating what these beliefs are. How might these beliefs influence your work with Lisa?

_____

_____

_____

_____

Case of Gary

1. What are your basic statistics?

Your name is Gary and you are a twenty-three-year-old, European-American male from an upper middle-class background. You have been attending college for the past seven months while living with your parents. At the present time, you are on an inpatient psychiatric unit. You have been there for two days. You were involuntarily admitted because you were considered "a danger to others."

2. How do you behave in the interview?

You are well groomed, intelligent, fast talking, and dramatic. In response to general questions, you don't have any trouble articulating your ideas, and you try to charm the interviewer. You sit in a relaxed fashion and smile a lot while looking directly at the interviewer. Your façade of friendliness is broken only if you perceive that the interviewer is ordering you around. If this happens, you quickly tell the interviewer to back off and stop pushing you around. If the interviewer doesn't immediately placate you, your voice gets loud and you become angry and agitated.

When the interviewer asks questions about what led you to be hospitalized, you start out smiling and say it was all a crazy mistake. If the interviewer presses you at all, you launch into a diatribe against your parents and the stupidity of the hospital doctors in believing your parents. You say this intensely but calmly unless you perceive that the interviewer is taking your parents' side. If this happens, you become angry and agitated.

If asked any questions about depression, anxiety, or suicide, you chuckle and say things like, "That's for losers. I'm a winner." If asked about aggression or violence, you insist you are an easygoing guy but if you have to, you can defend yourself. You show no signs of cognitive confusion, hallucination, or delusions during mental status screens. If assessed for substance use, you admit that you have often enjoyed using alcohol and stimulants, such as cocaine, for recreational purposes on the weekends and maybe sometimes during the work week. You are vague and unclear if asked if you ever supplied substances to other people.

3. Why are you being interviewed?

You were committed to a mental hospital for observation after a violent fight broke out between you and your dad at dinner. Your dad told you to stop drinking and you grabbed a wine bottle and hit him several times with it. Your mom called the police, who forced you to come to the emergency room of a psychiatric hospital. You heard the attending physician tell your parents that you should be hospitalized for an observation period. If asked why you attacked your father, say you were just angry because your dad was jerking you around. Your dad deserved what he got for acting like such a loser, and you are tired of people making such a big deal over it. If asked more about this, you tell the interviewer to back off.

If asked what you want from this interview, say you want the interviewer to get you out of the hospital and back home where you belong.

4. How do you feel?

You are very dramatic in your speech and exhibit lots of emotions, particularly anger. However, you are not used to talking about your feelings. Any comments by the interviewer that suggest he or she is interested in you or sympathetic to your experience lead you to feel happy, relaxed, and expansive. If you are feeling this way and the interviewer asks you about your parents, you say how lonely and depressed you always were as a child because your parents never had any time for you. You say how this sadness turned into anger in the last few years as you gained an adult perspective on your parents' behavior. You say that it is the last straw for you that your parents committed you to the hospital. Clearly, you will never get the love and support you crave from these cold and calculating people. If asked why they did this to you, say they decided to get rid of responsibility for you once and for all by accusing you of being dangerous. Now, they have an excuse to cut you off and not be bothered by you ever again. If asked if you can control your anger at your dad, say with disgust that you only lost control with your dad because he was acting like such a hypocrite. He was telling you that you had had too much to drink when he was the one who was an alcoholic. You appear not to have any strategies for controlling your anger. In your opinion, if others would treat you fairly, you would never lose control. You have never "lost it" with anyone but your parents because even strangers have more sensitivity to your needs than they do. If asked for more details about this, say that when you are feeling tension build up and warn people to back off or you will blow up, they always back off. Only your parents are selfish enough to push you past your limits. If you feel comfortable with the interviewer, you might ask the interviewer to call them for you and tell them to get you released from the hospital.

If the interviewer makes you feel comfortable, admit to being quite bored in the hospital. Say that none of the female doctors or nurses is attractive enough to flirt with and that none of the other patients has anything interesting to say. You feel caged in and stressed in such a small environment, and the tension rises with each day you remain cooped up. It would make you feel better if you could have something to drink or snort. If the interviewer seems understanding, hint that any drugs you take now, you could easily pay for once you get out of the hospital.

5. How do you think?

You are a fast thinker and respond quickly to any question you are asked. All of your thoughts are clear and follow logically from each other but you show poor judgment about the impact of what you say on other people. Anything that has gone wrong in your life is the fault of other people. You expect that other people will go along with your requests and help you. You consider yourself special and deserving of extra attention. You perceive that some people are more likely to help you if you act sad and anxious, so you will "play the game" to get what you want. If the interviewer shows signs of concern for you, you "milk this" for sympathy and then ask for help getting out of the hospital. You are outraged if told that to get out, you have to do anything that would take time or effort. You don't think you should be asked to waste your time. Rules are for other people, not for you.

6. What do you like about yourself?

You enjoy the fact that you can outthink most people, and you use this ability to be in control of your relationships. You consider yourself to be good looking, to have good taste, and to have an "unstoppable" attitude that usually gets you what you want. You laugh a lot in talking about yourself—it's a favorite topic. You enjoy drinking and taking drugs because being high feels great. You don't worry about withdrawal; some things are worth paying for.

7. How have you been doing at work?

You have a part-time job that takes about fifteen hours a week. You are hanging on the edge of losing it because your boss is very demanding and expects you to show up at the same time and same days every week whatever your personal plans might be. Your boss was willing to arrange your hours around your college schedule but not around your other "play" activities. If asked further work-related questions, say that your parents insisted that you work part time to help pay for your college bills because they were "letting you" live at home. You think they were insane to expect you to work and go to school at the same time; it is too constraining on your time. Sometimes you mess with your work schedule just to irritate your parents because your boss is a friend of your father and you know they "talk" about you. You have never gotten along with your fellow employees because they are like your boss and incredibly driven by boring rules.

8. How have you been doing in school?

You are enrolled in college, and this is your second attempt at a college education. You flunked out the first time because you never went to class or did any work. After that first time, your dad pushed you into the military. You lasted in service with the army for only three months. You hated all of the rules but enjoyed the socializing when you were off the base on a pass. On your last pass, you got into a bar fight with some other recruits over some "ladies." The military police arrested you. They put you in a small cell and it really freaked you out to be so shut in. You kept yelling at the guards that they needed to let you out. They ignored you. This led you to begin banging your head against the bars until your face and neck were covered in blood. When a guard noticed this, you were sent to the psychiatric ward of the base hospital. If asked questions about the incident, you say it was nothing. You just got freaked because you were coming down from an alcohol and cocaine high. You deny having any real desire to harm yourself; it was just the impulse of a bad moment.

After a brief evaluation, you were discharged from the service. You came close to getting a "dishonorable discharge," but your dad promised the base commander that you would receive psychiatric help, so your record remains "clean." You admire your dad as one smooth talker. He is a jerk, but he can be incredible. Your dad promised to help you try college one more time if you would take it seriously this time and get a part-time job. You agreed but never expected you would have to really "keep" the job for long. You have been attending more of your classes this time around, and you are getting passing marks. However, you are motivated to stay in college for the social life and not because you care about getting an education.

9. How is your health?

You feel great and you are tired of people telling you to back off of drugs and alcohol for health reasons. You are not worried about your liver; your liver is none of anyone else's business. At the hospital, you were given a full medical workup, and each nurse and doctor yapped at you about your liver; it was really annoying.

10. How do you relate to others?

You consider your relationship with your parents to be a total loss. You say things like, "My parents really stink. They're really stupid." They are just "loaded with money," but they refuse to give you any. You think it is "a load of crap" that your dad had you hospitalized for hitting him. If asked for details of this incident, you change the subject and criticize your parents. You say that your mother uses sedatives and alcohol to escape from your verbally abusive father. You say your dad has always been a heavy drinker who becomes hostile and verbally abusive when he drinks. You get restless and angry as you say your parents ignored you as you grew up. You say your dad is "full of it" when he says that you need to be in the hospital to learn self-control. Your dad has a split-second temper and swings his fists at a moment's notice. Therefore, he is a hypocritical bastard to lecture you on self-control. Early in your childhood, no one made these stupid demands on you. If your parents wanted to be left alone, they would just give you a few bucks so that you would go off to buy things. As a teen, you ran away from home a few times when your parents made life too boring for you. You would live off the credit cards you had stolen from them. Eventually, you would return home because your parents would cancel their cards, and this left you without easy money.

You have always been content with your parents' paving your way with their money. Since you "flunked" the military, however, your parents have begun to go through spurts of withholding money to "teach" you to be more "independent." You have no interest in being financially independent, and their behavior ticks you off. A month before you were forced into this hospital, you realized they needed a lesson. You broke all the windows in the house and left a note saying you would do more damage if they didn't stop being so cheap with you. They handed over a big check the next day and agreed to stop pressuring you.

You have always found people to hang out with, but the only long-term relationship you have had was with Brenda. You met her when you first came back to college. This was the "perfect" relationship at first. She had her own money and was always willing to fund your fun together. The two of you always had good laughs driving around in her sports car and taking vacations at her family's beach house. Gradually, she started to lose interest in drugs and she wanted you to stop too. This was too controlling for you and you dropped her. You miss the fun times you had together but figure you will find someone else to replace her when you are released from the hospital.

11. How do you view your life?

You are not motivated at all to change your current lifestyle. You blame all of your problems on others. You don't get it why other people always demand that you follow their rules. You just want to relax and party and wish your parents would shape up and make it easy for you.

EXERCISES FOR THE INTERVIEWER

Exercise 1: Develop a diagnosis for Gary

A. What criteria does Gary meet for a diagnosis of Intermittent Explosive Disorder and/or Substance-Related Disorders?

_____

_____

_____

_____

Name two other Axis I diagnoses that you might want to rule out for Gary and indicate what additional information might be needed to differentiate between the diagnostic choices for him.

_____

_____

_____

_____

Does Gary meet all the criteria for an Axis I disorder diagnosis? Should the diagnosis be deferred, or is a diagnosis not needed?

_____

_____

_____

_____

B. What criteria does Gary meet for an Axis II Disorder (Personality disorders and Mental Retardation)? Should a diagnosis be deferred, or is a diagnosis not needed? Explain and be as specific as possible.

_____

_____

_____

_____

C. Is there anything you might report for Gary on Axis III (General Medical Conditions that are potentially relevant to the client's mental disorder)?

_____

_____

_____

_____

D. List all specific psychosocial and environmental stressors that are influencing Gary at this time for Axis IV. Indicate if each stressor is mild, moderate, or severe.

_____

_____

_____

_____

E. What is your global assessment of Gary functioning for Axis V (current and highest in past year)?

_____

_____

_____

_____

F. Double-check your diagnostic choices starting at Axis V and proceeding backward through Axis I to determine if you may have overestimated or underestimated the impact of the situational, biological, or individual psychological factors on Gary's current functioning. Should you change anything? Be specific in describing why or why not.

_____

_____

_____

_____

G. Review your diagnostic choices again from Gary's point of view. Do your choices support the discussions you have had with him? Would he be disturbed by your choices? Be specific in discussing why or why not.

_____

_____

_____

_____

Exercise 2: Practice deepening interview with Gary

   A. As you sit in the room with Gary, he is becoming more and more agitated as he complains about his treatment from his parents and the hospital staff. As this happens, he has scooted his chair closer to yours, is leaning in toward you, and his voice is getting louder. How might this influence your attending behavior? Behaviors to consider include eye contact, orientation of your body, posture, facial expression, and autonomic behavior. If you are feeling uncomfortable, how might you broach this with Gary?

_____

_____

_____

_____

   B. Gary is making a series of remarks to you that show his level of arousal is too high for him to think. In the past, when this happened, he got violent. Make an empathetic comment that validates Gary's experience or lets him know you understand his experience in an attempt to decrease his arousal level and lower his risk for violence. Use information from Gary's profile to give you ideas of what you might say. An example is provided.

   Gary: When you ask about the bottle incident, you sound just like my blasted father! Why do you take HIS side?

   I can understand why you would feel so angry. You feel your dad has been very

   unfair to you and it adds insult to injury if I take his side (validating his right to be angry).

   Gary: I feel caged in at this hospital. I have no room to breathe. I am never alone. I can't tolerate this.

_____

_____

_____

_____

   Gary: You say you care about me, but you haven't done anything of any kind to help me. If you cared, you would get me released and fast!

_____

_____

_____

_____

   Gary: I am sick and tired of being told to stand on my own two feet. My parents are just full of it and so are you!

_____

_____

_____

_____

   C. Gary is on a destructive path. Use supportive confrontation in response to his comments in an attempt to get him to think more carefully about the negative consequences of his behavior. In your comments, remember to include empathy or support for Gary along with specific information about the negative consequences of what he is doing. Use information from Gary's profile to guide you in coming up with concrete examples of Gary's behavior to use in your confrontations. Use one of the following four styles: de-emphasize labeling, emphasize personal choice and responsibility, demonstrate that you have listened to his needs, or be honest with him about his problem behaviors in terms of the likelihood they will bring him positive or negative consequences. An example is provided that emphasizes his personal choice and responsibility for his behavior.

Gary: My parents are idiots to have put me here. They had no cause to have me locked up.

I can understand why you would hate to be forced to stay at the hospital. On the other

hand, you made the choice to attack your father with a bottle, and you could have

seriously injured him.

Gary: People keep asking me if I want to harm anyone. Everyone here is a fool.

_____

_____

_____

_____

Gary: I should be able to do what I want. My parents owe me.

_____

_____

_____

Gary: Drugs are just for fun. They have never hurt me and it's bull to say they have.

_____

_____

_____

_____

D. Gary never overtly threatens you, but whenever you make redirecting or supportive confrontation statements to him, he begins to use more aggressive nonverbal behavior. For example, he moves his chair in close to you, he leans close to you, and he talks right into your face. Whenever you indicate to him that his moving in so close makes you uncomfortable, he laughs, changes the subject to some complaint about someone, and pulls his chair further away from you. What process comment might you make to describe his manner of relating to you?

_____

_____

_____

_____

Exercise 3: Thought questions related to Gary

A. Consider who you are as an interviewer, and write down what you think might be most difficult about establishing rapport with Gary based on your age, ethnicity, gender, socioeconomic status, sexual orientation, religion, physical characteristics, and personality style. What specifically might happen?

_____

_____

_____

_____

_____

B. Is there anything you could do to enhance your ability to establish an effective working relationship with Gary? Be specific and detailed in describing your ideas.

_____

_____

_____

_____

_____

C. What information do you need to ask about to determine if Gary is an immediate or long-term danger to others? How dangerous do you think he is? Explain and be as specific as possible.

_____

_____

_____

_____

_____

D. What might you do to insure your own safety while you assess Gary?

_____

_____

_____

_____

_____

E. What role do you believe alcohol and illegal substances play in Gary's aggressive behavior?

_____

_____

_____

_____

CHILD AND TEEN PROFILES FOR USE IN INDIVIDUAL SESSIONS

Preface to Part III

If you have read the preface to the adult cases, you can skip the sections "Taking the Client Role" and "Taking the Interviewer Role."

TAKING THE CLIENT ROLE

Read the following cases and try to put yourself into the client's life. Remember that you aren't to memorize the details that are provided in the profile. The details are provided to help you bring the client alive for your collaborator in the interview process. You may change any demographics or details about a case that will help you more actively portray it. If the case is of Cathy and you are a male, feel free to make it the case of Carl and change whatever details you need to fit this gender shift.

Before the official interview starts, tell the interviewer what your basic demographics are, the reason that you were referred for the interview, and the location where the interview is taking place; all of this information is provided in the first section of the case profile. At the end of the interview, both you and the interviewer should reread the case profile as it was written and then put yourselves in the role of "interviewer" in order to complete the exercises on diagnosis, deepening the interview, and reflecting on the client interview from the perspective of the interviewer.

TAKING THE INTERVIEWER ROLE

Remember that before you begin to ask questions about why the client is here, you need to explain to the client who you are, how your clinic works, how your work is being supervised, and what the limits of confidentiality are. If you are being watched through a mirror or over videotape or audiotape equipment, this also needs to be explained to the client. Make sure that you are comprehensive in explaining how all client information will be kept confidential before asking clients for their written consent to be interviewed or engaged in treatment. In some states, minors of certain ages can consent to certain types of inpatient or outpatient treatment but not to others. In other states, minors cannot consent to any type of treatment. Therefore, the legal guardian of the minor is the one who needs to sign the consent form. You need to follow the Health Insurance Portability and Accountability Act (HIPAA) or your state confidentiality laws, in this regard. It is recommended that you follow whichever code has the stricter standard (APA, 2002; Newman, 2003). This is all part of helping clients understand what your role is and what their role is. This process of "role induction" can improve treatment outcomes when carried out effectively (Whiston & Sexton, 1993).

WHAT WILL BE KEPT CONFIDENTIAL?

In most circumstances, the information gained during the interview will be kept strictly confidential within the confines of your training program with a few highly specific exceptions. Confidentiality will need to be broken in the following situations: if the client threatens to do bodily harm to him or herself or to an identifiable other and if the client is the victim of child abuse or neglect. In these situations, you are required to put the safety of the client or others ahead of confidentiality and report the information to the appropriate authorities. Mandated reporting laws vary across states so you need to determine the exact parameters of reporting in your jurisdiction. For example, in Pennsylvania, a helper is only obligated to report to child abuse authorities if they have direct contact with a child who they suspect is being abused or neglected. In other states, if a helper hears about a potentially abused or neglected child from someone else, it is still a mandated report.

Confidentiality can also be broken if your clients want you to provide information to someone else such as a physician, school, the court, and so forth. According to the HIPAA privacy rule (1996) patients have specific rights and practitioners have specific responsibilities in how they use and disclose confidential health information. For more information on how HIPAA relates to psychologists and other mental health providers, go online to www.APApractice.org.

In practical terms, if a client wants you to reveal information about themselves to someone else, they need to sign a release of information documenting what information they want released and to whom they want it released. In working with minors, issues of consent to treatment, confidentiality, and release of records are more complex because some or all of these rights are only in the hands of the minor's legal guardian.

WHAT DO CHILDREN UNDERSTAND?

Cognitive abilities increase with age, intelligence level, and experience. Thus, the younger your clients are, the more their cognitive abilities set boundaries over how much they can understand about the interview and their role in it. If you want to be successful in gaining as much information as possible from young clients, you need to take their level of cognitive development into account in organizing the types of questions you will ask and the language you will use in asking these questions. The first step in carrying out a successful interview with children is to assess their understanding of language and key concepts. You want to do this before trying to ask them any important questions; you want to be confident that you can tell the difference between clients who don't want to respond and clients who don't know how to respond.

Boat and Everson (1986) provide practical guidelines for assessing children's understanding of questions that begin with who, what, when, where, why, and how. After determining what types of questions the child can understand, you can then adjust the type of questions you ask throughout the rest of the interview. Boat and Everson stress that questions beginning with "why" are often confusing to very young children because they are very likely to act without thinking. The older the child is the more adultlike the format and language of the interview can be.

This text makes three basic recommendations for adapting interviewing to the developmental needs of the client: use simple vocabulary, use directed and concretely focused questions, and focus on one clear issue at a time. These recommendations are now discussed in more depth.

Use Simple Language

The younger the child is, the more critical it is to use simple language in framing your questions and comments. Listen to how the child responds to you and try not to not use any vocabulary words that the child isn't using. For example, let us assume that a six-year-old girl is moving around a lot in her chair and looking tearful. If you say, "You look distressed," she may not understand you. *Distressed* is not a word that young children are likely to know. If you say, "You look sad," she is more likely to understand what you said and respond positively to your attention to her nonverbal behavior.

Use Directed and Concretely Focused Questions

Our ability to understand abstract concepts and engage in abstract reasoning is very much tied to our level of brain development. The research of Jean Piaget (1952) has demonstrated that children only begin to understand abstract concepts and engage in abstract reasoning as they enter the teen years. Children in the early school years need concepts to be expressed concretely or demonstrated with concrete aids in order to understand them. These school age children can then only apply logic to information when the reasoning involves something concrete. Children in preschool and younger are unable to apply logical reasoning whether the issues are abstract or concrete. Thus, whereas asking a teen a nondirective and very open-ended question such as, "What is happening at home?" may gain you a lot of information, it may only get you a blank stare from an eight-year-old. Young children can provide accurate information when the questions are framed in a more directive and concrete manner. For younger children, you may get more information by breaking down your large question into smaller, more concrete issues. For example, you might ask one question about the games they play at home to have fun, another question about the rules at home that make them mad, and so forth.

Some young children will be intimidated by the interview situation. This may lead them to come up with answers to your questions even if they don't understand what you are asking. When this happens, their answers won't make sense; this may make them seem unreliable or unable to provide accurate information (Saywitz, 1995). However, this conclusion is incorrect. Young children can give you accurate information if you are careful to ask for it in a developmentally appropriate manner (Saywitz, 1995).

Focus on One Clear Issue at a Time

The younger the child is, the more important it is to ask questions that focus on only one issue at a time. It may confuse a young child to ask complex questions that force them to consider several things at one time and organize their answers. For example, if you ask, "Tell me what you do at home for fun with your parents, your brother, and your friend Sam," the young child may feel confused. Who should they talk about first? What are they supposed to say? They don't do the same things with all of these people so why are you asking about them all together?

To get at this type of information more effectively, start with one relationship, such as the relationship between themselves and their father, and ask, "What do you do for fun with your dad?" After discussing this information, move on to another question such as, "What do you do for fun with your mom?" By breaking down your original complex question into smaller pieces, you are now making it clearer to the child what you are asking for. If each of your questions is directed and concretely focused, the child should be able to clearly answer each one.

It can be a challenge to adopt your interviewing skills to the developmental needs of the client. For further guidance in this process, consult some of the exercises that follow chapters 11–20, which provide you with examples of how you might want to modify your responses to clients based on their developmental level.

HOW ARE CHILDREN AND TEENS GOING TO COMMUNICATE WITH YOU?

The older the child or teen is, the more they will use language to communicate with you. Conversely, the younger they are, the more they may communicate through their physical behavior. If angry, they may respond to your questions by withdrawing and refusing to talk, or they may act up by swearing, kicking, and so forth. Clearly, this will require you to be particularly observant of their nonverbal cues if you want to understand their mood states.

Because a young child, or an angry teen, may physically act out, be strategic in your use of your physical self. In general, keep an arm's length away from your client during the interview, so if you perceive that a client may be about to hit you, you have time to protect yourself by moving out of the way. Similarly, arrange the interview situation so that you are sitting closer to the door than they are. If a client gets the urge to run away from the interview, you want to be in control of the door.

For a more in-depth look at skills for effective interviewing with children and teens, see Suggestions for Further Reading (p. 251).

DOES THE CLIENT DIFFER FROM YOU IN IMPORTANT WAYS?

Adequate role-induction discussion at the beginning of the intake often needs to go beyond explaining who you are and the procedures of the setting in which you work. You may need to discuss the clients' expectations and perceptions for the intake. Both you and the setting procedures may be quite different from what the client expected. Discuss these differences with your client and listen carefully to what the client has to say. In addition to sharing your expertise with your clients, be prepared to discuss the limitations of your knowledge (Hays, 2001). Practice this during the role plays.

After the role play is complete, do not go directly to the didactic exercises. First, review the client profile to insure that you understand the client's thoughts, feelings, and patterns of relating. It is possible that the intake wasn't thorough enough to help you develop an accurate diagnosis, so let the client profile fill in any knowledge gaps you may have. As you complete the exercises that help you practice interviewing skills, try to adapt your thinking and the style of your comments to the client's cultural context in terms of age, ethnicity, gender, religion, socioeconomic status, and so forth. This can be a challenge. To help you with this challenge, each profile provides cues as to how a client might respond to different aspects of the interviewing situation. For some of the exercises, an example of how you might adapt your comments has been provided.

Case of Cynthia

1. What are your basic statistics?

Your name is Cynthia, and you are a thirteen-year-old European-American female in eighth grade. You live with your single mother, who works in a department store and also attends college classes part time. You do not have any siblings. You are being interviewed by a practitioner in private practice at the request of your mother.

2. How do you behave in the interview?

You are of average weight and are dressed in casual but expensive (name-brand) clothing. You have highlights in your hair, and your nails are painted with sparkling nail polish. You do not sit still but play with your hair, dig into your purse to find a comb or brush, inspect your fingernails, and generally seem focused more on grooming yourself than talking to the interviewer. At several points during the interview, you ask how much longer this will take and seem impatient to be done with the interview.

You are of average intelligence and not very introspective. You answer questions concretely and may act confused when the interviewer asks open questions which make it harder for you to guess what answer would be "right." You become irritable or even rude if you perceive the interviewer to be questioning choices you have made or criticizing you in any way. You frequently refer to your mother as "dumb" and to the interview as "pointless."

If asked mental status questions, you complain that the questions are "stupid" and accuse the interviewer of thinking you are "psycho." You deny suicidal ideation but laugh sarcastically and say you have often felt like "killing" your mother. If the interviewer probes further on these feelings, you deny any intention to harm your mother but say that she just makes you so mad sometimes you want to scream. If asked about drug or alcohol use, you say, "Wouldn't you like to know?" However, when pressed, you deny experimenting with drugs or alcohol but indicate that if you wanted to, it would be easy to get high because there are plenty of kids in your school who do and you could easily get drugs from them. If asked about your mood, you say, "Of course I'm depressed. Who wouldn't be, with a mother like mine trying to control your whole life." However, you deny any actual symptoms of depression if asked specific questions.

3. Why are you being interviewed?

You are being interviewed because your mother has become concerned recently about your eating habits. You no longer eat breakfast before you go to school, and she had noticed that you are not eating very much at the few dinner times when the two of you can sit down and eat together. She was surprised recently when you turned down her invitation to go to McDonald's, which used to be a favorite outing for the two of you on days when she had worked late and had not had time to cook a meal. When she asked you about why you were eating less, you told her that you were tired of being fat and were never going to have a chance of getting on the cheerleading squad unless you lost weight. She seemed to understand this because she herself has been on numerous diets throughout her lifetime and is currently somewhat overweight. She offered to help out by buying diet soda instead of regular soda and getting fruit and diet bars for you to pack for your school lunches. However, she became alarmed a couple of weeks ago when she heard you throwing up in the bathroom. You tried to tell her you weren't feeling well, but she didn't buy it. She contacted the school guidance counselor, who recommended treatment and made you an appointment. Although your mother had spoken with the private practitioner on the phone prior to this appointment and accompanied you to the appointment, you said you wouldn't talk if she was present for the interview, and so she agreed to let you be interviewed alone.

You have never been in treatment before, and you do not think you need to be here now. If asked what you expect to get out of the interview, you say, "Nothing." However, if the interviewer makes you feel comfortable and seems genuinely interested in your point of view, you say that you could use some help getting your mother off your back. You feel she interferes in your life way too much, that you should have a lot more freedom to make your own decisions, and that she just doesn't understand you at all. You say that "everybody" at school does stuff to lose weight, that your mom clearly doesn't know anything about this because she is overweight, and that she should just stop bugging you about it. You long to be more popular, especially with guys at school, who don't seem to notice you at all. If you thought the interviewer might be able to help you figure out how to do this, you might actually be interested in treatment, but you do not express these feelings unless you feel really understood and accepted by the interviewer.

4. How do you feel?

You feel angry at your mother for making this appointment for you and "interfering" in your life. You feel as if no one really understands you. You spend a lot of time alone after school while your mother is working, and you resent this. Yet, you don't really feel comfortable with your peers either. You have tried to fit in by wearing the right clothes or doing your hair or nails the way other girls do, but you have the feeling that your peers can see right through this exterior image to the "real" you, and you don't really feel that the real you is cool, or stylish, or someone other kids would want to hang out with. Your mother has tried to increase your social involvement by getting you into Girl Scouts or the church choir or encouraging you to join extracurricular activities like band or chorus at school. If the interviewer asks about these activities, you say you aren't really interested in them or that they are "boring." The truth is, you haven't felt accepted by the other kids when you have attended these activities. You don't know what to say or how to act in order to fit in, but you do not admit this to the interviewer and instead complain about the activities themselves. You think you would like to be a cheerleader because these seem to be the popular girls and they are the ones who seem to have boyfriends. You think a lot about boys these days, and sometimes the feelings you have when you think about boys make you want to "jump out of your skin."

5. How do you think?

You think you are old enough to make more of your own decisions, and your mother doesn't seem to understand this. You think that she treats you "like a child." You think that if you could just look the way you want to look and be a cheerleader, then everything else would fall into place and you would be happy. You have tried restricting your eating to lose weight, but were never very successful. Now you think you have a possible solution. You were in the restroom at school after lunch one day when you heard someone throwing up in the stall next to you. You noticed that one of the cheerleaders came out shortly afterward, and you asked her if she was okay. She laughed at you and said she was fine. Another one of your classmates was in the restroom, too, and after the cheerleader left, she made a comment about "stupid things people do to stay skinny and be popular." You learned about eating disorders in health class, but this was the first time you ever knew someone who actually threw up to manage their weight. When you learned about eating disorders in school, you thought the whole idea was "gross," but you had never put this idea together with someone you perceive to be popular and pretty. You thought a lot about this and one day when you were home alone, you decided to see if you could make yourself throw up. To your surprise, it worked, and you didn't really feel all that bad afterward. In fact, it felt good to be in control of your body and to make it do something you wanted it to do. Suddenly a whole new way of controlling your weight seemed possible, one that did not require you to be so stringent about what you ate or to feel deprived. You figure you can control this behavior and use it only when you need it. You do not believe you are at risk for an eating disorder, and you become very defensive with the interviewer if he or she seems to imply that you might be at risk or might need help with this behavior. You have lost a few pounds since you started using this strategy and love the way you felt when you recently were able to buy a pair of jeans a whole size smaller than you used to wear.

6. What do you like about yourself?

You like feeling that you can control what happens to your body. You feel as though you don't have a lot of control over your life in general, and it is exciting to think you can control what you weigh or how you look. If the interviewer asks you what you like about yourself, however, you have trouble answering the question. You say that you like your new clothes and your choice of hairstyle and fingernail polish. You have a harder time identifying internal qualities or personality traits that you like.

7. How have you been doing at work?

This question is not relevant for this client.

8. How have you been doing in school?

Your grades are average, B's and C's. You believe you probably could do better in school, but you aren't really motivated to work harder. You like classes in which your teachers seem to pay attention to you, but dislike classes in which the teacher corrects or reprimands you. You especially seem to have love–hate relationships with your male teachers, whom you either idolize or despise, depending on whether they are nice to you or not. You are having trouble with math right now, but you don't mind because the math teacher, who is young and male, has offered to stay after school to give you extra help. You would much rather be hanging out after school getting help on math from him than at home alone, feeling bored and lonely.

9. How is your health?

You haven't been to a physician lately, but you don't have any major health complaints. You last got a physical exam for school in sixth grade. Your mother takes you to the doctor for colds and viral infections, but you have never had any long-term illness and are not currently on any medications. You have been feeling more tired than usual lately. You have been taking naps in the afternoons and still have trouble getting up in the morning in time for school. But you figure this is normal because you read somewhere that teenagers need more sleep than other people anyway.

10. How do you relate to others?

Your relationship with your mother has become tenser lately. You used to be very close and spent a lot of her time off from work doing things together, just the two of you. You never knew your father, and your mother has told you that she was not married to your father when she became pregnant with you, but you don't know any details about this time in her life. As long as you can remember, your family has consisted of just you and your mother. Your mother has tried dating a few men over the years, but these relationships have not lasted long, and you have always been relieved when they ended and she had more time to devote to you again. You expect her to take you on outings, to spend money on you when shopping, and to devote her spare time to you. You resent it when she has to work late or study for one of her classes or is too tired to do something with you after work. You do not do any chores at home and do not see this as your responsibility. After all, it's her house, so she should take care of it. You resent it when she tries to tell you what to do or gets "in your face" about your choice of clothes, music, or strategies for losing weight.

You have one or two girlfriends with whom you like to go to the movies or spend the night. You don't like having them over to your house because your mother always seems to be hanging around listening to your private conversations. You prefer to go to their houses because their mothers seem more relaxed and let you do what you want without monitoring you much. Your friends are like you, in that they are not very popular and have trouble fitting in at school. Lately, you have been trying to distance yourself from them by sitting at another table at lunch and refusing invitations to spend the night. You have decided that maybe hanging out with them is part of why you are not popular at school and that you need to make friends with more popular girls if you are going to "move up" in popularity at school.

You are interested in boys but don't know how to approach them. You spend a lot of time looking at teen magazines and fantasizing about young singers and movie stars, but you generally avoid boys your own age. You tell the interviewer that they are just too "immature" for you, and this is why you avoid them. In reality, you are afraid you will say something stupid or they will laugh at you if you try to have a conversation with them.

11. How do you view your life?

You will say your life "sucks." Your mother is "an idiot" who tries to "control" you. School is "boring," staying at home alone with nothing to do is "boring," and this interview is "boring." If your mother would just stop interfering and let you become the person you want to be (by losing weight, trying out for cheerleading, and moving up the popularity ladder), things would be great. The one arena where you have felt successful lately is in losing a little weight, and you don't want the interviewer, your mother, or anyone else to take that away from you.

EXERCISES FOR THE INTERVIEWER

Exercise 1: Develop a diagnosis for Cynthia

A. What criteria does Cynthia meet for a diagnosis of Bulimia Nervosa or Eating Disorder NOS on Axis I?

_____

_____

_____

_____

_____

Name two other Axis I diagnoses you might want to rule out for Cynthia and indicate what additional information might be needed to differentiate between the diagnostic choices for her.

_____

_____

_____

_____

_____

Does Cynthia meet all the requirements for an Axis I disorder, should the diagnosis be deferred, or is a diagnosis not needed?

_____

_____

_____

_____

_____

B. What criteria does Cynthia meet for an Axis II diagnosis (Personality Disorders and Mental Retardation)? Should a diagnosis be deferred, or is a diagnosis not needed? Explain and be as specific as possible.

_____

_____

_____

_____

_____

C. Is there anything you might report for Cynthia on Axis III (General Medical Conditions that are potentially relevant to the client's mental disorder)?

_____

_____

_____

_____

D. List all relevant categories of psychosocial and environmental stressors for Cynthia and specify examples of each one on Axis IV. Indicate if each stressor is mild, moderate, or severe.

_____

_____

_____

_____

_____

E. What is your global assessment of Cynthia's functioning for Axis V (current, highest in past year)?

_____

_____

_____

_____

_____

F. Double-check your diagnostic choices starting at Axis V and proceeding backward through Axis I to determine if you may have overestimated or underestimated the impact of the situational, biological, or individual psychological factors on Cynthia's current functioning. Should you change anything? Be specific in describing why or why not.

_____

_____

_____

_____

_____

G. Review your diagnostic choices again from Cynthia's point of view. Do your choices support the discussions you have had with her? Would she be disturbed by your choices? Be specific in discussing why or why not.

_____

_____

_____

_____

_____

Exercise 2: Practice deepening interview with Cynthia

A. In order to pinpoint an accurate diagnosis for Cynthia and to establish a baseline for treatment, you need to obtain more detailed information about her eating practices, self-image, and attitudes about gaining weight or becoming fat. Generate a list of both open-ended and closed questions that will help you obtain a fuller picture of Cynthia's behavior, thoughts, emotions, imagery, and physical sensations with regard to these three areas. Use the following prompts to help you. An example of one open-ended question and one closed question is provided for each area relevant to prompt 1.

Prompt 1: Cynthia's eating practices

(Behavior) What do you do to control your eating? Do you throw up after you eat?

(Thoughts) What do you think about as you eat? Do you tell yourself to vomit?

(Feelings) How do you feel as you are eating? Do you feel in control or out of control as you

vomit? (Imagery) What image comes to mind as you consider eating something? Is the image

pleasant or unpleasant for you? (Physical Sensations) What sensations do you feel in your

body as you begin to eat? Do your body sensations tell you it is important to eat or not to eat?

Prompt 2: Cynthia's self-image

Prompt 3: Cynthia's attitudes about gaining weight or becoming fat

B. Cynthia has presented herself in a somewhat hostile fashion and is resistant to the idea of changing her eating practices. Respond to each of the following statements by Cynthia with an empathetic comment that might help her to feel understood and comfortable sharing her feelings more openly in the interview. Use information from Cynthia's profile to guide you in making these comments. An example is provided.

Cynthia: I wish my mother would just get off my back. She keeps interfering in my life and she thinks she knows what's best for me, but she's totally wrong. Things just aren't the way they used to be when she was my age. Anyway, it's my life, not hers.

You feel like she keeps trying to impose her ideas on you and somehow it doesn't fit your

experience. It's frustrating that she doesn't seem to understand the way you see things.

And you want to have more of a say in making your own choices.

Cynthia: If you were me, you'd want to lose weight too. Look at me. I'm wearing the right clothes, I'm doing my hair and nails the way the popular girls do, but I might as well be invisible at school. But if I lose weight, then they'll have to notice me. It's the only way I'll ever make it as a cheerleader. Just knowing the chants and drills isn't enough. You have to be noticed; you have to be popular to get on the squad.

Cynthia: I loved it when I got these new jeans that were a whole size smaller. It made me feel strong, like I could do anything I wanted to, make myself into anything I wanted to be. Nobody, not you, not my mom, not the guidance counselor or my teachers is going to take that away from me.

Cynthia: Everybody at school who's anybody does something to control their weight. My mom obviously is too dumb to understand this. I mean, look at how overweight she is! It's no big deal. It's my body, and I should be able to choose what I do with it.

C. Despite her resistance to changing her eating practices, Cynthia has identified a number of things she wants. Look back over the statements made by Cynthia in the preceding exercise and come up with a summarizing statement you could say to her that will include all of the things she most wants. State your conclusion in such a way as to have it serve as a transition to the topic of what Cynthia might need to do to attain her goals without damaging her body.

Exercise 3: Thought questions related to Cynthia

A. Consider who you are as an interviewer and write down what you think might be most difficult about establishing rapport with Cynthia based on your age, ethnicity, gender, socio-economic status, sexual orientation, religion, physical characteristics, and personality style. What specifically might happen?

_____

_____

_____

_____

B. Is there anything you could do to enhance your ability to establish an effective working relationship with Cynthia? What specifically might you do?

_____

_____

_____

_____

C. Consider the role of development in the case of Cynthia. What specifically do you know about Cynthia's current developmental stage that might help to explain some of her current difficulties?

_____

_____

_____

_____

D. Specifically, what might you do in the interview or say to Cynthia or her mother with regard to the role of developmental influences on Cynthia?

_____

_____

_____

_____

E. Consider the role of Cynthia's absent father in contributing to her current difficulties. How might the absence of a father have affected Cynthia, her mother, Cynthia's relationship with her mother, Cynthia's ability to relate to males, Cynthia's self-image, and so forth?

_____

_____

_____

_____

G. Consider the role of cultural influences in Cynthia's current difficulties, specifically, cultural values regarding thinness. Does Cynthia's eating behavior truly reflect individual pathology or is it actually a "normal" reaction to a toxic cultural norm? What is the role or responsibility of the practitioner in intervening to change toxic cultural norms in society at large versus treating individuals who are affected by that cultural norm?

_____

_____

_____

_____

14

Case of Jeffrey

1. What are your basic statistics?

You are a 16-year-old, European-American male, in 11th grade. You live with your father, John (age 49), your mother, Sandra (age 48), an older brother, James (age 18), and a younger brother, Jason (age 14). Your parents are both teachers in the same high school you attend. You also have an older sister, Sarah (age 20), who attends college in another state. You are being interviewed by a practitioner in a private practice setting.

2. How do you behave in the interview?

You sit slouched in your chair and do not make eye contact with the interviewer. Your hair is long, and when you bend your head forward, it conveniently screens your face. You speak quietly and mostly in monosyllables. When asked closed questions, you give one-word answers. When asked more open questions, you may shrug or answer, "I don't know." For some questions, you may not answer at all until the interviewer repeats the question. Your demeanor is more one of studied indifference than hostility, however, and if the interviewer is successful in establishing rapport, you may sit up a little, make occasional eye contact, and put more effort into answering the questions.

When the interviewer asks about the problems that led to your being interviewed, you initially shut down and withdraw even more. Depending on the interviewer's skill in getting past your defenses, you may show flashes of anger and emotional pain, expressed in a raised voice, agitated movements, and clenching your fists, but when this happens, you quickly try to cover it up by getting quiet again and breaking eye contact, slumping forward in your chair to hide your face from the interviewer.

If asked mental status questions, you do not demonstrate any difficulties with memory, concentration, or attention. You deny any symptoms of depression or anxiety. You also deny drug or alcohol use, although you may initially fend off such questions about use of these substances by saying, "Doesn't everybody my age try something if they get the chance?" If asked about suicidal or homicidal ideation, you hesitate a long time before answering. If the interviewer presses you to answer, you say that you don't have any plans for this at the moment. Pressed further, you say that sometimes you get angry enough to think about doing something to "let off steam," but you again deny any current plans to harm anyone or yourself. If the interviewer probes further, you say something like, "I'm not stupid. If I was planning something,

153

I sure wouldn't tell someone like you. But don't worry. I'm not going to do anything in the near future. Now can we talk about something else?"

3. Why are you being interviewed?

Your parents made the appointment for you at the urging of the school principal and guidance counselor. You are currently in danger of failing eleventh grade. Your grades are mostly D's and F's, although you currently have a B in your computer class. Your parents and teachers are frustrated with you, and no one seems to know how to reach you or motivate you. Your parents tried hiring a tutor, but you were so rude and uncooperative with the tutor that he quit.

In addition to your poor grades, the school has recently suspended you for ten days because one of your teachers found a notebook you had left in her classroom, in which you had written some song lyrics with references to guns and dying. You had illustrated these lyrics with what appeared to be drawings of people bleeding and dying. Even more alarming to the teacher was a list of "People I Love to Hate," which included the names of several of your teachers and classmates. The teacher turned the notebook over to the school principal, who called you in for a conference with the teacher, the guidance counselor, the assistant principal, and your parents. Asked for an explanation, you just shrugged and said you were bored in class and this was your way of entertaining yourself. The principal kept questioning you, and finally you got mad and yelled that you thought there were plenty of people in this school you'd be glad to see "gone," including everyone in the room. The school suspended you and strongly advised your parents to take you for a psychological evaluation.

You previously saw a psychologist when you were in elementary school because your teachers were concerned that you seemed to be having trouble fitting in socially. You got teased a lot and didn't have any friends except for one or two other kids who, like you, didn't seem to fit in. The psychologist talked to you about how to make friends and encouraged you to join a club or other after-school activity. You weren't interested in sports or learning to play an instrument in the band, so it was hard for you to find an activity that suited you. However, when you moved up to the junior high school in seventh grade, there were more activities available. You got involved in a computer club, and seemed happier, so your parents stopped taking you to the psychologist.

All you really want to get out of the interview is to get through it without letting the interviewer get past the "wall" that you put up to keep people away from your feelings. You don't trust adults, who always seem to want to control you, and you don't like most of your peers, who either ignore you or make fun of you. You just want to "be left alone," to listen to your music, play your video games, mess around on the computer, and generally shut the world out.

4. How do you feel?

You feel angry at your parents and at the school for making you come here. You feel your parents will never understand you because as teachers, the school is their "whole world" and it embarrasses them to have you doing so poorly and getting in trouble. You assume they will always take the perspective of the school over your feelings or needs.

You feel alienated from your peers, who seem superficial, shallow, and judgmental. All they seem to care about is getting good grades, doing well in sports, or pairing off with boyfriends or girlfriends. School to them seems to be one big game, whereas to you it seems like torture. You don't like your classes or teachers and have basically taken the attitude that school is something to be endured until you are old enough to drop out. The threat of being expelled or made to repeat a grade doesn't really seem like a threat to you because you don't plan to finish school anyway. In fact, being suspended has been a relief because you can stay in your room at home and play your video games without having to think about school for a while.

Deep down, you are in a lot of pain because you have the feeling that everyone else has figured out how to "play the game" of life better than you have. You sometimes feel as though you would be better off dead, just because then you wouldn't have to deal with getting up every day and feeling the same feelings of loneliness and alienation again. You hated elementary school because the other kids made fun of you for being clumsy, for being smaller than the other kids, for having a big nose, for anything they could think of that made you "different." Junior high school wasn't much better, except for the computer club, where you were as good as or better on the computer than anyone else and could become completely absorbed in projects on the computer that let you block out anyone and anything that bothered you. You still got teased, but at least you had one place you could get away from it all. In senior high school, you don't get teased as much because you have figured out how to be "invisible." You keep to yourself or hang out with one or two other friends who are also "misfits" and who would rather play video games, mess around on the computer, or listen to music than do anything else. Sometimes you and these friends like to imagine what it would be like to pull something like the Columbine incident. It feels good just to imagine the looks on everyone's faces if you showed up one day with a gun and took control. In fact, you do not have access to a gun and have never seriously contemplated turning this fantasy into action, but the one time you really feel good and powerful is when you imagine such a scenario.

You are jealous of your brothers, who excel at sports. James is the football star quarterback, and Jason excels at hockey. Your parents attend all their games and talk a lot about how proud they are of your brothers. Your older sister was at the top of her graduating class and won all kinds of scholarships to attend college. Your parents are also very proud of her. You sometimes think it's not your parents' fault that they don't understand you. It has been easier for them to feel proud of their other children, who excel in such obvious ways. You can't really think of any reason why they should be proud of you, and you don't expect that they ever will be, but it still hurts to think you'll never measure up. When you were younger, you used to wonder if maybe you had been adopted because you seem so different from everyone else in your family.

5. How do you think?

You do not demonstrate any evidence of hallucinations or delusions. Although you perceive others to have a rather negative opinion of you, this perception is basically accurate. Your parents are worried about you, your teachers are frustrated with you, the school administration is afraid of you, other kids think you are weird, and your siblings ignore you except when there is a conflict over who has access to the computer, television, or something else they want. You expect to be rejected by others, and this is often the case. What you do not recognize is how you contribute to bringing about this rejection.

You expect the interviewer to reject you or become frustrated with you, also. You try to keep the interviewer at a distance by revealing as little as possible. However, if the interviewer persists in probing at sensitive areas, or actually seems interested in getting to know how you think about things, you attempt to scare him or her away by getting angry, using foul language, or saying provocative things about what you'd like to see happen to some of those kids at school.

6. What do you like about yourself?

There is not much you really like about yourself. You are proud of your computer skills and your video game skills. You are happiest when you can lose yourself in the world of a challenging video game or computer project. You are loyal to your one or two friends who share these interests, and you pride yourself in the fact that they can trust you to keep their secrets.

7. How have you been doing at work?

This question is not applicable to this client.

8. How have you been doing in school?

You got good grades in elementary school, and in fact, were identified as gifted in second grade. However, by junior high school, your grades had started dropping, and your parents reluctantly took you out of the advanced classes and placed you in average classes. You barely passed tenth grade and are now failing eleventh grade. You are getting B's in your computer class, and the teacher says you could easily have an A except that you tend to spend your time on projects that interest you rather than meeting the class requirements. You are failing math and English, and you currently have a C in both science and history classes. You are not taking a heavy schedule and have study halls which you could use to get extra help from the math lab, but you choose either to go to the computer room or do nothing in study hall rather than seek extra help. Your parents wanted you to get your learner's permit for your driver's license but told you that you would have to have passing grades before they would let you do this. You decided you didn't care enough about driving to bring your grades up, and you have not made any effort to get your permit. The bottom line for you is that you are just waiting to turn seventeen years old so you can drop out of school, and you don't really care what kind of grades you get in the meantime.

9. How is your health?

You do not currently have any significant health problems. You had a physical last summer, prior to entering eleventh grade, and were in good health at that time. You had problems with asthma in elementary school, which was yet another cause for teasing by other kids, who called you "Whistle-breath," and made fun of you when you had to leave class to go to the nurse to use your inhaler. This has gotten better as you have gotten older, and you seldom use an inhaler anymore.

10. How do you relate to others?

You relate to others primarily by keeping your distance from them. This is a strategy that developed over the years as a reaction to the distress and disappointment you experienced when others made fun of you or ignored you. You prefer to withdraw into your room to listen to music, play video games, or get on the computer. You resist your parents' efforts to start conversations with you. You seldom go to either of your brothers' sporting events, preferring to stay home alone. You also resist your teachers' efforts to have discussions with you about how you are doing in school. You get along with your computer teacher, as long as he lets you pursue projects that interest you. He is the only teacher who ever has anything positive to say about your school work.

You hang out with one or two friends who are also into video games and computers, and who seem to share your feelings of alienation from their peers. You feel they understand you and you can trust them. They are the only friends with whom you talk about your feelings about school and your classmates because they feel the same way.

11. How do you view your life?

You view your life as pretty meaningless and unsatisfying. You have the feeling that you are just "waiting it out" until you can get away from the school environment and be on your own. Yet in reality, you have no clear picture of what life on your own might be like because you have no plans to finish school and no real skills to get a job except your computer skills. Sometimes you imagine creating a new video game or computer program and making lots of money from its sale. Most of the time, you focus more on escaping your current unsatisfying situation than on what might come afterward. You don't really picture a future. Your motivation right now is centered on getting away from your current circumstances rather than moving toward something more positive.

EXERCISES FOR THE INTERVIEWER

Exercise 1: Develop a diagnosis for Jeffrey

A. What criteria does Jeffrey meet for a diagnosis of Oppositional Defiant Disorder or Major Depressive Disorder on Axis I?

_____

_____

_____

_____

Name two other Axis I diagnoses that you might want to rule out for Jeffrey, and indicate what additional information might be needed to differentiate between all possible diagnoses for him.

_____

_____

_____

_____

_____

Does Jeffrey meet all the requirements for an Axis I disorder? Should the diagnosis be deferred, or is a diagnosis not needed?

_____

_____

_____

_____

B. What criteria does Jeffrey meet for an Axis II diagnosis (Personality Disorders and Mental Retardation)? Should a diagnosis be deferred, or is a diagnosis not needed? Explain and be as specific as possible.

_____

_____

_____

_____

C. Is there anything you might report for Jeffrey on Axis III (General Medical Conditions that are potentially relevant to a client's mental disorder)?

_____

_____

_____

_____

D. List all relevant categories of psychosocial and environmental stressors for Jeffrey and specify examples of each one on Axis IV. Indicate if each stressor is mild, moderate, or severe.

_____

_____

_____

_____

E. What is your global assessment of Jeffrey's functioning for Axis V (current, highest in past year)?

_____

_____

_____

_____

F. Double-check your diagnostic choices starting at Axis V and proceeding backward through Axis I to determine if you may have overestimated or underestimated the impact of the situational, biological, or individual psychological factors on Jeffrey's current functioning. Should you change anything? Be specific in describing why or why not.

_____

_____

_____

_____

G. Review your diagnostic choices again from Jeffrey's point of view. Do your choices support the discussions you have had with him? Would he be disturbed by your choices? Be specific in discussing why or why not.

_____

_____

_____

_____

Exercise 2: Practice deepening interview with Jeffrey

A. Jeffrey tries hard to present an attitude of indifference and detachment in the interview, but his nonverbal behavior often provides clues to the inner emotions he is not verbalizing. For each of the following scenarios, respond to Jeffrey's nonverbal behavior by tentatively commenting on the emotions they seem to reflect. Use information from Jeffrey's profile to guide you. An example is provided.

Jeffrey says, "I don't care about fitting in. Most of the kids in my school are dumb anyway. All they care about is showing off by getting good grades, being jocks, or getting laid by somebody popular. I'm not into any of that." He raises his voice, clenches his fists, and pounds them on the arms of his chair. "I wish they'd just quit bugging me and leave me alone."

I hear you saying you don't care about fitting in, at least not in the way most other kids try

to fit in. But I hear you raising your voice, I see you clenching your fists, and I get the

impression that you have some pretty strong feelings about it after all, that deep down you

may be really angry that those seem to be the only ways to measure up or fit in.

Jeffrey: I'm used to being teased. In elementary school, it was my big nose, or my asthma, or the fact that I wasn't any good at sports. In junior high, I didn't wear the right clothes or sit at the right lunch table. It used to hurt (voice breaks, he leans forward so his hair covers his face), but I'm over that now. I just do my own thing and stay away from everybody.

_____

_____

_____

_____

Jeffrey: Sometimes I imagine pulling something like that Columbine thing. It would be so totally awesome to show up one day with a gun and just take control. Like, I can just see the looks on all their faces as they realize that I have all the power and it's too damn late to go back and fix the way they treated me.

_____

_____

_____

_____

B. Although Jeffrey is uncomfortable sharing his emotions with others, he does mention his feelings in a superficial way from time to time in the interview. Help Jeffrey feel understood and safe to explore his emotions by making two types of responses to his comments. Make the first comment a simple, reflective listening comment, and make the second a more complex, empathetic comment that goes beyond the surface of what Jeffrey has said to invite him to share the deeper emotions behind his statements. An example has been provided.

Jeffrey: To other kids, school is this big game, where they're all after some kind of prize. To me, it's more like this torture chamber to just get through until I can escape.

1. *It's like they're playing a game, and you're going through hell (reflective listening).*

2. *It feels like you're living in two totally different realities. Theirs is a game to be played,*

   with prizes to win. You're just barely hanging on, trying to endure one day at a time,

   waiting for the torture to end (empathetic comment).

Jeffrey: School is my parents' whole world. You have to do well in their world for them to be proud of you. I suck at their world. It embarrasses them.

1. _____

_____

2. _____

_____

Jeffrey: It's different in computer class. I get to leave the torture chamber for a while. I get into something on the computer, and I'm getting it, and I know I'm probably as good as or better than anybody in the class, and time just flies by.

1. _____

_____

2. _____

_____

Jeffrey: I'm just putting in time until they kick me out or I'm old enough to drop out. Sometimes I think I can't stand it another day. That's when I think about checking out, that it might actually be a relief to be dead.

1. _____

_____

2. _____

_____

Exercise 3: Thought questions related to Jeffrey

A. Consider who you are as an interviewer and write down what you think might be most difficult about establishing rapport with Jeffrey based on your age, ethnicity, gender, socioeconomic status, sexual orientation, religion, physical characteristics, and personality style. What specifically might happen?

_____

_____

_____

_____

_____

B. Is there anything you could do to enhance your ability to establish an effective working relationship with Jeffrey? What specifically might you do?

_____

_____

_____

_____

_____

C. The school has recommended that Jeffrey's parents have him evaluated because they are concerned about the risk of violence. His parents may be concerned about the risk of suicide. Jeffrey admits that he fantasizes about behaving violently and that he sometimes thinks he would be better off dead. But he denies any intent to do anything "in the near future." And he actively resists talking about these issues. Pursuing them further may jeopardize rapport and make him even more resistant to treatment. You are responsible as an interviewer to address both the concerns of Jeffrey's parents and the school, on the one hand, and to establish the necessary rapport with Jeffrey to engage him in treatment, on the other hand. How would you balance these two potentially conflicting tasks? Be specific in identifying what you think is most important to accomplish in the interview and what, specifically, you might say or do in the interview to assess the risk of suicidal and/or violent behavior while trying to develop rapport.

_____

_____

_____

_____

_____

_____

_____

_____

Case of Melissa

1. What are your basic statistics?

Your name is Melissa, and you are a ten-year-old, European-American female in the fifth grade. Your parents have recently divorced, and are engaged in a bitter custody battle for you and your sister, Jessica, age four. Your parents, Jack (age thirty-eight) and Denise (age thirty-six), both live in the same town. Jack is a car salesman, and Denise works part-time at a beauty salon. The judge has recently ordered that you and your sister divide your time equally between both parents, spending alternating weeks at each parent's home. The interviewer obtained this information about your basic statistics prior to meeting with you, in phone conversations with both parents. You are being interviewed in a private practice setting.

2. How do you behave in the interview?

Your hair and clothes are neat and clean. You sit quietly and speak softly, in a subdued voice. You are cooperative, and it is clear from your efforts to answer all questions fully that you want the interviewer to like you. If you are not sure that you know the right answer to a question, you hesitate, apologize, and ask for the question to be repeated.

Your vocabulary is good and demonstrates intelligence. You brought a book with you to read in the waiting room before the appointment. If the interviewer asks you about this, you say that you love to read and often have a hard time putting a book down if you are really interested in it.

If the interviewer asks about your living situation and your feelings about your parents' divorce, you speak even more softly. Your voice may quiver, and your eyes may fill with tears. You may also rub your stomach as if in pain and may interrupt the interview to ask if you can take a break and go use the restroom.

You admit that you often feel sad and worried and that you sometimes lie awake at night thinking about your parents' divorce and wondering if they will ever get back together again. You cry often when you think about this. Your mother has spoken with your teacher at school, and she has been very understanding. She told you that you could leave the room to go talk to the nurse or the guidance counselor any time you felt too upset to stay in class. If asked mental status questions, you deny any suicidal ideation or aggressive impulses. You also show no signs of having confusing thoughts or strange ideas.

3. Why are you being interviewed?

Your mother called to make the appointment for you. She told you she thought you needed someone besides your parents to talk to about the divorce. She had noticed that you were complaining a lot about stomachaches and were not eating or sleeping well. Your stomachaches have gotten so bad recently that you asked your mom if you could stay home from school. She was surprised because you love school and never want to miss a day. The next week, when you were staying with your dad, you had such a bad stomachache at school that you asked the school nurse to call your dad, and he came and took you home. Your dad told your mom about this the next time he brought you back to her house. Your mom took you to your pediatrician, who said there was nothing medically wrong with you and suggested you were "stressed." After this, your mom told you that she had talked to your father about bringing you to see someone, and that he had agreed as long as he could speak to the interviewer on the phone before the appointment and make sure he would be informed of what took place. Both your parents have told you that they understand it is hard for you to be "stuck in the middle" and that they think it might be a good idea if you had someone to talk to who wasn't on either parent's side.

4. How do you feel?

You feel sad and anxious most of the time. It scares you when your stomach hurts because you think there might be something really wrong with you. You are afraid that you might get really sick or even die while you are with one parent and not be able to see the other parent ever again. You get really frightened when you overhear one of your parents arguing with the other over the phone because they scream at each other and say scary things about getting custody of you and your sister and never letting the other parent see you again. You don't really think they mean this because they always try to reassure you if they notice you have been listening to the conversation, but it is frightening to see your parents become so angry and emotional.

You try very hard not to let either parent think that you have chosen sides with the other. When you are with your father, he often questions you about things your mother has said and done. When you are with your mother, she does the same thing, asking questions about your father. You feel scared that you are going to say the wrong thing and get in trouble with someone. You don't want your parents yelling at you the way they yell at each other.

Living in two houses is also confusing because your parents have such different rules for you. For example, your mother will make you do homework before you can play or watch television, but your father sometimes lets you do your homework later at night or forgets to ask about homework at all. You have just begun to learn to play the flute, and whereas your mother wants you to practice every day, your father tells you it's up to you whether you practice. The last time you went to your father's house, you forgot your flute, and you didn't want to ask him to go back and get it because he seemed busy and might get mad at you. When your mother realized you had forgotten it, she called and yelled at your dad, who then yelled at you anyway, so he still ended up mad.

You also feel responsible for your little sister, who keeps asking you why you have to live in two houses now, or when mommy and daddy are going to be together again. When you are at your father's house, Jessica cries for your mother, and you have to comfort her at night so she won't wake your dad. When you are at your mother's house, Jessica has tantrums when mom makes her do things that she doesn't have to do at dad's house, and you feel you have to try to calm her down so mom won't get upset. Sometimes you try to correct her behavior so mom won't have to, and you feel hurt when mom doesn't seem to appreciate this but instead criticizes you for acting like Jessica's parent. You don't blame Jessica, who has a lot of your same feelings and is too little to understand what is happening, but you feel very responsible for helping her through this, as you are the one person who really understands what she is going through.

5. How do you think?

You are bright and express yourself well, although you worry about giving "wrong answers." You do not demonstrate any evidence of disordered thinking. You expect to be able to please others and work hard to do so. You think that if you try really hard to figure out what other people want from you and how to keep from upsetting or disappointing them, you should be able to keep everyone happy. It bothers you when you find your mom crying in her room or when your dad seems preoccupied and angry. You want everyone you love to be happy, and you believe you should try your best to make this happen.

You have noticed some positive changes in your parents since the divorce, and this surprises you when you think about it. For example, your father has started cooking and doing laundry, things you never saw him do when he lived with your mother. Your mother, on the other hand, has begun thinking about opening up her own beauty salon instead of working for someone else. You think it is a good thing that both your parents are making some positive changes, but you don't understand why they had to get divorced in order for this to happen.

You have mixed feelings about the interviewer. On the one hand, it is nice to have someone listen to your side of the story and show an interest in how the divorce and custody battle are affecting you. On the other hand, you are suspicious of how the information you are giving the interviewer might be used. After all, you have already been interviewed by a custody evaluator, who told your parents things you had said which you wish they had not known, and by a judge, who told you that the courts would make the decision about where you lived but still wanted to know how you felt about it. You are afraid that if you say anything negative about either parent, that parent will find out what you said and think that you want to live with the other parent. You do not want to have to choose between your parents, but you also do not like going back and forth each week to a different house. You will seek a lot of reassurance from the interviewer about keeping your feelings "private" before opening up in the interview.

6. What do you like about yourself?

You like that you are a good student and a good reader. You like that you try to help take care of your little sister. You like being a "helper" to your mom and dad. You also like being a good friend, and you have several friends at school who trust you with their secrets because they know you would never tell them to anyone.

7. How have you been doing at work?

This question is not applicable to this client.

8. How have you been doing in school?

You get mostly A's at school. You like school. You enjoy learning new things, you get along well with your teachers and your classmates, and you like the fact that school is predictable and people seldom yell at each other. You feel comfortable going to the school nurse or guidance counselor when you are upset, and you feel your teacher understands you and is "nice." Recently, however, it has been harder to enjoy school because you get your stomachaches. You don't want to miss school, but you can't concentrate on what the teacher is teaching you when your stomach hurts, and it just seems easier at those times to go to the nurse's office.

9. How is your health?

According to your pediatrician, there is nothing wrong with you except "stress." You have stomachaches several times a week, especially at the beginning of a week after you have just transferred from one house to the other or at the end of a week when you are thinking about moving back to the other house. You have no other medical concerns.

10. How do you relate to others?

You get along well with adults and with your classmates. Your eagerness to please others and "keep the peace" make you very likeable. You are thoughtful and sensitive, and you often notice when someone needs to be cheered up or encouraged. Your friends find you to be loyal and dependable. Your little sister relies on you for security in the moves back and forth between your parents' homes. Your parents would also describe you as helpful and cooperative. However, your mother has sometimes told you that you are "overresponsible," and your father has said that you are "too sensitive." You are not sure why they said these things, as you think these are good things.

11. How do you view your life?

Your life is currently confusing and upsetting to you. You can't make everyone happy, and the "rules" seem to keep changing. You wish everyone could just "get along with each other." You really wish your parents would get back together, but you don't see how this can realistically happen with all the mean things they have said to each other. If they can't get back together, you just wish they could stop fighting with each other. You don't like living in two houses, but you think you could deal with this if you just didn't have to worry all the time about making either parent mad by saying or doing something that made it seem as if you had chosen sides. You want things to settle down for everyone, and you want to stop having stomachaches. Most of all, you want to know what you can do to make things better for everybody.

EXERCISES FOR THE INTERVIEWER

Exercise 1: Develop a diagnosis for Melissa

A. What criteria does Melissa meet for a diagnosis of Adjustment Disorder on Axis I?

_____

_____

_____

_____

Name two other Axis I diagnoses that you might want to rule out for Melissa, and indicate what additional information might be needed to differentiate between an Adjustment Disorder and each of these diagnoses.

_____

_____

_____

_____

Does Melissa meet all the requirements for an Axis I disorder? Should the diagnosis be deferred, or is a diagnosis not needed?

_____

_____

_____

_____

B. What criteria does Melissa meet for an Axis II diagnosis (Personality Disorders and Mental Retardation)? Should a diagnosis be deferred, or is a diagnosis not needed? Explain and be as specific as possible.

_____

_____

_____

_____

C. Is there anything you might report for Melissa on Axis III (General Medical Conditions that are potentially relevant to a client's mental disorder)?

_____

_____

_____

_____

D. List all relevant categories of psychosocial and environmental stressors for Melissa and specify examples of each one on Axis IV. Indicate if each stressor is mild, moderate, or severe.

_____

_____

_____

_____

E. What is your global assessment of Melissa's functioning for Axis V (current, highest in past year)?

_____

_____

_____

_____

F. Double-check your diagnostic choices starting at Axis V and proceeding backward through Axis I to determine if you may have overestimated or underestimated the impact of the situational, biological, or individual psychological factors on Melissa's current functioning. Should you change anything? Be specific in describing why or why not.

_____

_____

_____

_____

G. Review your diagnostic choices again from Melissa's point of view. Do your choices support the discussions you have had with her? Would she be disturbed by your choices? Be specific in discussing why or why not.

_____

_____

_____

_____

Exercise 2: Practice deepening interview with Melissa

A. Melissa internalizes her feelings and experiences them in the form of physical symptoms (stomachaches). Help Melissa become aware of the connection between her emotions and her physical sensations by sensitively commenting on what her nonverbal behavior may be communicating in the following scenarios. Use Melissa's profile to guide you in making these connections. Be careful to use developmentally appropriate language. An example has been provided that uses simple vocabulary.

Melissa: I don't like living in two houses. (Her voice drops, she speaks almost in a whisper, and her eyes fill with tears.) I liked it better when we were all together, except for the yelling and fighting.

I hear the way your voice gets quiet and I see your eyes filling up with tears and I wonder

if you feel very sad about living in two houses.

Melissa: When I am at my dad's, I miss my mom. But when I am at my mom's, I miss my dad. (She rubs her stomach, as if in pain.) Do you have a restroom here somewhere?

_____

_____

_____

Melissa: Could you repeat that question? I'm sorry, I didn't understand it. (She rubs her hands together, frowns, bites her lip, and looks down at the floor.)

_____

_____

_____

Melissa: I don't like to talk about this stuff. After I talked to that other person, she told my parents what I said, but she made it sound like I was mad at my dad and mom and that's not what I meant at all. . . . (She breaks off, drops her eyes to the floor, and taps her foot nervously against the chair leg.)

_____

_____

_____

B. Establishing a baseline with regard to Melissa's symptom of stomachaches in terms of their frequency, intensity, and duration will help you chart her progress in treatment over time. Generate a list of open-ended and closed questions that will help you obtain more detailed information about her stomachaches using the following prompts. Examples of one open-ended and two closed questions are given for prompt 1.

Prompt 1: Stomachaches at her mom's house

What were the stomachaches like the last time you stayed with your mom? How many

stomachaches did you have? How long did your first stomachache last?

Prompt 2: Stomachaches at her dad's house

_____

_____

_____

Prompt 3: Stomachaches at school

_____

_____

_____

Prompt 4: Times she doesn't have stomachaches

_____

_____

_____

C. Melissa has trouble trusting the interviewer because, during the custody evaluation, the evaluator told her parents things that made them mad at her. She does not want this to happen again. Use reflective listening in response to Melissa's comments to help her view you as someone who understands her experience and will be trustworthy. In responding to Melissa, be careful to use simple language that she can easily understand. An example has been provided.

Melissa: I try to help my mom by making sure Jessica behaves. But then mom yells at me and says I'm not the mom. I'm just trying to help!
You try to help your mom with Jessica but mom just yells at you for helping.

Melissa: That other lady told my parents stuff I said. But she didn't understand what I really meant. And I didn't know she was going to tell them, or I wouldn't have said what I said!

_____

_____

_____

Melissa: Everybody keeps asking me where I want to live, with my mom or with my dad. I just want us all to be a family in one house. I don't like going back and forth, but I can't choose just one parent all the time and never see the other.

_____

_____

_____

Melissa: I have to be so careful what I say, so neither one of them thinks I'm on the other one's side. Mom asks me about stuff dad says, and dad asks me about stuff that happens at mom's house, and I don't want to say anything to make anybody mad.

_____

_____

_____

D. For each of the following statements from Melissa, respond with an empathetic comment that will help deepen her emotional awareness. Use an empathetic comment that shows you understand the meaning of her experience, that validates her experience, or that helps her regain emotional control. Use information from Melissa's profile to guide you in determining what emotions lie underneath the surface of her words. An example has been provided of an empathetic comment that underscores the meaning of her experiences.

Melissa: I want my parents to be together. Sometimes at night I can't sleep because I'm wishing so hard for them to get back together. But then I remember lying awake and listening to them fight with each other, and I used to pull the covers over my head and just wish it would stop. I never meant for it to stop like this, though, by them divorcing.

You are torn between wanting your parents to get back together and being afraid of

the fighting that happened when they were together. And maybe a little tiny part of you

is afraid that somehow by wishing for the fighting to stop, you caused them to divorce?

Melissa: Sometimes I hear my mom and dad yelling at each other on the phone, stuff about getting custody and not letting the other one see us again. And sometimes when my stomach hurts, I get afraid that if something happens to me when I'm at one house, I might never see the other one again. I don't like saying goodbye to either of them when I go to school. I never thought about stuff like this before.

_____

_____

_____

_____

Melissa: When we're at my dad's, Jessica sometimes cries for my mom, and I have to comfort her so my dad doesn't wake up. I don't want him to feel bad. But I don't tell my mom when I see her because I don't want her to worry about Jessica. I just want everybody to be okay.

_____

_____

_____

_____

Melissa: It's weird to see my dad doing laundry and cooking and stuff. His spaghetti is pretty good! And my mom is changing, too. She's doing a lot of stuff she always let my dad do before. I didn't know either one of them could change so much. It's kind of cool, but I wish they could've done it without divorcing.

_____

_____

_____

_____

Exercise 3: Thought questions related to Melissa

   A. Consider who you are as an interviewer and write down what you think might be most difficult about establishing rapport with Melissa based on your age, ethnicity, gender, socio-economic status, sexual orientation, religion, physical characteristics, and personality style. What specifically might happen?

_____

_____

_____

_____

_____

   B. Is there anything you could do to enhance your ability to establish an effective working relationship with Melissa? What specifically might you do?

_____

_____

_____

_____

_____

   C. What are the specific advantages and disadvantages of joint physical custody for Melissa based on her profile?

_____

_____

_____

_____

_____

   D. Based on Melissa's profile, what are the advantages and disadvantages of her attending services for herself versus being seen along with her sister Jessica and her parents?

_____

_____

_____

_____

_____

   E. What confidentiality does Melissa have from her parents?

_____

_____

_____

_____

_____

16

Case of Edward

1. What are your basic statistics?

Your name is Edward, and you are a twelve-year-old, African-American male in sixth grade. You live with your mother, Melita, and your younger brother, Manuel, age ten. Your mother is a first-generation immigrant from Angola, having fled as a refugee with your father, Antonio, during the Angolan revolution. Your father and mother separated when you were two years old, shortly after the birth of your brother, and you neither remember him nor know anything about where he is now. You and your brother were born in this country and are American citizens. Your given name was Eduardo, but you prefer Edward, or Eddie, because it seems less foreign. You are being seen in an outpatient community mental health center.

2. How do you behave in the interview?

You are neatly but shabbily dressed. You sit relatively still during the interview, but squirm from time to time in your chair as if uncomfortable. Your gaze wanders around the room, taking in the pictures on the wall, the view from the window, and the door, especially when your attention is distracted by sounds from the hall or nearby offices.

You give concrete answers to questions and do not exhibit much insight. You do not volunteer much information, and your answers to questions are as brief as possible. You are uncommunicative, but not uncooperative.

If the interviewer asks about why you are here, you say that you do not know. If pressed, you say that your mother told you that you had to come and talk to a doctor, but you don't know why. If the interviewer asks if this has anything to do with your poor grades in school, you acknowledge that this could be the reason why you are here, but you really aren't sure.

You deny any symptoms of depression or anxiety. If the interviewer asks whether you have ever threatened to kill yourself, you admit that you have, but say that this was just because you were mad at your mother at the time. You deny any use of drugs or alcohol. You give adequate answers to mental status questions. You struggle a bit, however, if asked to do any mental arithmetic. If the interviewer uses big words, you may look confused, hesitate, or say that you "don't know."

3. Why are you being interviewed?

Your mother brought you to the community mental health center on the advice of the school guidance counselor. You were identified as having a learning disability in first grade. In

175

fact, you repeated first grade because the school believed you might be more successful if you had more time to master the basic skills necessary for reading and math. You receive learning support at school, but still do very poorly in spelling and reading. Your math skills are somewhat better, but you have trouble when doing word problems, which require you to be able to read and understand the problem before attempting to solve it. Although you cooperate with the learning support teacher at school and seem to benefit from one-on-one attention, your mother has not been able to work with you at home because you have temper tantrums when she tries to get you to practice spelling or reading. You complain that she doesn't pronounce the words properly, because of her accent, and this "messes up" your spelling even more.

Of more concern to your mother is the fact that you have recently begun to hang around with some older children whom she believes will get you into trouble. You live in subsidized housing, and there are a lot of kids in the development who are unsupervised much of the time. Your mother works as a clerk in a grocery store and has to take whatever hours she is given. This means she is usually at work when you get home from school, and you are on your own for several hours before she gets home. Recently, the landlord gave your mother a written warning because he had caught you with some older boys who were lighting fires with cigarette lighters in some tall grass in back of the apartment complex. Getting a warning really upset your mother, as she doesn't know what she would do if she lost her subsidized housing. When she tried to discipline you by grounding you, you got very angry and threatened to kill yourself. This alarmed her. She contacted the school guidance counselor, who told her that the local community mental health center might be able to help.

You have never been in mental health treatment before. You have been to medical doctors and assume that this is another "doctor" like those. You may wonder why this doctor is not examining you physically and is asking so many questions.

4. How do you feel?

You do not talk to anyone about your feelings, and in fact, if asked about your feelings, you have a hard time identifying them. You do recognize the feeling of anger, but the feelings you have about school are harder to label. You say that you feel "bored," but you appear sad and discouraged when you say this. However, if the interviewer specifically probes for feelings of sadness or worry, you deny any awareness of these feelings.

You feel ashamed that you upset your mom, but even more ashamed that she has an accent and customs that make her different than your friends' mothers. When she comes to an event at school, you try to ignore the curious way people look at her when she starts to talk. You can't stand to study spelling or practice reading with her because when she pronounces the words in her strange way, it confuses you even more. Even without her help, reading is confusing for you. You have to work so hard just to sound out the words that you can't remember what you just read when you get to the end of a line or a sentence. You would rather avoid reading or spelling for as long as possible, although this means you often get big red F's on your spelling tests. You try to hide these tests from your mother, but she always finds out eventually when report card time comes or she gets a call from your teacher. Lately, you have begun to dread school, which just seems like one long experience of failure and helplessness for you.

You are much happier when you and your brother can hang out with your friends after school. They don't like school much either, and they don't care about their own grades or yours. You can run fast and jump high and climb any tree around, and these skills earn you admiration and acceptance from these kids. Much of your time with them is spent daring each other to see who can run the fastest, climb the highest, or catch the most snakes from the swampy area around the stream that runs across the back of the apartment complex. You excel at these activities and feel like you are well accepted among these friends. You know that some of what they do is stuff your mother would not approve of, but as long as she is at work and you don't get caught, no one needs to know. If pressed by the interviewer, you admit that these boys also smoke, sneak beer from their parents' refrigerators, and occasionally shoplift small items like cigarette lighters or candy from the nearby department store. You deny doing any of these things yourself, but may squirm uncomfortably while being questioned about these activities.

5. How do you think?

You think very concretely. You are not a good liar, and if the interviewer persists in questioning you closely or confronts you about something your mother has already told about you, you admit the truth. You have noticed that although your friends seem to be able to get away with all kinds of behavior, you always seem to get caught, but you are not sure why this is. Your teachers and your mother are always telling you that you should think about the consequences of your actions before you do something. You have never been able to think beyond the immediate situation and what is most appealing to you in that moment, or what seems to win the approval of your friends.

You think you are stupid when it comes to reading and spelling. You don't expect to get any smarter, and when you think about being in school for six more years until you graduate, it seems like an impossibly long time to be so frustrated.

6. What do you like about yourself?

The things you like about yourself have to do with your physical or athletic abilities. You like that you can run faster, jump farther, and climb taller trees than any other boy in your neighborhood. You enjoy watching sports on television and sometimes fantasize about becoming a star football player. You like that you look out for your younger brother, and you are fiercely loyal to him. You would never let anyone hurt him or make fun of him, and you like that he relies on you for protection.

7. How have you been doing at work?

This question is not applicable to this client.

8. How have you been doing in school?

Your grades are mostly C's and D's. You are currently getting an F in spelling. At a recent parent conference, you heard your teacher tell your mother that school will get even harder for you if you do not learn to read because your other subjects, like science and social studies, will demand more reading skill as you move on to higher grades. The teacher wants you to take a reading class in summer school. You hate school as it is and really look forward to summer vacation as a break from school. You are really hoping your mother will not agree with the teacher and make you go to summer school. In fact, when you got home after the parent–teacher conference, you told your mom that if she tries to make you go to summer school, she'll be sorry because you will either run away or kill yourself. You said this because you knew this would scare her, and you hoped she would give up the idea of summer school if you scared her enough.

9. How is your health?

You are in good health. You go to a pediatrician several times a year for the usual colds and sore throats, but are not under treatment for any chronic conditions. Your mother complains that you do not eat the food she cooks for you, but you say you do not like African food and wish she would learn to cook hotdogs, hamburgers, and "sloppy joes" like other mothers.

10. How do you relate to others?

You get along well with your brother. Even your occasional sibling battles are usually good-natured, and since you are bigger than he is, you can usually win these contests anyway. You enjoy hanging out with your friends in the neighborhood, but these relationships consist mostly of daring each other to take on physical challenges or playing outdoor games, rather than talking to each other about what you think or feel. You don't even talk to your brother about how you feel. It's not that you are trying to hide your feelings from him or from anyone else, but you really are not introspective and do not have words for your inner experience.

You are cooperative with your teachers at school and do what is asked of you. However, if the in-class work is difficult and you do not understand it, you sit and draw cartoon doodles on your paper until either the class ends or the teacher comes and makes you do the work. You do not ask questions when you are confused, and the teachers seldom know if you are understanding what is being taught until they check on the work you have actually done or find you doing nothing. You are not a behavior problem in school, and your teachers generally like you but are frustrated that you do not seek help when you need it. The only time you become difficult to manage is during a test, when you sometimes give up and refuse to even try to fill in the answers. If the teacher sends you down to the learning support teacher to take the test, however, he can usually get you to persevere, if he sits there and prompts you to answer each question or rephrases the questions for you to make them easier to understand.

Your relationship with your mother is not close. You are happiest when she is at work and you and your brother are on your own at home. You do not help out around the house, and she often complains that she has to do everything for you and for your brother. She asks you to take out the garbage and clean your room, but you have learned that she will ask several times and then do it herself if you just wait and ignore her long enough. You don't talk to her about what is happening at school, and in fact, you try to hide your bad grades from her for as long as possible. You actively resist any efforts she makes to help you study or practice your spelling words. When she gets angry with you or tries to enforce rules or study time, you have temper tantrums and threaten to run away or kill yourself. This is usually effective in getting her to back off.

11. How do you view your life?

You don't think your life is all that bad, except for school. You have fun hanging out with your friends and your brother when you are not in school. You sometimes wish your mom were like other moms and less "African," and you often wish your family had more money so you could have more of the things you see advertised on television. When you are not being pressed by your teachers or your mother to think about school, you are "fine." You just wish school would disappear and you could forget all about it. Although you would like your mom to be proud of you, instead of upset with you, you don't believe this is possible. You don't think there is any way you can be successful at school, and so you would rather avoid it than try to change what you are doing.

EXERCISES FOR THE INTERVIEWER

Exercise 1: Develop a diagnosis for Edward

A. What criteria does Edward meet for a diagnosis of a Learning Disorder (specify which one) on Axis I?

_____

_____

_____

_____

Name two other Axis I diagnoses that you might want to rule out for Edward, and indicate what additional information might be needed to differentiate between a Learning Disorder and each of these diagnoses.

_____

_____

_____

_____

Does Edward meet all the requirements for an Axis I disorder? Should the diagnosis be deferred, or is a diagnosis not needed?

_____

_____

_____

_____

B. What criteria does Edward meet for an Axis II diagnosis (Personality Disorders and Mental Retardation)? Should a diagnosis be deferred, or is a diagnosis not needed? Explain and be as specific as possible.

_____

_____

_____

_____

C. Is there anything you might report for Edward on Axis III (General Medical Conditions that are potentially relevant to a client's mental disorder)?

_____

_____

_____

D. List all relevant categories of psychosocial and environmental stressors for Edward and specify examples of each one on Axis IV. Indicate if each stressor is mild, moderate, or severe.

_____

_____

_____

_____

E. What is your global assessment of Edward's functioning for Axis V (current, highest in past year)?

_____

_____

_____

_____

F. Double-check your diagnostic choices starting at Axis V and proceeding backward through Axis I to determine if you may have overestimated or underestimated the impact of the situational, biological, or individual psychological factors on Edward's current functioning. Should you change anything? Be specific in describing why or why not.

_____

_____

_____

_____

G. Review your diagnostic choices again from Edward's point of view. Do your choices support the discussions you have had with him? Would he be disturbed by your choices? Be specific in discussing why or why not.

_____

_____

_____

_____

Exercise 2: Practice deepening interview with Edward

A. Edward is not introspective and is generally unable to identify his emotions, except for anger. He tends to use words like "boring" when he is experiencing unpleasant emotion for which he lacks a more accurate label. However, his body language conveys clues to his emotions, which you can use to help him become aware of his inner experience and develop a richer vocabulary for that experience. Respond to the following scenarios by commenting sensitively on Edward's nonverbal behavior to help him identify and label his feelings more accurately. Use information from Edward's profile to guide you in identifying his feelings. An example is provided.

Edward: School is boring. (He jiggles his feet impatiently, drums his fingers on the arm of the chair, and sighs loudly.)

The way you are jiggling your feet and drumming your fingers on the chair, and that

big sigh just now, makes me think that school frustrates you, and you're tired of

feeling frustrated.

You have asked Edward how he feels when he gets back another spelling test with a big red "F" on it. He says, "It's boring." When he says this, he breaks eye contact, puts his head in his hands, frowns, and looks down at the floor.

_____

_____

_____

_____

Edward tells you he has another big spelling test tomorrow. You ask how he feels about this. He shrugs, says, "I don't know." Meanwhile, he squirms in his chair and rubs the palms of his hands on his pants as if they are sweaty.

_____

_____

_____

_____

You have asked Edward what happens when his mother tries to help him practice his spelling words. He says, "Nothing. I get mad, that's all. I just don't want to do it with her. It's stupid, the way she says the words. She doesn't say them right, that's all." He squirms and breaks eye contact; his face flushes.

_____

_____

_____

_____

B. Generate both open-ended and closed questions that will help Edward to open up and share more about his life using the following prompts. Make these developmentally appropriate. An example of two open-ended questions and one closed question for prompt 1 are provided that use the directed and concrete language that will aid Edward in responding.

Prompt 1: Behavior when having academic problems at school
What did you do the last time you were asked to read out loud in class? What did you do the

last time you had a spelling test? Can the other students tell if you are having trouble with

school work?

Prompt 2: His feelings toward his mother

_____

_____

_____

_____

Prompt 3: His feelings toward his brother

_____

_____

_____

_____

Prompt 4: His feelings about his "African-ness"

_____

_____

_____

_____

Exercise 3: Thought questions related to Edward

A. Consider who you are as an interviewer and write down what you think might be most difficult about establishing rapport with Edward based on your age, ethnicity, gender, socio-economic status, sexual orientation, religion, physical characteristics, and personality style. What specifically might happen?

_____

_____

_____

_____

B. Is there anything you could do to enhance your ability to establish an effective working relationship with Edward? What specifically might you do?

_____

_____

_____

_____

C. Consider Edward's situation as one of two brothers being raised by a single mother, who has to work long hours to support her sons, has limited financial resources, and no husband or extended family nearby to provide support. How do you think this situation may have contributed to the development of Edward's problems? Be specific.

_____

_____

_____

_____

D. How might the situation be different if Edward had a father in the home or grandparents nearby to provide support to his family?

_____

_____

_____

_____

E. How could your treatment plan and choice of interventions address the specific problems faced by a low-income, single-parent household? Be specific.

_____

_____

_____

_____

F. Discuss how acculturation conflicts have contributed to Edward's difficulties. Be specific and give examples.

_____

_____

_____

_____

Case of Raoul

1. What are your basic statistics?

You are a seventeen-year-old, Mexican-American male. You live with your single mother and two younger brothers in a three-bedroom rental house in a small rural farming community. You haven't seen your father in three years. You have a grandmother and a grandfather who also live in the United States but who are not citizens. You have an extensive family network that still lives in Mexico. Your mother became a citizen ten years ago. You and your brothers were born in the United States. Your rental house is within the "Mexican" neighborhood of a predominately European-American community. You are a senior at a local high school. You are being interviewed at a community mental health center.

2. How do you behave?

You are well groomed, quiet, and reserved. Your pay careful attention to what the interviewer says to you and weigh each word carefully. You answer questions but only with very brief answers. For example, if asked who is in your family you say, "Mom and my two brothers." If asked if you are uncomfortable being interviewed, you say, "yes." You are angry at being interviewed and view the interviewer as "another outsider who thinks he or she knows everything." Despite this hostile attitude, you have a lot of self-control and behave respectfully. The only sign of your anger is the overemphasis you may give to certain words in your answers. For example, if asked if you know why you are being interviewed, you say, "Yes, SIR" or "Yes, MA'AM." While answering questions, you stare into your lap. If the interviewer makes enough supportive comments to you, you gradually open up and become more talkative.

If the interviewer asks you questions about drugs, you get agitated. You state that you are being persecuted because of your Mexican background and that many white students are involved with drugs and the teachers ignore it. Even though angry, you do not yell or use bad language. You show your tension through the intensity with which your words come out. Your internal turmoil is also evident in your nonverbal behavior; your legs bounce and your fists clench. If the interviewer shows sensitivity to your feeling of victimization, you calm down immediately. You look up at the interviewer and say something like, "Thanks for believing me." If you perceive the interviewer is showing signs of not believing you or of "minimizing" your negative experiences, your tension and anger intensify and you bang your fists against your legs. However, you do not say or do anything threatening.

In a mental status screen, you deny suicidal thoughts or depressive symptoms but admit that you feel like an "outsider" in town and you don't like this. You admit grudgingly to some anxiety over your current situation. Your anxiety stems from the fact that the police handled you very roughly when you were arrested. One of the officers hit you in the stomach while the others weren't looking, and you were threatened by another arrestee while you were waiting in the police station for your mother. Your thought content is consistently coherent and clear, but you are suspicious of the motives of all the whites in your town and this may come off as "paranoid." You admit to daily use of marijuana, but deny it has had any harmful effects on you. If asked to talk more about your drug usage, you say something like, "Everyone smokes back home in Mexico and the law against it in the United States is just plain stupid." If asked screening questions about violence, you deny any homicidal thoughts or aggressive outbursts. These questions anger you, and you look very tense and upset because you think the questions show that the interviewer considers all Mexicans as dangerous.

3. Why are you being interviewed?

Your mother has insisted that you come to the interview. You have come out of respect for her. She is worried because you were arrested for having drugs at school, and a police hearing is coming up in two weeks. If the interviewer is supportive, you admit that the hearing makes you nervous. The police handled you roughly when you were arrested and you wonder if it will be even worse at the hearing. You don't know anyone who has been in court before, and you would appreciate some advice about what to say at the hearing. You do not want to be sent to jail, but you do not want to admit to doing something wrong when you don't think you did. You do not question the interviewer directly about this; instead, you try to feel the interviewer out to determine if he or she might know something that would be helpful to you. For example, you may look up briefly and say, "Have you been to one of these police hearings?"

You have never received any psychological services before. You are not "crazy," and you figure you have been sent here because your probation officer thinks all Mexicans must be crazy. You resent this but are also curious about what is going to happen. Your mom told you the interviewer will want you to promise to stop smoking dope. You have no intentions of making this promise, and you become slightly belligerent if the interviewer seems to be asking you for this.

4. How do you feel?

You feel a lot of deep anger against the white community. You believe all the whites in town are disrespectful and condescending when they interact with your family. Employees of stores follow you around and "watch you." You notice all the looks you get whenever you shop and assume they all think you are a thief. You often leave a store without buying anything, saying as you leave, "You can all go on your coffee break now, the thief is leaving." Your mom works really hard to support your family, and you really respect her for this. You are angry because you think the whites in town don't show her proper respect. For example, you think her male boss stares at her and has improper feelings for her. You are angry most of the time at school because you feel picked on.

The only time you really feel relaxed is when you smoke dope with your friends. The world seems calmer, and you like to be calm and relaxed. These friends hang out with you at school and give you a sense of belonging. You don't see them outside of school because you have too many family obligations.

5. How do you think?

You don't feel like being rushed into making choices or decisions. When asked a question, you want to mull it over carefully before answering. You expect to be treated like an adult and perceive most adults outside your family as condescending. You believe you are ready to take on adult decisions and responsibilities. You consider your mother's and brothers' welfare to be your responsibilities because you are the eldest son and because you "made" your dad leave when you were fourteen. You watched your dad physically abuse your mom for years. One weekend, after you saw your mother take a bad beating, you came to the conclusion that you could not respect a man who would mistreat his wife. This was a painful conclusion for you to reach. You took action the very next time you saw your dad losing control. One day, you walked in the house to find your dad beating your mother. You jumped in between them and punched your dad in the face. Your dad stared at you for a moment and then walked out without a word. He never came back.

As the "man of the house," you thought long and hard about the financial problems your mother was having, and you have done your best to help. At first, you contributed by taking over many responsibilities within the home for caring for your siblings. Then, you took on a part-time job with your grandfather. When you realized how much your grandfather needed to keep most of the money you made, you came up with the idea of selling dope to make ends meet. It seemed like a simple solution to an overwhelming problem. If you had dropped your work with your grandfather and taken some other time-consuming job, your grandparents would have suffered. It takes very little time to sell dope because you can do it at school between classes.

6. What do you like about yourself?

You see yourself as a good son and older brother. You often make meals for your siblings and help them with their homework when your mom is late coming home from work. Your brother had a lot of trouble learning to read, and it was your help after school that led to his current mastery of reading. You always look for ways to help your mother around the house without being asked. You are proud that you have brought needed money home to help your mother pay the bills.

7. How have you been doing at work?

You work part-time as a gardener with your grandfather. He has an active business taking care of a number of homes in the affluent section of your town; he is having trouble pushing the lawn mower now that he is older. You have taken over cutting the grass at these homes while your grandfather trims bushes and takes care of the gardens. You only accept a little money for this because you know your grandparents need the money for themselves.

You have a small side business selling marijuana. You got loads of it last summer when you visited your relatives in Mexico. You use all the money you make to help your mom pay bills. Until the arrest, she assumed all the money came from the gardening business and didn't ask any questions. She was just relieved to get your help. Until the arrest, your grandfather was proud of how hard you worked just to help him. He didn't know how much money you were giving your mother, so he hadn't asked how you were able to pay her when he knew you weren't taking much for your work with him. Since the arrest, your grandfather has been very quiet around you. He hasn't said anything to you about the marijuana, but he has forced you to accept more of the gardening money and has said things to you such as, "Take this to help your mother."

8. How have you been doing in school?

At the present time, you are a first-semester senior in high school. Whereas in the past you were an average student with a good record of attendance, in recent months you have been cutting classes and not handing in homework assignments. Over the course of this year, you have become more and more a part of a group that is considered "delinquent" by the principal.

Your group, while never engaging in any physically aggressive behavior within the school, often insults other students as they enter and leave the building. The group also smokes cigarettes and marijuana. You never had any group to "hang" with at the school before. Prior to now, you were a quiet student who did his work and then left promptly at the end of the day.

9. How is your health?

You have never had routine medical or dental care except for the free screenings available at school. You are currently in good health.

10. How do you relate to others?

You family situation used to be financially stable but emotionally stormy. This was because your father was a good provider, but he was also an alcoholic who became very violent after drinking. You never had any direct problems with your father and often spent your free time with him. Three years ago, however, you came home from school to find you father beating your mother; you got in between them and struck your father. After this one blow, your father walked out of the house and has never returned. He has never contacted the family or sent any money to provide financial support. You miss him, but feel that his treatment of your mother was unacceptable. You have always been close to your mother. Your earliest memories are of her constant care for you, your siblings, and your elderly grandparents who live down the street from you. She always puts family members ahead of herself. You have a lot of respect for her and view her as an ideal mother. You do a lot to help her around the house. You are a favorite of your grandparents and spend a lot of your free time with them. They are very proud of you and don't think your mother needs to worry about your marijuana usage. They know about your arrest, and they are worried about the court hearing because they are afraid you will be handled roughly.

You are close to your younger brothers. They often come to you for help with their chores or homework. You play with them a lot and they respect you. You tell them stories about the relatives back in Mexico and encourage them to speak Spanish at home. Your mother knows she can rely on you to watch them if she needs to leave the house.

You only socialize with peers at school. There are no Mexican males your age in your neighborhood. You have a lot of cousins your age in Mexico that you hang out with whenever you get to visit. You feel lonely for the companionship of young men your own age who can understand what it is like to be a Mexican in your town.

11. How do you view your life?

You feel very frustrated that you have to live in an area that is disrespectful of Mexicans. However, you see the extreme poverty of your relatives back home and realize your family has much more in the United States. Although you fully intend to stay in the United States, you enjoy criticizing it to your peers at school. You don't feel as comfortable with your group at school as you do with your cousins in Mexico, but it is better than being alone. In Mexico, last summer, you stayed up until 3 a.m. each night running around with your cousins. It was great to feel so free and so accepted. No one acted like you were a troublemaker or drug addict. You just don't know why you can't be treated like this in the United States.

EXERCISES FOR THE INTERVIEWER

Exercise 1: Develop a diagnosis for Raoul

A. What criteria does Raoul meet for an Axis I diagnosis of Conduct Disorder and/or Substance-Related Disorders?

_____

_____

_____

_____

Name two other Axis I diagnoses that you might want to rule out for Raoul and indicate what additional information might be needed to differentiate between the diagnostic choices for him.

_____

_____

_____

_____

Does Raoul meet all the criteria for an Axis I disorder? Should the diagnosis be deferred, or is a diagnosis not needed?

_____

_____

_____

_____

B. What criteria does Raoul meet for an Axis II diagnosis (Personality Disorders and Mental Retardation)? Should a diagnosis be deferred, or is a diagnosis not needed? Explain and be as specific as possible.

_____

_____

_____

_____

C. Is there anything you might report for Raoul on Axis III (General Medical Conditions that are potentially relevant to the client's mental disorder)?

_____

_____

_____

_____

D. List all specific psychosocial and environmental problems on Axis IV that are influencing Raoul at this time. Indicate if each stressor is mild, moderate, or severe.

_____

_____

_____

_____

E. What is your global assessment of Raoul's functioning for Axis V (current and highest in past year)?

_____

_____

_____

_____

F. Double-check your diagnostic choices starting at Axis V and proceeding backward through Axis I to determine if you may have overestimated or underestimated the impact of the situational, biological, or individual psychological factors on Raoul's current functioning. Should you change anything? Be specific in describing why or why not.

_____

_____

_____

_____

G. Review your diagnostic choices again from Raoul's point of view. Do your choices support the discussions you have had with him? Would he be disturbed by your choices? Be specific in discussing why or why not.

_____

_____

_____

_____

Exercise 2: Practice deepening interview with Raoul

A. Raoul has faced serious discrimination and prejudice in his community and feels very humiliated by it. In response to his remarks, write two types of comments. Have the first be a simple, reflective listening comment and the second be a more complex, empathetic comment to either validate his experience, let him know you understand what he is experiencing, or help him regain emotional control. Use information from Raoul's profile to guide you in developing these comments. An example is provided of empathy used to validate Raoul's reactions to his experiences.

Raoul: Everyone at the stores stares at me and treats me like a shoplifter!

1. *They treat you like a shoplifter (reflective listening).*

2. *It would feel humiliating to most people to be treated like that. You have a right to expect*

   people to treat you with respect (empathetic comment).

Raoul: The teachers all treat me like I am retarded just because I don't blurt out answers in class!

1. _____

2. _____

   _____

Raoul: The police hit me even though I didn't resist arrest. They know I have no money to use in defending myself against them.

1. _____

2. _____

   _____

Raoul: You just pretend to listen because I'm your money in the bank. You think Mexicans are dirt, just like everyone else around here.

1. _____

2. _____

   _____

B. Raoul is using and selling marijuana which is against the law in the United States. In response to each of his comments, write a supportive confrontation. Remember to include in your comment both an affirmation for Raoul or emotional support as well as specific information about the negative consequences of what he is doing. Use information from Raoul's profile to help you do this. Use one of the four styles of supportive confrontation including: de-emphasizing labeling, emphasizing personal choice and responsibility, demonstrating that you have listened to what Raoul needs, or being honest with Raoul about his problem behaviors and the likelihood that they will bring him positive or negative consequences. An example is provided using the style of emphasizing his personal choice and responsibility for his actions.

Raoul: This whole situation is just stupid! I'm only on drug charges because I'm not white!
It stinks that there is a lot of racism against Mexicans in this community. But, racism
aside, you did choose to break the drugs laws of the United States. You describe yourself
as the "man" of your family. As the man, you have to take responsibility for what you
have done.

Raoul: My friends and I just have lots of laughs. We have never done anything wrong.

_____

_____

_____

_____

Raoul: My mother is afraid that I'll go to jail and then have a criminal record. She always worries about nothing.

_____

_____

_____

_____

Raoul: My Mexican cousins think I'm so lucky to go to school. I don't need school. I can make good money now.

_____

_____

_____

_____

C. Every time you ask Raoul a question related to drugs, the police, or his declining school performance, he looks briefly up at you and then snorts as his eyes return to his lap. What process comment might you make to point out this pattern to him and ask him what he is trying to tell you by doing it?

_____

_____

_____

_____

Exercise 3: Thought questions related to Raoul

A. Consider who you are as an interviewer and write down what you think might be most difficult about establishing rapport with Raoul based on your age, ethnicity, gender, socioeconomic status, sexual orientation, religion, physical characteristics, and personality style. What specifically might happen?

_____

_____

_____

_____

B. Is there anything you could do to enhance your ability to establish an effective working relationship with Raoul? Be specific and detailed in describing your ideas.

_____

_____

_____

_____

C. What might you say to Raoul if he said, "You say you respect me as a Mexican. Prove it by telling my mother I don't need to come here. You know I don't need it."

_____

_____

_____

_____

D. What might you say if Raoul said, "You're just a student. If I was white, I would have gotten a real professional to help me."

_____

_____

_____

_____

E. Raoul is seventeen years old. He doesn't want you to share anything he tells you with his mother. What might you say? Remember that as a minor, Raoul has no legal confidentiality from his mother in many treatment situations.

_____

_____

_____

_____

F. What role do you view poverty has in the problems that Raoul is facing within his community?

_____

_____

_____

_____

Case of Erica

1. What are your basic statistics?

Your name is Erica and you are a seven-year-old, European-American female. You are currently living in a rural, farm community with your mother and maternal grandmother. Your father was killed recently in an automobile accident. Your mom was badly hurt in the accident and is still recovering. You were in the car at the time of the accident but are unhurt. Your grandmother moved into your home immediately after the accident to care for you and your mom. You don't know your grandmother very well because she always lived very far away and you only saw her once a year. You attend first grade at a nearby elementary school. You are being interviewed by a practitioner in private practice.

2. How do you behave in the interview?

You are clean and well dressed in what you consider to be special clothes. You try hard to sit like a "lady" and not get messed up. You try to keep your knees tightly together with your feet on the floor and your ankles together; your mom told you this was polite behavior. You are a bright girl and won't have any trouble understanding the interviewer unless he or she talks using vocabulary that you don't understand. You grandmother forced you to come to this appointment even though you begged her to let you stay at home. So, you are pouting and being passively resistant to the interviewer. When asked questions, at first you just look down, shrug your shoulders, and swing your legs. If the interviewer tells you to look up or shows any signs of irritation with you, you press your lips together and say nothing. If the interviewer tries to be soothing and kind, you nod and start to cry.

If the interviewer asks any questions about your mom and dad, you look down, play with your feet, and try not to cry. You sniff a lot. You don't have any Kleenex and you want to blow your nose. If the interviewer notices and offers you one, you are very grateful and say thanks several times. Then, you ask if the interviewer has children. If the interviewer says yes, you ask what they are like. If the interviewer says no, you ask, "Do you like little girls?" If the interviewer says yes to this, you start trying to really please the interviewer so that he or she will care about you.

You may find the mental status questions that screen for psychosis, violence, or cognitive confusion to be confusing. You do not display any thinking problems or inappropriate affect. You display age-appropriate sadness and anxiety about your current life situation. You have no thoughts of harming yourself or others.

3. Why are you being interviewed?

Your school recommended that your grandmother make this appointment for you. Your grandmother told you about this after you overheard her talking to your teacher on the phone. She said that your teacher called because she was worried about your stomachaches. The teacher told your grandmother that you are complaining about your stomach every day at school and asking to be sent home. Your grandmother's voice sounded very serious when she told you about this, and you found this scary. You think the teacher is telling your grandma to bring you to this appointment as a punishment.

You heard your grandma tell the teacher that your family was involved in a terrible car accident four weeks ago in which your father was killed and your mother was seriously injured. You were secured with a lap belt and shoulder harness in the middle of the back seat of the vehicle during the accident. The accident occurred late at night. You couldn't see much of anything because it was so dark and you were too short to see over the front seat of the car. You had fallen asleep right before the accident happened. The car flipped over during the accident and when you were rescued, you had been hanging upside down for about an hour. Your parents had been thrown from the car as they had not been wearing seat belts. Your dad hit the road and died right away. Your mom landed in the grass and broke a lot of her bones. Your mother was hospitalized for three weeks, and you were not allowed by your grandmother to visit her in the hospital. Your mom is now home but bedridden.

If asked how things are going, you sigh and say that your grandmother moved into your home after the accident in order to take care of your mother and you. Your mom is supposed to be healing okay, but you are worried. She is always in bed because both of her arms and legs were broken in the accident. At the present time, your mom cries all the time but you aren't allowed to take care of her. Your grandmother lets you come into your mom's room twice a day to talk but only for ten minutes at a time. Your grandma is always saying that your mom hurts really bad and gets tired easily.

If asked about your grandma, you say she is old, grouchy, and always says she is too tired to play. If your mom goes to sleep, your grandma goes to sleep. Grandma told you that she would be napping while you are here. This makes you even madder about this appointment. You are here just to get you out of the house so your noise won't wake anyone up.

If asked about school, you say your teacher hates you. She says you are mean to all the other kids and keeps sending you to time out. Because she is unfair, you don't want to do your homework. You did very well last year in school, and you had heard your old teacher tell your mom that you were friendly and well behaved. Your teacher this year never says this and punishes you all the time.

4. How do you feel?

You are very angry at your dad for not coming home. Grandma said he would return on judgment day, but she says this is a long way off. You want him to come home earlier because you need him. You are also very angry at grandma for not letting you see your mom at the hospital. Grandma kept saying it was a rule of intensive care. This sounds stupid to you, but grandma just yelled when you said this.

You are very sad about your mom and often cry out for her. If asked further about this, you say that you just really miss your mom. Grandma doesn't cook anything right. Grandma has dumb stinky rules. Grandma falls asleep in the living room chair and leaves you feeling lonely. If the interviewer asks if anyone is helping you, you say Grandma prays a lot but you won't. You hate God because he took your dad away. If the interviewer says kind things to you about this, you start to cry or whisper forlornly about how sad everything is.

5. How do you think?

You can be quite thoughtful and serious for your age. You have decided that God took your dad from you because God is selfish and doesn't care that you miss your dad. Your mom has always said, "God wants us to be good and if we are, God will take us to Heaven." You were good for a few days because you thought then God would take you to see your dad in Heaven. But then later, you got scared because if you went to heaven, you would leave your mom. You decided to be bad so God wouldn't want you.

You perceive everyone to be angry at you, and you expect the interviewer to yell at you for not being a good girl. You perceive that everyone is very busy and doesn't have time for you anymore. You also worry that the accident was your fault. Your parents had often told you to stop talking during car trips because trying to answer your questions distracted them from driving. The last thing you clearly remember about the accident is asking your dad how long it would be before you got to sleep in your own bed. When your mom told you to be quiet, you fell asleep. The next thing you knew, you were upside down and really scared. You called out to your parents, but neither one answered you. If the interviewer is very attentive to you and kind during the interview, separating from him or her at the end of the interview will be difficult. You might ask the interviewer not to leave you because you need someone to take care of you. You might ask if the interviewer would please take you home because you hate where you live now.

6. What do you like about yourself?

You think you are smart at school and that you used to be a good friend. You loved to play on the swings during recess. There are only two swings. Kids liked you because you knew how to take turns and share the swings. You don't really like yourself anymore. So much makes you mad these days and you get mad so fast you can't seem to stop yourself from being mean. You have even pushed other kids off the swings when you wanted to take a turn.

9. How is your health?

You only received a few minor bruises in the car accident and did not need medical treatment for them. You say that you feel fine except for stomachaches every morning when you have to leave for school. You also admit to feeling tired a lot. Your grandma has told you that it is because your nightmares are spoiling your sleep. You aren't sure what this means, but you remember your nightmares: They are all about your mom and dad. In the nightmares, you are standing next to your grandma by the graves of your mom and dad. Grandma looks at you and says you are a brat who killed your parents by being selfish. When you start to cry in the dream, your grandma says your mom cried herself to death because of you. If the interviewer asks you if you think your mom is going to die, admit that you worry about this a lot. You have heard your mom crying but whenever you try to go help her, your grandma tells you to go off and play and then she goes in to be with your mom. When you do see your mom, she strokes your hair and says she loves you. You aren't sure if she means it because she always looks sad as she says it. If asked if you caused your dad's death, you might nod your head yes. No one has ever accused you of this, but you believe it's true because your parents often said you distracted them with your talk when they were driving. Although you went to sleep before the accident happened, you figure something you said before you dropped off may have caused the accident.

10. How do you relate to others?

At home, you used to be the family "chatterbox." Your family always had breakfast and dinner together, and your parents encouraged you to talk about your day with them. Your mom and dad used to be proud of everything you said and did. If asked how you know this, you might say that your mom and dad both said you were their perfect little princess. After dinner, you always played games outside with your mom and dad or board games inside the house. Your dad always put you to bed by carrying you on his shoulders and pretending to drop you so that you would land in bed with a bounce. Your dad was so funny he always made you laugh until your tummy hurt. Your mom didn't play such fun games with you. She was always worried that you would get hurt. But she was great about making you fun snacks and letting you have friends over to play with. Your grandmother used to visit once a year at Christmas. She brought great presents but always seemed more interested in talking to your mom than to you. Once, when you started crying about this, she said, "Didn't your mommy ever tell you that SHE was MY perfect princess?" Your mom would always laugh at this and this confused you. How could your mom be a perfect princess? You were the perfect princess.

You used to really enjoy talking to the other kids at school. You were really good at sharing and taking turns. Since the accident, you pout or cry at school. You just don't feel like talking, and you yell at other kids if they come up to you and try to talk. You watch your old friends playing games without you. You were mean to them first, but it still makes you sometimes angry and sometimes sad that they play games without you. You might ask the interviewer why kids are so mean. You hate them all now.

You hate your teacher, so you don't do your homework and you daydream in class. At least once a day, your teacher comes up to you and asks if you are okay. You always answer in a mean voice and just say your stomach hurts. She then starts yelling at you to be respectful. Last year you liked school; the teacher was nice and read good books out loud. This year is awful.

11. How do you view your life?

You are very confused about what happened the night of the accident. You think about it constantly, but it doesn't help. You just can't figure things out. Your grandmother says a deer caused the car accident, but you don't understand how a deer could cause a car accident. Your parents used to explain stuff to you when you were confused, but now you don't have anyone to turn to for explanations. You don't know what to do. Why is everything so awful? Why doesn't anyone care?

EXERCISES FOR THE INTERVIEWER

Exercise 1: Develop a diagnosis for Erica

A. What criteria does Erica meet for an Axis I diagnosis of Adjustment Disorder with Mixed Disturbance of Emotions and Conduct or Bereavement?

_____

_____

_____

_____

Name two other Axis I diagnoses that you might want to rule out for Erica and indicate what additional information might be needed to differentiate between the diagnostic choices for her.

_____

_____

_____

_____

Does Erica meet all the criteria for an Axis I disorder? Should the diagnosis be deferred, or is a diagnosis not needed?

_____

_____

_____

_____

B. What criteria does Erica meet for an Axis II diagnosis (Personality Disorders and Mental Retardation)? Should a diagnosis be deferred, or is a diagnosis not needed? Explain and be as specific as possible.

_____

_____

_____

_____

C. Is there anything you might report for Erica on Axis III (General Medical Conditions that are potentially relevant to the client's mental disorder)?

_____

_____

_____

_____

D. List all specific psychosocial and environmental problems on Axis IV that are influencing Erica at this time. Indicate if each stressor is mild, moderate, or severe.

_____

_____

_____

_____

E. What is your global assessment of Erica's functioning for Axis V (current and highest in past year)?

_____

_____

_____

_____

F. Double-check your diagnostic choices starting at Axis V and proceeding backward through Axis I to determine if you may have overestimated or underestimated the impact of the situational, biological, or individual psychological factors on Erica's current functioning. Should you change anything? Be specific in describing why or why not.

_____

_____

_____

_____

G. Review your diagnostic choices again from Erica's point of view. Do your choices support the discussions you have had with her? Would she be disturbed by your choices? Be specific in discussing why or why not.

_____

_____

_____

_____

Exercise 2: Practice deepening interview with Erica

   A. Erica is depressed because of her current circumstances. This may be reflected in her sad facial expression, her slumped body posture, and her lack of body movements. How might this influence your nonverbal attending behavior? Behaviors to consider include eye contact, orientation of your body, posture, facial expression, and autonomic behavior.

_____

_____

_____

   B. Erica is very young and may have trouble responding to open-ended questions that are too general or abstract. While making questions very general and abstract may give adults a lot of choice in how to respond to the question, it may leave young children confused and unable to respond. Young children, like Erica, may be able to respond more easily to more directed, open-ended questions that are tied to something that is specific and concrete. Rewrite the following open-ended questions to make them more appropriate for a seven-year-old. An example is provided that breaks the first "adult" question into several "child" questions.

Example appropriate for an adult: What is happening in your life right now?

(Rewritten for seven-year-old) *What did you do in school today? What do you do with*

your grandmother when you are at home? What do you do with your mom when you are

at home?

What is your relationship like with your grandmother?

_____

_____

_____

How has life changed since your dad died?

_____

_____

_____

How are you feeling at home?

_____

_____

_____

   C. Erica may have trouble identifying her feelings due to her young age. Deepen her emotional awareness by making comments on her nonverbal behavior that tie them to a feeling she may be experiencing. Use information from Erica's profile to guide you. An example is provided:

Erica clenches her fists and frowns as she says her grandmother didn't let her visit her mom in the hospital.

Looking at that big frown on your face and your tight fists, I wonder if you are feeling mad

at your grandmother for not taking you to visit your mom in the hospital.

Erica slumps in her chair, chews on her hair, and says her mom is mean and never plays with her.

_____

_____

_____

Erica's face turns red and her eyes tear up as she says her dad left her and won't come back.

_____

_____

Erica's legs bounce around and she looks away as she says that her teacher always yells at her for no reason.

_____

_____

_____

D. Whenever you try to get Erica to talk about her misbehavior at home or at school, she responds with confusing information. Write a redirecting comment that supports Erica emotionally but tries to help her give clearer information. Be careful to phrase your redirect so that it doesn't sound like a criticism. An example is provided.

Interviewer: Tell me why you were sent to time-out in school today.

Erica: I got cold at recess and the teacher sent me to time-out.

It feels icky to be cold. Tell me what happened that got you sent to time-out.

Interviewer: Your teacher called and told me you lost your homework. What happened?

Erica: I did bring my homework home. I hate school!

_____

_____

_____

Interviewer: Your grandma said that you threw your lunch in the trash. What happened?

Erica: My mom made good stuff. Grandma won't let my mom make my lunch.

_____

_____

_____

Interviewer: How did you get that bruise on your leg?

Erica: Grandma says curiosity kills the cat so I went outside.

_____

_____

_____

Exercise 3: Thought questions related to Erica

A. Consider who you are as an interviewer and write down what you think might be most difficult about establishing rapport with Erica based on your age, ethnicity, gender, socioeconomic status, sexual orientation, religion, physical characteristics, and personality style. What specifically might happen?

_____

_____

_____

_____

B. Is there anything you could do to enhance your ability to establish an effective working relationship with Erica? Be specific and detailed in describing your ideas.

_____

_____

_____

_____

C. What might you say to Erica if she asks you, "When is judgment day?"

_____

_____

_____

_____

D. What might you say to Erica if she asks, "Why do you think God is so mean?"

_____

_____

_____

E. What might you say to Erica if she asks, "Will my mom die?"

_____

_____

_____

F. How will you explain who you are to seven-year-old Erica?

_____

_____

_____

G. What might you say if Erica asks you to take her home with you?

_____

_____

_____

Case of Joseph

1. What are your basic statistics?

You are a ten-year-old, biracial Puerto Rican and European-American male. Your father and grandmother are European American, and your mother and her family are Puerto Rican. You have just been placed in foster care by Children and Youth Services (CYS). This placement occurred because your grandmother had to go into the hospital and had no one to care for you while she was there. You have no memories of your mother or her family, as you have not seen them since you were three years old. You have had extremely limited contact with your father. He works on an oil tanker and only comes home once a year. He calls your grandmother once or twice a year and speaks briefly to you. You are being interviewed at a community mental health center.

2. How do you behave?

You are dressed in clean clothes that your foster mother bought for you. These are your first "brand new" clothes; your grandmother provided you with used clothing from Good Will Industries. You are feeling very good about how you look and respond with pleasure if the interviewer compliments you on your appearance. At the beginning of the interview, you are quiet and subdued, replying only in monosyllables. However, if the interviewer is patient and compassionate, you slowly open up more and more. You eventually show yourself to be an intelligent person who can be very expressive and charming.

If any of your "problems" come up, you shut down and become sullen. You sink into your chair and stare down in your lap. You avoid questions you don't like by simply looking down and pretending to examine your clothes. Anything that relates directly to your grandmother is very hard for you to talk about. If the interviewer is persistent in trying to discuss her, you become very agitated. You say things such as, "I want to see her. If you really care like you say you do, you will get me back with my grandmother."

You pass any mental status screens that assess memory and concentration. You show no signs of cognitive confusion, hallucinations, or delusions. You are irritated by any assessments of "homicide" or "anger control" because these imply to you that the interviewer considers you a bad seed. You lose your temper if asked about drug or alcohol use because you view these as accusing you of being an addict. You might jump out of your chair and say something like, "Stop accusing me of stuff I haven't done." If the interviewer responds to this behavior with empathetic and supportive statements, you immediately calm down and just shake your head no to show you don't use alcohol or drugs.

If asked about depression and anxiety, you withdraw into your chair and get very quiet. You are afraid your grandmother will die and have nightmares about this. You miss her a great deal and feel lonely and forlorn at your foster home. You respond positively to any empathy expressed by the interviewer by giving eye contact and answering questions more fully.

3. Why are you being interviewed?

Your grandmother told the CYS worker that she is permanently revoking custody because she feels she is too old to be responsible for raising you. She has not talked to you since that day she called for an ambulance. The CYS worker told you earlier this week that your grandmother does not want to talk to you again because she believes this will make things worse; she steadfastly believes that a clean break is best. She told the CYS worker to tell you this because "she was being paid by the state to handle this sort of thing." Your reaction to the news was to go into a rage, which included swearing and throwing furniture. You told the CYS worker that she was a liar. This incident led to your referral to this interview. The CYS worker would like you to receive help understanding why you aren't living with your grandmother anymore and adjusting to your new living situation. The worker also thinks you need help with anger management. This is the first time you have ever been involved with a mental health professional. You don't know what to expect, but you know you aren't crazy and think it is stupid to be here. You absolutely do not believe what the CYS worker told you about your grandmother revoking custody.

4. How do you feel?

You are extremely angry at Children and Youth Services for placing you in foster care. You want to go home to your grandmother. When people try to explain she is ill, you either become really quiet and subdued or you freak out and start swearing and throwing things. Neither strategy is getting you anywhere. Why is everything so out of control? Why can't anyone see that you need to be with your grandmother? When you try to be aware of your feelings, you explode. You seem to have the choice of ignoring your feelings or freaking out.

You have had many nightmares involving your grandmother being hurt and calling out to you. In each dream, you try to reach your grandmother, but some evil force stops you. You stand paralyzed and watch your grandmother die. You are terrified by these dreams and think they are telling you to get to your grandmother or she will die. The CYS worker has told you that your grandmother is in the hospital and recovering, but you are suspicious because you haven't heard from her.

5. How do you think?

You did not believe the CYS worker when she told you that your grandmother was revoking custody. Your grandmother has threatened this many times, and you are almost positive that she will get over it like she has before. On the other hand, you do have the general expectation that bad things are going to happen to you. You figure that if you care enough about someone, they are going to just up and leave you at some point. You cope with this by trying to avoid thinking about it. However, on some level, you can never forget about it and it affects the way you view other people's behavior. You often misperceive neutral comments as being a form of rejection. For example, your foster parents remind you each day to make your bed and put your dirty clothes in the hamper. You believe this is a sign that they value the clothes more than you. You go along with the hamper routine only because you figure if you damage the clothes, your grandmother will be stuck with a clothes bill you know she can't pay. Similarly, while your foster parents are encouraging you to eat as much as you want, you are sure they will actually complain to CYS that you eat too much. You try to hold back but you can't stop yourself from eating until you are no longer hungry. While part of you says, "Don't eat too much or they will get mad," part of you says, "Eat up while there is food to eat." You figure paying the bills from the hospital may prevent you and your grandmother from eating enough for a long time.

Most of your daily thoughts concern your grandmother. You worry a lot that no one is looking after her at the hospital because she isn't rich. You expect poor people to be ignored and rich people to get anything they want.

6. What do you like about yourself?

You hate yourself. If you were more loveable, your dad wouldn't have dumped you. You are grateful that your grandma will take care of you despite the fact that you are such a loser. If pressed about finding something good to say, admit that you are proud you learned how to make home repairs yourself and that you are able to make friends easily. You do enjoy sports, but you don't think that much of your abilities. You figure you just have an advantage over most of the other ten-year-olds because you are bigger. You worry that these ten-year-olds don't really like you for "yourself." Your strategy has been to supply them with gum and candy bars to keep them interested in you. This has worked great so far.

7. How have you been doing at work?

This question is not relevant to Joseph.

8. How have you been doing in school?

You have always done badly in school even when you were in kindergarten. You don't know why. You figure you are basically an idiot. The school has recently placed you in a learning disabilities classroom although there has been no formal testing of your abilities. Your new teacher likes you but says you are unreliable. You never follow through in completing your homework, and you always have an excuse for why you didn't do it. You just find the whole school thing boring. If a teacher is nice to you, you initially start doing work to please him or her. However, at some point, you always lose interest and stop trying. Your grandmother has never seemed to care whether you do your school work or not, so you just don't worry about it.

You are very interested in the other kids at school. You live in a neighborhood that doesn't have anyone your age to hang out with, so school is a welcome change. This is why you never make a fuss about going to school. Your foster parents live in the same school district as your grandmother, so you haven't lost contact with your school friends. These are boys that you talk to in class and that you play games with on the playground at recess. You have given them candy bars and other treats to keep them interested in you. You have overheard the teachers talking about you. The teachers wonder how you can afford to hand out treats, as they know your family is very poor. The teachers have noticed some thefts from the teacher's lounge, but no one has ever seen you in the lounge or anywhere near it. Some teachers have found money missing from their classroom desks, but no one has seen you in one of these rooms unsupervised. You get questioned now and again, but the teachers never find anything out. You don't feel bad about taking the money because you only take it from teachers who seem to have plenty.

9. How is your health?

You have received no routine medical or dental care beyond the minimum requirements set by the school system. Now that you have entered foster care, you have had your first comprehensive physical and dental workup. You weren't given any medicine at the doctor's office, so you figure you must be doing okay. However, the dentist told you that you have five cavities that have to be drilled. You don't like this idea at all.

10. How do you relate to others?

Your general style with adults is to be quiet and sullen. You expect them to be unpredictable and uncaring. You are polite to your neighbors and the teachers at school, but you have no real interest in them. You only real attachment is to your grandmother. You have heard "the story of your life" many times, as your grandmother has shared it with neighbors and teachers. Your dad just appeared one day at grandma's house and dumped you there when you were three. You had been badly hurt by your mother. Your dad had asked your grandma to take care of you while he "took care of" that witch who had hurt you so bad. You have no memories of your mother, but you kind of know your dad because grandma has lots of his things at her house and she has talked to you about him. Every year, your dad visits once. He never gives any warning that he is coming. He spends most of his time talking to his buddies at the local bars, but he lets you hang around. He also calls around your birthday to say hello to you and speak with your grandmother. The conversation is usually over in about five minutes. Dad always promises to come get you some day, but it never happens. Grandma has explained that your dad loves the ocean and works on an oil tanker; it is against the rules to have children on the tanker.

Your grandmother owns a tiny house in town and barely gets by living off her social security benefits. The house you live in is falling apart. You have tried to fix some stuff, but no one ever taught you to do this so lots of your repairs have been disasters. You have learned some things by watching a home repair show on TV. You are proud that you have learned how to paint, spackle, and repair holes in walls. The problem is that although you can fix some of the holes you have made in walls, you usually can't come up with money to pay for materials. Your neighbor has a well-stocked garage. You have stolen some stuff from him. One Saturday morning, he caught you doing this. He asked what you were up to, and you slammed him hard in the stomach with the wood you had planned to make off with and ran as fast as you could away from him. You hid in the woods for a while. When you got home around 3:00 p.m., your grandma locked you in the garage as a punishment. You scared her by showing up at the dinner table that night; you had used some tools to dismantle the back of the garage so that you could get out. Your grandma screamed at you that you were a chronic thief and would end up in jail some day because you wouldn't learn your lessons from her.

You have been stealing for a long time. You can't even remember how young you were when you first started. You remember that the first thing you ever stole was food. Grandma had always lectured you about how you shouldn't eat "more than your share." Whenever you left a meal still feeling hungry, which was quite often, you would sneak into the kitchen and try to get more to eat when grandma wasn't looking. This had been a continuing source of conflict between you and her. Last month, she had finally "solved the food-stealing problem" by putting a lock on the kitchen door so you couldn't sneak in and steal food to snack on.

Throughout your conflicts with grandma, in addition to locking you in your room or in the garage, she would always threaten to dump you in an orphanage if you didn't learn to "behave." These threats had never scared you because you could tell that she was lonely and needed you just like you needed her. This year, however, things seem to have gotten worse. She says your temper has gotten too hot for her to handle, and she seems more serious when she threatens to dump you than she did before. This scares you, and you have reacted to this fear by threatening to beat her up if she doesn't stop saying she will dump you. Actually, you would never hurt her, but you have lost enough control that you have put your fist through the wall a few times. You have also begun to destroy things but only after really being hurt by something. For example, last month the phone rang and, to your surprise, it was your dad. He wanted to talk with your grandmother, but she wasn't home; she was trying to convince the electric company not to turn off the electric service to your house. The heating bill was too high for grandma's budget because the winter was so harsh. She made small payments each month, but the last few notices for full payment were very threatening. You asked your dad if he could please send some money to help with this. He got mad quickly. You tried to placate him by saying it wouldn't happen again, but grandma had just been so sick this past year that the bills had gotten out of control. Your dad hung up on you when you were in mid-sentence. After this happened, you stormed into the room where his stuff was stored, took his leather jacket out of the closet, and cut it to shreds with a scissors. Your grandma really flipped out over this when she came home to find you doing it. She spent two weeks screaming at you and asking how she was going to explain this to your dad when he came home.

The biggest crisis occurred in your home last week; your grandma fell down the stairs and injured her leg. You helped her up and half-carried her to bed. You took the key out of her pocket, so you could get into the kitchen and make meals for her. Grandma seemed pleased with you, but she kept saying that you couldn't really help and that she knew something was seriously wrong. By the next day, her leg had swollen to the point where she could barely move it. She knew she needed to go to the emergency room. She called an ambulance for herself and Children and Youth Services for you. You heard her tell CYS that she had no one to take care of you while she was in the hospital because you dad wouldn't come home to get you. She also said that she was afraid of you. You were puzzled by this. You would never hurt her and you don't get why she would really believe any of your threats to do so. At CYS, you spent the day being bored watching stupid people rushing by and ignoring you. At the end of the day, you were shipped off to live at the Carlsons' house.

You view the Carlsons as very weird people. They keep getting in your face and trying to get you to talk about stuff. You do not want to talk to them. After all, you won't ever see them again once your grandmother takes you back. When they talk to you, it is just a series of questions that you don't want to answer. You respond to their questions by looking at the floor while mumbling "yes" or "no" to whatever they have said. They do have a warm house and lots of nice stuff, but you want to get back to your grandmother's place.

11. How do you view your life?

Your life stinks. You are both angry and depressed about your mom and dad dumping you. You love your grandma, but you have never told her that. She takes care of you but never says she loves you either. You have never heard her say loving words to anyone.

EXERCISES FOR THE INTERVIEWER

Exercise 1: Develop a diagnosis for Joseph

A. What criteria does Joseph meet for an Axis I diagnosis of Conduct Disorder or Separation Anxiety Disorder?

_____

_____

_____

_____

Name two other Axis I diagnoses that you might want to rule out for Joseph and indicate what additional information might be needed to differentiate between the diagnostic choices for him.

_____

_____

_____

_____

Does Joseph meet all the criteria for an Axis I disorder, should the diagnosis be deferred, or is a diagnosis not needed?

_____

_____

_____

_____

B. What criteria does Joseph meet for an Axis II diagnosis (Personality Disorders and Mental Retardation)? Should a diagnosis be deferred, or is a diagnosis not needed. Explain and be as specific as possible.

_____

_____

_____

_____

C. Is there anything you might report for Joseph on Axis III (General Medical Conditions that are potentially relevant to the client's mental disorder)?

_____

_____

_____

_____

D. List all specific psychosocial and environmental stressors that are influencing Joseph at this time on Axis IV. Indicate if each stressor is mild, moderate, or severe.

_____

_____

_____

_____

E. What is your global assessment of Joseph on Axis V (current and highest in past year)?

_____

_____

_____

_____

F. Double-check your diagnostic choices starting at Axis V and proceeding backward through Axis I to determine if you may have overestimated or underestimated the impact of the situational, biological, or individual psychological factors on Joseph's current functioning. Should you change anything? Be specific in describing why or why not.

_____

_____

_____

_____

G. Review your diagnostic choices again from Joseph's point of view. Do your choices support the discussions you have had with him? Would he be disturbed by your choices? Be specific in discussing why or why not.

_____

_____

_____

_____

Exercise 2: Practice deepening interview with Joseph

A. Joseph withdraws and responds in monosyllables whenever he is asked to talk about his problems. Due to his emotionally impoverished background, he may have trouble identifying his feelings. Deepen his emotional awareness by making comments on his nonverbal behavior and asking him if this represents a certain emotion state. Use information from Joseph's profile to guide you. Use simple vocabulary to insure that he understands you. An example is provided.

You asked Joseph to talk about his dad. Joseph is staring at the clenched fists in his lap and saying nothing. His face is red.

I see your hands are in fists and your face is red. I wonder if you are mad.

You asked Joseph if he knows how his grandmother is doing. Joseph's face looks white. He has responded to your comment by sinking more deeply into his chair.

_____

_____

_____

_____

You just told Joseph that you understand he is not going to be returning to his grandmother after she leaves the hospital. He throws his head backward against the chair and stares at the ceiling. His hands are clenched on the arms of the chair.

_____

_____

_____

_____

B. Joseph has many feelings bottled up inside him because none of his caregivers have given him emotional nurturance and helped him understand his feelings. Practice giving him emotional nurturance through making two types of comments to what he has said. Make the first comment a simple, reflective listening comment and the second a more complex, empathetic comment to either validate his experience, let him know you understand what he is experiencing, or help him gain emotional control. Use information from Joseph's profile to guide you. An example is provided of using empathy to let Joseph know he has been understood.

Joseph: My grandmother keeps asking me why I cut up my dad's jacket. I just felt like it. That's all there is to it.

1. *You just felt like it (reflective listening).*

2. *I can understand why you would be very angry at your dad. He didn't help you and you*

   needed help. Your anger may have grown so strong that you couldn't keep it inside any

   longer (empathetic comment).

Joseph: I yelled at that Children and Youth Services worker so she would listen when I said I want to see my grandmother.

1. _____

2. _____

_____

Joseph: These foster parents are so weird. I can't figure out why they are always looking at me. They always ask me so many questions. They just don't make sense.

1. _____

2. _____

_____

C. Whenever you bring up important issues Joseph needs to work through, he minimizes their importance. Use supportive confrontation in an attempt to help him became more aware that he needs to work through these issues. Remember to include empathy or support for Joseph within your comment, as well as specific information about the negative consequences of what he is doing. Use information from Joseph's profile to guide you. Use one of the four styles of confrontation including de-emphasizing labeling, emphasizing personal choice and responsibility, demonstrating you have listened to his needs, or being honest with Joseph about the positive or negative consequences of his behavior. An example is provided of being honest about the consequences of his behavior.

Interviewer: Have you thought about your grandmother recently?

Joseph: She will be okay. I don't have time to think about her.

It is hard to talk about your grandmother because you miss her and don't know when or if

you will be able to see her again. While it hurts to think about her, she is seriously ill and

you will hurt even more if we pretend her welfare is not important to you.

Interviewer: When is the last time you heard from your dad?

Joseph: Who knows and who cares. I don't need him for anything.

_____

_____

_____

Interviewer: How are you getting along with your foster parents?

Joseph: They will either keep me or kick me out. I have nothing to say about it.

_____

_____

_____

Interviewer: How are you doing with your school work?

Joseph: Homework is boring. I won't waste my time with it.

_____

_____

_____

Exercise 3: Thought questions related to Joseph

A. Consider who you are as an interviewer and write down what you think might be most difficult about establishing rapport with Joseph based on your age, ethnicity, gender, socioeconomic status, sexual orientation, religion, physical characteristics, and personality style. What specifically might happen?

_____

_____

_____

_____

_____

B. Is there anything you could do to enhance your ability to establish an effective working relationship with Joseph? Be specific and detailed in describing your ideas.

_____

_____

_____

_____

_____

C. At a court hearing next week, Joseph's grandmother will permanently revoke custody. She does not want to speak to Joseph. During your interview, Joseph asks you to arrange for him to talk to his grandmother. What might you say?

_____

_____

_____

_____

_____

D. Joseph was raised without any understanding of his Puerto-Rican heritage except for the fact that his mother "abused" him. He is now living with European-American foster parents who are unlikely to consider his biracial heritage in their attempts to parent him. Should you raise this issue with Joseph and/or with his foster parents? Be specific in giving reasons for yes or no.

_____

_____

_____

_____

E. What role do you think poverty is playing in the problems Joseph is having with his grandmother?

_____

_____

_____

_____

20

Case of Sabina

1. What are your basic statistics?

Your name is Sabina and you are a sixteen-year-old, Bangladeshi-American female. Your parents were born and raised in Bangladesh and came to the United States to go to medical school. You and your two younger sisters were born in the United States after your parents graduated from medical school. They settled in a large metropolitan city, and you and your sister attended public school. Last year, you left home to move in with a boyfriend. He was arrested for embezzling money from his employer and is currently awaiting trial in the county jail because you couldn't raise his bail money.

You are now in the custody of Children and Youth Services (CYS), and you are residing in a group home. Your caseworker has started the process of making you an emancipated minor. You plan to rejoin your boyfriend once he is released from jail. You are being interviewed at a community mental health center.

2. How do you behave in the interview?

You are highly intelligent and highly expressive in your responses. You are used to being told by others that you are highly attractive and charming. You are well groomed and wearing typical clothes for an inner-city teenager. You have several earrings in each ear, a nose ring, and belly-button ring. You do not initiate any conversation because you consider this disrespectful, but you sit on the edge of your seat and emanate energy and enthusiasm. You respond quickly to any question coming from the interviewer.

When the interviewer asks questions about your family or your boyfriend, you suddenly lose your energy and collapse physically into the chair. It is as if you are a balloon that has suddenly popped. If this is pointed out to you, you quickly get back on the edge of your chair and change the subject. If brought back to your family and/or boyfriend, you state sadly that things are quite bad in these areas and you would prefer to put them out of your mind.

In response to mental status questions, you show no signs of cognitive confusion, hallucinations, or delusions. You deny homicidal and suicidal ideation, but your eyes take on a funny glaze in response to suicide questions. If probed gently about this, you sigh and say something like, "It is hard to go on. Everything feels too hard and painful these days." You do not have a suicidal plan. You admit to some anxiety and sadness about your boyfriend's current legal situation. You feel some responsibility for his plight because he got into money trouble when you moved in with him, and this may have contributed to his decision to steal. You didn't know he was stealing, and you have been having trouble falling asleep ever since you found out; you also haven't felt like eating.

3. Why are you being interviewed?

Your CYS caseworker sent you to this interview because she is concerned that you are seriously depressed. You are estranged from your parents, and your only social tie is with your boyfriend who is currently in jail. You were recently evicted from the apartment you shared with him. You feel that your landlord disapproved of your relationship and had been looking for an excuse to eject you both. He stormed over to the apartment after reading of your boyfriend's arrest and demanded you pay in full the three months' back rent that you owed. You had nothing to give him. You tried to bluff your way through it by telling him your boyfriend would be home later and would pay the rent. Your landlord wasn't fooled, and he sent the police over to evict you. You asked the officers to let you stay in the apartment, explaining that you were estranged from your parents and had nowhere to go. The officers realized that you were a minor and contacted Children and Youth Services. These people placed you in a group home and encouraged you to start working on your GED. Once you have achieved this high school equivalency, you will be able to get a job. At that point, CYS will take you to court and have you declared a legally emancipated minor. You have never received psychological services before and do not know what to expect.

4. How do you feel?

You are feeling desperate now that your boyfriend is gone because you have no one to turn to. You haven't been considering suicide, but you do feel very lonely and depressed and unsure how to go on. Your life has always revolved around your family relationships, and being so disconnected is a new and terrifying experience for you. You try never to allow negative emotions to show because you consider this inappropriate. You are sensitive to the feelings of other people and are very used to putting their needs ahead of yours, particularly if they are your elders.

You try not to let anyone know how bad you feel because you believe that you should always please others and try to make them feel good. For this reason, you try to act upbeat, be very attentive to the cues of the interviewer, and seek to be pleasing. You also try to be entertaining as you are used to trying to entertain your parent's guests with your conversation and your music. However, out of respect to the interviewer, you talk about your parents and your boyfriend if pressed to do so. Then, you speak very softly and frequently become choked up and tearful. After discussing family issues for a while, you may end up with your face in your hands because you are feeling too overcome with sorrow to speak.

When discussing your future legal emancipation, you become quite anxious. You do not want to live all by yourself, but you understand that you can't just keep living in the group home. You are soothed and respond with gratitude to any empathetic comments from the interviewer.

5. How do you think?

You are of above average intelligence and have no trouble understanding anything asked of you by the interviewer. You believe that your family will never forgive you for having a relationship with your boyfriend and never accept you back into the family. You recognize that you have gone against their values in many ways and consider yourself a "bad daughter." In your cultural and religious background, it is taboo to have premarital sex, and marriages are arranged by the elders in the family. You knew your parents had plans for your future career and future marriage. Therefore, you have to accept what has happened to you for ignoring their wishes.

You have always been a religious person, and you have tried to turn to prayer to help you with your current difficulties. You are praying alone at home. Even though you could go to a different mosque than your parents, you are sure that somehow everyone will know who you are and what you have done; somehow your lack of personal modesty and disobedience to authority will be visible to everyone. You briefly considered going to a mosque and asking a religious leader to advise you, but decided not to do this because you are afraid he will condemn you for what you have done and then you will know for sure that you can never pray at a mosque again.

Now that your boyfriend is gone, you have had a lot of time to reflect on what you have done. You have come to realize that you acted too quickly in leaving home, and you sincerely regret some of what you have done. You can be very introspective but you have been trying hard recently to NOT think about how much your life has changed for the worse in the past year. Sometimes, you fantasize that you have gone back in time and are still working hard in school to please your parents. But, you believe that you can never go back. Who would want you as a daughter-in-law now that you have had sex with a man outside wedlock? Would you even be allowed back in the mosque to pray if people knew what you had done?

When these critical thoughts begin to overwhelm you, you shake yourself with determination and face the facts. You have made a serious commitment to your boyfriend by having sex with him, and thus your future must be with him. You have such strong feelings for him that it must be true love. You and your girlfriends used to go to movies and talk of how "true love" conquered all. The dilemma for you is that true love has not conquered all for you. You are in serious trouble, and you are ashamed of your current lifestyle. You try to avoid meeting anyone who knew you before. If you see a friend from school, you run away. You know the friend will condemn you and you can't face this.

You think that many people in the United States stereotype all Moslems as Arabs and as terrorists. You find this very offensive and expect that you will be mistreated by most people because they are Christians and don't respect your beliefs. Your sense of isolation now is very acute. You have always been "different" from the mainstream, but now you are also "different" from your own people.

6. What do you like about yourself?

You used to be proud of your high record of school achievement. You are also pleased that you have never forgotten to do your daily prayers despite the fact that, in other ways, you feel you have betrayed your religious faith. You are good at reading the emotions of others and feel that you have helped some of the other girls at the group home by recognizing when they were sad and helping them cheer up; your parents often praised you for your ability to do this for family members. You also love music and the arts and feel confident in your skills. You know your parents believed you were talented.

7. How have you been doing at work?

This question is not relevant to Sabina.

8. How have you been doing in school?

You have been a straight "A" student throughout your childhood and the beginning of high school. You dropped out of high school at the beginning of your junior year when you moved in with your boyfriend. Since living in the group home, you have been studying for the GED.

9. How is your health?

You have no health problems.

10. How do you relate to others?

In the past, you were very close to both of your parents; you know they loved you very much. You are their eldest child, and they focused a great deal of attention on your education, your music and arts training, and your cooking skills. You were also very close to your sisters. You tried hard to set a good example for them in turns of filial obedience and academic excellence. Your parents put a great deal of emphasis on family traditions and expected you to study hard and enter medical school when you were older. They trained you from a young age to come directly home from school, do your homework, and then watch over your sisters. Your parents were quite proud of your intellectual and artistic abilities. Your family was very religiously observant and went frequently together to a mosque near your home.

Your relationship with your parents began to deteriorate when you began puberty at the age of twelve. You became interested in boys, and your parents were dismayed by your immodest and open attraction to boys at your school. None of these boys were Moslems. Some of them tried to call you at home to invite you out. Your parents would never allow you to talk with them on the phone and always rejected their invitations. This led you to start actively rebelling against their standards, first by wearing clothes that they considered immodest and later by actively deceiving them.

Your mother and father told you that since you were so interested in boys, they would begin arranging your marriage earlier than they had planned. Rather than having you marry after you went to college, as had been their original plan, you would marry first and then go to college. You had always known that an arranged marriage was in your future. Your parents and all of your relatives had been married in this way. But you had pushed it out of your mind and fantasized, along with all of your girlfriends, about finding your "true love." When your mother first brought up marriage, you tried to tell her about a romantic movie you had seen over the weekend with your friends and how you had always hoped that you would find love in this romantic way. Your mother was horrified and told you that from now on, she didn't want you going to the movies or watching any TV shows without her approving them in advance. She reminded you that many of your girlfriends came from divorced families and that she and your father would never want you to be a victim of such a terrible thing as a divorce. She spoke eloquently of how the Bangladeshi way led to greater happiness and contentment. You felt your mother's love for you as she told you this. You were horrified by how many of your friends' parents were divorced. You had listened as your friends talked of their troubles as they felt tossed back and forth between their estranged parents. But, while you felt that divorce was horrible, you just couldn't imagine that this would happen to you and your "true love." Thus, rather than calming you down, this talk with your mother actually increased your feelings of rebellion, and you put your first foot down on the path of deceit.

A boy you found very attractive had been asking you out for weeks. He worked as a junior manager at the local department store where your mother bought most of the family clothes. He was only a high school graduate, and your mother didn't consider him a proper person for you to know. In returning some clothing that hadn't fit your younger sister, you whispered to him that you would meet him at the library on the next Saturday. Your stolen date on Saturday blossomed into a secret life from your family. As far as your parents knew, you were spending extra hours in the library studying hard to excel in a science course that you told them you were finding very difficult. In actuality, you were spending time with your new boyfriend. You had never been prepared for how strong sexual feelings could be. As you were expected to have no sexual contact with males until you were married, you had been considered too young to be informed about your sexuality. This made you an easy target for your boyfriend. While he was intelligent, he had never thought of attending school after high school; no one in his family had ever done this. He had had many girlfriends before you and was a smooth talker. He found your looks exotic and extremely attractive. With each date, he pressed for more and more sexual contact with you. Finally, on one stolen date, he brought you to his apartment to pick up his wallet, which he said he had forgotten at home. Once in the door, his sexual pressure on you intensified. While he did not physically force you to have intercourse, he did exert a lot of psychological pressure on you to give in. He aroused your sexual desire to such an intense level that you could barely think of anything beyond the fact that he must be your "true love" and that you must give in to whatever he wanted. Once the deed was done, you panicked. He was concerned with how upset you became and tried to help you calm down by giving you alcohol to drink. He kept stroking you and telling you that everything was all right. You had little tolerance for the alcohol, and it put you to sleep.

The next morning you woke up in his apartment. It was the beginning of the end. Your family had been terrified by your absence and had called the police to search for you. When you returned home, there was a huge scene. You tried to brazen it out by declaring you were in love and planning to marry this man you had been secretly dating. Your parents restricted you from leaving the house for days and wouldn't let you use the phone. In desperation, you told them of your sexual encounter and while they sat in the living room in shock, you fled the home. You went directly to your boyfriend and told him you had nowhere to go. He comforted you in your distress and told you that everything would be all right and you could live with him. Although he never said he would marry you, you always assumed he would sometime in the future.

You avoided school because you believed everyone would ostracize you and you couldn't face that. You were unable to find a job because you had no work experience, and potential employers were very suspicious because you would never talk about your parents. Your boyfriend said he would take care of you, and he had indeed started working longer hours to bring in more money. Your first few months with him were wonderful. Every night, the two of you went out to a movie or out to a restaurant. Recently, there didn't seem to be enough money to do anything. You missed your family dreadfully. You would always dissolve in tears when your boyfriend was gone, but you worked hard to hide your pain from him. The last time you were with your boyfriend, he had come home unexpectedly from work and found you crying. He tried to comfort your distress and asked you to tell him what was wrong. You then told him how much you missed your family and the sense of "belonging" to them. He said he had an idea and ran out of your apartment; he had gone to look for a CD of Bangladeshi music including your favorite artists Palash and Shakila. He wanted to help you with your homesickness. The next time you heard his voice, he was calling you from the police station. He had been caught shoplifting; he hadn't had enough money to buy the CD. He asked you to get money to bail him out. There was none left in the apartment. In desperation, you called his boss. This turned out to be a mistake; by coincidence, his boss had just discovered that there was a lot of money missing from petty cash at work. When his boss showed up at the jail, the first thing he did was ask your boyfriend if he knew where the missing money was. Your boyfriend tried to deny it because he was so scared. However, when confronted by the police, he admitted to borrowing money from work in order to make ends meet at home. He told his boss and the police that he had been sure he could eventually come up with a way to replace the money he had taken. His boss pressed charges, and your boyfriend remained in jail. When you visited your boyfriend at the police station, he begged you to forgive him for stealing and asked you to wait for him to get out of jail. You are scared to be alone, but you do plan to wait for him.

11. How do you view your life?

You feel that you have betrayed your family and that they will never stop suffering because of what you did. You fear that your younger sisters will have trouble marrying because you have besmirched the family's reputation. You did steal into the schoolyard once to try and grab a few moments with them to beg for their forgiveness. They cried and begged you to find an intermediary to talk for you with your parents. They said your parents have stopped sleeping since you left. Your parents always talk about you when they think your sisters are asleep and with every talk, your mother ends up in tears. This visit with your sisters left you even more depressed than before. They said that your parents are considering sending them to live with relatives in Bangladesh so that they won't be ruined by the culture in the United States like you have been.

EXERCISES FOR THE INTERVIEWER

Exercise 1: Develop a diagnosis for Sabina

A. What criteria does Sabina meet for an Axis I diagnosis of Child or Adolescent Antisocial Behavior or an Identity Problem?

_____

_____

_____

_____

Name two other Axis I diagnoses that you might want to rule out for Sabina and indicate what additional information might be needed to differentiate between the diagnostic choices for her.

_____

_____

_____

_____

Does Sabina meet all the criteria for an Axis I disorder? Should the diagnosis be deferred, or is a diagnosis not needed?

_____

_____

_____

_____

B. What criteria does Sabina meet for an Axis II diagnosis (Personality Disorders and Mental Retardation)? Should a diagnosis be deferred, or is a diagnosis not needed? Explain and be as specific as possible.

_____

_____

_____

_____

C. Is there anything you might report for Sabina on Axis III (General Medical Conditions that are potentially relevant to the client's mental disorder)?

_____

_____

_____

_____

D. List all specific psychosocial and environmental stressors that are influencing Sabina at this time for Axis IV. Indicate if each stressor is mild, moderate, or severe.

_____

_____

_____

_____

E. What is your global assessment of Sabina on Axis V (current and highest in past year)?

_____

_____

_____

_____

F. Double-check your diagnostic choices starting at Axis V and proceeding backward through Axis I to determine if you may have overestimated or underestimated the impact of the situational, biological, or individual psychological factors on Sabina's current functioning. Should you change anything? Be specific in describing why or why not.

_____

_____

_____

_____

G. Review your diagnostic choices again from Sabina's point of view. Do your choices support the discussions you have had with her? Would she be disturbed by your choices? Be specific in discussing why or why not.

_____

_____

_____

_____

Exercise 2: Practice deepening interview with Sabina

A. Sabina may expect you to shun her as she feels that her family has. What might you do, as you listen to Sabina, to try and let her know, with your nonverbal behavior, that you are attending closely to what she is experiencing and not judging her? Behaviors to consider include eye contact, orientation of your body, posture, facial expression, and autonomic behavior.

_____

_____

_____

_____

B. Write a series of open-ended and closed questions to the following prompts in order to assess the role of acculturation issues in Sabina's current difficulties with her family. Use information from Sabina's profile to guide you. An example is given of two open-ended questions and one closed question for prompt 1.

Prompt 1: Her view of the role of a teen and her parents' view of this role
What do you see as your role in the family now that you are a teen? How do your parents view
your role now that you are a teen? Has your role in the family changed since you became
a teen?

Prompt 2: The meaning of being from Bangladesh for herself and for her parents

_____

_____

_____

_____

Prompt 3: Her view of the role of a woman and her parents' view

_____

_____

_____

_____

C. Sabina is in a great deal of emotional turmoil due to her current situation. In response to her remarks, write two types of comments. Have the first be a simple, reflective listening comment and the second a more complex, empathetic comment to either validate her experience, let her know you understand what she is experiencing, or help her gain emotional control. If Sabina is expressing more than one feeling, or is ambivalent about a situation, make sure your comments take this into account. Use information from Sabina's profile to guide you in making your comments. An example is provided of using a series of empathetic comments to help Sabina feel in control of her emotions.

I am okay at the group home, but I can only live there for six months. My boyfriend won't be getting out for years. I am so alone.
1. _You feel okay now but so alone (reflective listening)._
2. _Right now you feel okay, but it is scary to think about the future because your boyfriend is_
   going to be gone for a long time. You are going to have to make decisions about your future
   before he gets out of jail. It is hard to make these plans all by yourself (empathetic
   comments).

I am used to always being around family. There was always someone there with me. My sisters and I always talked about everything. Even the smallest things going on were discussed. I can't even remember why I used to complain about sharing a room with my sisters. If only I could be surrounded by them again. I want to belong.

1. _____

_____

2. _____

_____

I don't mind hard work. I can work hard, but no one wants to hire me because I don't have a high school diploma. Even my boyfriend's job, which is boring and repetitive, requires a high school diploma. My family was going to send me to college. They had such wonderful plans for me.

1. _____

_____

2. _____

_____

D. Sabina keeps saying that she must have a life that is completely separate from her parents and sisters. Yet, she also seems eager to gain your opinion about whether she is making the right decision or not. She has repeatedly asked for your advice about every decision she needs to make concerning her education, her living situation, her relationship with her boyfriend, and her relationships with her family members. She seems overly awed by your expertise. What process comment might you make to draw her attention to this pattern? What specifically are the pros and cons of Sabina relying heavily on your opinions?

_____

_____

_____

_____

_____

Exercise 3: Thought questions related to Sabina

A. Consider who you are as an interviewer and write down what you think might be most difficult for you in establishing rapport with Sabina based on your age, ethnicity, gender, socioeconomic status, sexual orientation, religion, physical characteristics, age, and personality style. What specifically might happen?

_____

_____

_____

_____

_____

B. Is there anything you could do to enhance your ability to establish an effective working relationship with Sabina?

_____

_____

_____

_____

_____

C. What might you say if Sabina asks you what you know about the Moslem faith?

_____

_____

_____

_____

_____

E. Do you believe that Sabina's religious beliefs need to be addressed within the treatment relationship? Be specific and concrete in responding to this.

_____

_____

_____

_____

_____

F. What role do acculturation issues play in Sabina's current situation?

_____

_____

_____

_____

_____

Case of Alex

1. What are your basic statistics?

You are an eight-year-old, European-American male who has been brought in for treatment by your stepmother and biological father. Your father remarried six months ago. When you came for visitation three months ago, your stepmother noticed that your leg had a festering sore. At the hospital, the physician stated that your leg was highly infected and that if treatment had been delayed a few more days, amputation might have been necessary. The physician called Children and Youth Services (CYS), who investigated and determined that your biological mother had seriously neglected you. Your stepmother encouraged your father to assume custody, and you moved in with them. You have been living with them for the last two months. You are being interviewed at a community mental health center.

2. How do you behave in the interview?

You are dressed in clean clothes, and you frequently look down at your pants or the sleeves of your shirt to check to see if they are still looking good. You might stand up periodically to smooth the back of your pants and then sit back down. You are doing this to prevent wrinkles. If the interviewer notices how much attention you are paying to your clothes and asks you about it, say that these are brand new school clothes and your stepmom warned you not to ruin them like you did your last new outfit. You are very talkative and engage easily in extensive conversations with the interviewer. You are very curious about the interviewer and the place you are being interviewed and may interrupt the conversation repeatedly in order to ask questions about these things. For example, you may ask where the interviewer got his or her cool shoes or why the interviewer decided to buy one of the pictures that is on the wall or the type of chair in the room.

If asked about why you are here, you sink into the chair, sigh, and look very sad. You may tear up or begin to cry quietly. If asked what is wrong, you say that your stepmother hates you. When asked why, you change the subject or ask if the interviewer hates you also. You may try to get the interviewer to discuss his or her own life. If the interviewer gets very firm with you and insists that you answer a question, you cringe, apologize, and get very quiet. If the interviewer is firm but supportive, you say that your stepmom wants you to come here because she thinks you are a compulsive liar who is selfish and destroys everything you touch. If asked about your father's opinion, you say that he seems to think you are okay, but your stepmother is the boss. If you are asked why your stepmother calls you a liar, selfish and so forth, you work hard to change the subject. You are indirectly uncooperative. You never refuse to answer a question, but you always manage, somehow, to get off track onto another subject. You apologize several times if you think you have angered or disappointed the interviewer, and you look down into your lap.

You don't understand mental status questions unless the interviewer asks them in a very concrete manner. For example, you are confused by things such as, "Have you ever had any unusual experiences?" You understand things like, "How do you feel when your stepmother yells at you?" If you understand the interviewer's questions, you admit to feeling fearful, sad, and angry at certain times. You don't express any desire to hurt yourself or others. You don't have any concentration problems or other signs of a thought disorder except you are easily distractible. For example, if you are in the middle of answering something and the interviewer looks up at a clock or picture, you stop talking for a moment and then ask the interviewer a question about the clock or the picture.

3. Why are you being interviewed?

You were referred by your CYS caseworker after your stepmother complained to this individual about your behavior. She described you to the caseworker as lazy, a pathological liar, and destructive. You know this because your stepmother made you stand by the phone while she made the call. Your stepmother told you that the CYS caseworker thinks your behavior is due to your prior history of neglect. Your stepmother is giving you a few more months to shape up or she is kicking you out. You cried about this while your dad was home, and he put his arms around you and gave you a big hug. At the same time, he said that your stepmother knew best and you had to learn to do what she said. Your stepmother has told you many times that she blames your biological mother for your problems, but now that you are in a good home, you should be able to shape up. You give this information to the interviewer but only after initially trying to avoid doing so by changing the subject.

If the interviewer asks you specifically what is going wrong at home, you admit that you never remember to change out of your school clothes before going out to play. You get home at 3:30 but your stepmother doesn't get home from work until 5:30. You are supposed to go to your room, change clothes, then go into the kitchen and get your snack out of the refrigerator. Your stepmother leaves it for you in a special container. When you are done eating the snack, you are supposed to put your dirty dishes into the sink and then start in on your homework. Once your homework is done, you are allowed outside.

Rather than following this schedule, you always go out to play in your school clothes and get them all ripped and dirty because you play too rough. Then, you eat your snack, but you get food all over the floor and never remember to put your dirty stuff in the sink. You never do your homework unless she stands over you and makes you. If asked how you are punished, you admit, after initial attempts to avoid doing so, that your stepmother has sent you to your room without dinner, taken away your TV privileges, and refused to let you go out to play. When she does this, you get really mad and start breaking anything you can get your hands on. You get very sad when you give this information and ask repeatedly if the interviewer hates you now.

You have never received any mental health services before. If asked what you expect to happen from coming to the interview, say your stepmother expects you to be punished by the interviewer if you act up. You are also supposed to come home with ideas from the interviewer on good ways to punish you when you don't behave at home. Your stepmother is frustrated that nothing she does makes you behave; she wants ideas that will work.

4. How do you feel?

You may have trouble responding to feeling questions because you aren't used to thinking about your feelings. You are used to being active and doing stuff. If asked if you are ever happy, for example, you might not know what to say. However, if asked about what you do after good stuff happens, like your dad playing with you, you are able to say you smile and laugh and jump a lot. Then, if asked how you feel when you jump and smile and laugh, you say you feel happy. If asked if you are ever anxious, you do not know what anxious means. If the interviewer says something like, "Do you ever worry about stuff at home?" you say you worry about making mistakes whenever your stepmother is around. She seems to notice every mistake you make. If asked for a specific example, you say that you thought you cleaned up your room good yesterday, but something was wrong with it and you weren't allowed to go outside. Going outside is your favorite thing, and she is always taking it away from you. So now you get worried whenever you do a chore and she is watching you. You sigh a lot as you talk about this stuff. If asked what your dad says about this, say he has told you that you will have to leave if you can't make your stepmother love you. Sometimes, if you worry too much, you get clumsy and fall on things or drop things, and then these things break. This seems to happen a lot when you are supposed to bring your plate to the sink. If the dishes get broken, your stepmother gets really mad.

If asked if you are ever sad, you say that you are sad most of the time because your stepmother does not love you and she has told you that your real mom doesn't love you either. Your stepmother used to say that it was wrong the way your real mom raised you. Now she says you are bad and she can understand why your real mom ignored you most of the time. When she says this to you, it makes you cry.

If asked about what you do when you are angry, say that maybe you want to smash things. Sometimes you smash your own toys. When you are smashing stuff, you feel better, but then later you get sad because you don't have that toy anymore. Your stepmother makes you mad all of the time now and so you don't have many toys left. So you yell at her and call her names instead of breaking your toys. It really makes her mad when you call her a witch. You are glad she is mad because then she feels the way you feel. If asked why she makes you so angry, you might say she has too many rules and they all stink. If asked what you want to happen, say you really want to kick your stepmother, but you know you can't. If asked why not, say because she would take all your stuff away from you.

Your dad has told you that you will be out of the house if you don't shape up. You have been told by CYS that you will never go back to your real mom and so there is nowhere to go if your stepmother kicks you out. As much as you hate her, you don't know what will happen to you if she kicks you out. You think about this sometimes and feel really scared.

If the interviewer is being nice to you during this discussion, you might say you think you could be happy forever if the interviewer would take you home.

5. How do you think?

You expect adults to like you at first because they have always seemed to. You also expect that somehow, for some unknown reason, the adults will go from liking you to hating you. You don't understand what it is that goes wrong but it always does. You don't have any ideas about what you might do that gets adults mad at you. You know adults own the world and you do, initially, try hard to please them. You want them to approve of you and love you. You don't spend much time thinking. You like to be on the move. You have a hard time sitting still, so even when eating your snack, you tend to wander around the kitchen looking at stuff while you eat. You don't understand why you should do your homework before playing. Playing is fun and homework is boring, so obviously you should play not do homework.

6. What do you like about yourself?

You like the pictures you draw. You make a lot of drawings in your free time and give them to your dad or the teachers at school. You used to make drawings for your stepmother. She used to put them on the refrigerator, but now she rips them up and tells you to get back to your homework. If given the opportunity, you draw a picture of a heart, put the interviewer's name in the middle, and then give the heart to the interviewer.

7. How have you been doing at work?

This question is not relevant to Alex.

8. How have you been doing in school?

You moved two months ago into a new school as a result of your change in custody. If asked about school, say your real mom didn't send you to school very often. Your stepmother makes you go every day. In school, your teacher has told you that she likes you but that she wants you to try harder to learn things. She says you are behind everyone else in reading and math and that you need to learn to be organized and not hand in such messy work. Your teacher says she thinks you are smart. She thinks you aren't doing your work because you haven't learned to be responsible.

If asked how you relate to other children at school, you say that the boys let you play with them on the playground but none of them plays with you outside of school.

9. How is your health?

When you were living with your mother, you had no contact with doctors beyond the stuff that is handled at school. You recently spent the whole day at a doctor's office having loads of tests. Children and Youth Services paid for it, but you know your stepmother requested it. The doctor told your stepmother that you are not growing as well as you should. He thinks you need to eat more and eat lots of healthy stuff so you will grow more. You liked this advice because you were hungry a lot at your real mom's place and it didn't feel good. Your stepmom does feed you a lot, but she ruins it by yelling at you for not having good table manners. The doctor gave you some special cream for your leg. It is healing well, but your stepmother says you will always have a scar because your real mom took such bad care of you.

10. How do you relate to others?

At first, your stepmother seemed to like you. She would cuddle you at night and read you stories. She bought you all new clothes and toys. She was very pleased that you moved in. Problems started as soon as school started. She was very angry that you ruined all your school clothes. She has told you over and over that you can't wear dirty and torn clothes to school and that she can't afford to keep buying you new stuff. You used to cry when she said this stuff to you, but now you get mad and yell back at her. You think her rules are stupid and she can't make you follow them.

Your father is a salesman who travels all over the country on business. He is only home once in a while. He has told you that he believes that all of your problems are your old mom's fault. He used to see you a few times a year before you came to live with him. He was nice during these visits, but he never seemed to notice that things were bad at your mom's house. He does think your stepmother yells at you too much, and you have heard him telling her that. You have also heard him telling her that any real woman would know how to handle a seven-year-old boy. You don't know what he means by "real woman," but you can tell it really upsets your stepmother. When she begins to scare you with threats of kicking you out, you say, "You aren't a real woman anyway. Dad says so." This always makes her run off and cry.

You think your new teacher is okay. She is trying to help you learn to read and she likes your pictures. You wish she would stop checking your homework so carefully. Your teacher last year didn't do that. You don't know why she has to be so picky about your homework. Once, when she sent you to the corner for not doing your work, you started to cry. She then took you out of the corner and comforted you. You really liked it when she gave you a tissue and helped you blow your nose. You asked her if she would like to take you home. She gave you a hug and just sent you back to your desk. You overheard her having an argument with your stepmother on the phone. Your stepmother was really mad when she saw you later that night. She told you that it was your responsibility to get your homework done and that she wasn't going to be pushed around by your school teacher.

11. How do you view of your life?

You are glad you are with your dad. You eat much better at his house. You can admit that your stepmother is a good cook and has bought neat stuff for you. If she would stop being mean, you would be glad to be living with her.

EXERCISES FOR THE INTERVIEWER

Exercise 1: Develop a diagnosis for Alex

    A. What criteria does Alex meet for an Axis I disorder of Oppositional Defiant Disorder or Parent-Child Relational Problem?

_____

_____

_____

_____

    Name two other Axis I diagnoses that you might want to rule out for Alex and indicate what additional information might be needed to differentiate between the diagnostic choices for him.

_____

_____

_____

_____

    Does Alex meet all the criteria for an Axis I disorder, should the diagnosis be deferred, or is a diagnosis not needed?

_____

_____

_____

_____

    B. What criteria does Alex meet for an Axis II diagnosis (Personality Disorders and Mental Retardation)? Should a diagnosis be deferred, or is a diagnosis not needed? Explain and be as specific as possible.

_____

_____

_____

_____

    C. Is there anything you might report for Alex on Axis III (General Medical Conditions that are potentially relevant to the client's mental disorder)?

_____

_____

_____

_____

    D. List all specific psychosocial and environmental stressors that are influencing Alex at this time on Axis IV. Indicate if each stress is mild, moderate, or severe.

_____

_____

_____

_____

E. What is your global assessment of Alex's functioning for Axis V (current, highest in past year)?

_____

_____

_____

_____

F. Double-check your diagnostic choices starting at Axis V and proceeding backward through Axis I to determine if you may have overestimated or underestimated the impact of the situational, biological, or individual psychological factors on Alex's current functioning. Should you change anything? Be specific in describing why or why not.

_____

_____

_____

_____

G. Review your diagnostic choices again from Alex's point of view. Do your choices support the discussions you have had with him? Would he be disturbed by your choices? Be specific in discussing why or why not.

_____

_____

_____

_____

Exercise 2: Practice deepening interview with Alex

A. Alex acts out his feelings without really being aware of them. Help Alex deepen his emotional awareness by identifying his possible feeling state and how he may be expressing it through his nonverbal behavior. Use information from Alex's profile to guide you. An example is provided.

Alex: She sent me to my room again. I showed her. I broke that truck she just gave me!

You were mad that she sent you to your room, so you showed her that you were mad by breaking the toy she gave you.

Alex: My dad didn't come home to play with me like he promised, so I hid in the closet and she couldn't find me.

_____

_____

_____

Alex: She yelled at me for being dirty, so I flushed my homework down the toilet.

_____

_____

_____

Alex: The kids next door never let me play ball with them. Yesterday, I saw their ball in our yard. When no one was looking, I grabbed it and hid it in our garage.

_____

_____

_____

B. Alex tries to change the subject whenever a sensitive topic comes up. Write a redirecting comment that supports Alex emotionally but encourages him to face the issue he is trying to avoid. Be careful to phrase your redirect so that it doesn't sound like a criticism. Use information from Alex's profile to guide you. An example of a redirect, to prevent avoidance, is provided.

Interviewer: What did you say that led your stepmother to call you a liar?

Alex: Did you ever get called a liar when you were a kid?

I know it feels bad to talk about your stepmother calling you a liar. What did you say that she called lying?

Interviewer: Did you do your homework today?

Alex: The teacher was so unfair to me today. I was sitting in my seat like everyone else but then David, who sits behind me, poked me with a pencil, so I had to turn around and poke him back. The teacher blamed me for not paying attention and made me sit in time-out during recess!

_____

_____

_____

Interviewer: Tell me what happened when you saw your mother yesterday at Children and Youth Services.

Alex: My stepmother says my real mom doesn't love me. Do you think she loves me?

_____

_____

_____

_____

Interviewer: Did you follow your schedule today when you got home from school?

Alex: What was your schedule like when you were a kid?

_____

_____

_____

_____

B. Alex often feels that no one listens to him. In response to his comments, make a summarizing statement that demonstrates you are listening, that highlights a theme, that serves as a transition, or that decreases his emotional intensity. Use information from Alex's profile to guide you. An example of using summarizing, as a transition to a related issue, is provided.

Alex: My stepmother hates me. No matter what I do, she thinks I am bad. She yells at me after everything I do. I tell her that she is the one who is bad, not me. Even my dad thinks she is bad because I heard him tell her she isn't a real woman because she can't control me. But even though it is her fault, my dad says I have to listen to her or I will have to leave.

She yells and yells no matter what you do. You don't want to listen, but your dad says

you will have to leave if you don't. Did you do anything today because she asked you to?

Write another summarization in response to Alex's previous comments that highlights a theme that comes through in his comments.

_____

_____

_____

_____

Alex: At school all the other kids sit in their seats all the time, but I don't like to. I don't want to sit. I like to move around. The teacher has a lot of great stuff in her room. I like best to get there before everyone else so I can look around at all the shelves and touch stuff. The teacher doesn't seem to mind me touching the stuff before class, but she gets really mad when I do it during reading or something. Why does everyone have to pick on me?

_____

_____

_____

_____

Exercise 3: Thought questions related to Alex

A. Consider who you are as an interviewer and write down what you think might be most difficult about establishing rapport with Alex based on your age, ethnicity, gender, socioeconomic status, sexual orientation, religion, physical characteristics, and personality style. What specifically might happen?

_____

_____

_____

_____

_____

B. Is there anything you could do to enhance your ability to establish an effective working relationship with Alex? Be specific and detailed in describing your ideas.

_____

_____

_____

_____

_____

C. How might you react internally if Alex grabs something in the interviewing room and threatens to throw it through the window? What if he starts coming toward you while threatening to kick you?

_____

_____

_____

_____

_____

E. Alex has a history of acting out aggressively in response to his negative emotions. Assume that you have been talking about his relationship to his biological mother and you can see the tension building up inside him from his nonverbal cues. What might you say to Alex if he threatens to do something aggressive in the session?

_____

_____

_____

_____

F. What might you do if Alex starts throwing objects at you?

_____

_____

_____

_____

Case of Cathy

1. What are your basic statistics?

Your name is Cathy, and you are an eleven-year-old, European-American female. You have been residing in foster care for the past four months. This placement was made after you revealed you were a victim of sexual abuse to one of your teachers at school. Your foster home consists of a married couple who have encouraged you to call them mom and dad. They have no children of their own. You are currently attending the fifth grade in a rural, elementary school. Your biological family consists of your mom, your grandfather, your sister Karen, and two adult cousins who sometimes live with your family and sometimes live with other extended family members in another state. Your mother also has boyfriends who come and go. You are being interviewed at a community mental health center.

2. How do you behave in the interview?

You are well groomed and fuss with your hair and pull on your clothes. During the interview, you are quiet and shy but intelligent and have no trouble understanding any questions from the interviewer. You do not initiate any conversation but respond immediately to any questions that are asked because you wish to please the interviewer. You answer softly, looking down in your lap most of the time but periodically looking up furtively at interviewer. The more the interviewer says things to help you feel comfortable, the more you open up and give more eye contact. If you feel criticized in anyway, you shut down.

When asked why you are being interviewed, you become very tearful and almost incoherent. If the interviewer gives you a lot of support, you calm down. If asked specifically about the sexual abuse, you ask the interviewer if you could please talk about something else. You lean back into the chair as if it can protect you. You cross and uncross your ankles and give other nonverbal signs of anxiety.

If asked mental screening questions by the interviewer, such as whether you are ever anxious, sad, or angry, your first response is denial. If the interviewer probes gently saying it's okay to talk about these things, you admit to really missing your mom and siblings, being angry at yourself for admitting the sexual abuse, and being terrified of your foster father. You find any questions about hallucinations or delusions difficult to understand and you apologize to the interviewer repeatedly for being so stupid. If asked about whether you have ever hurt anyone or thought of hurting yourself, you say no.

3. Why are you being interviewed?

Four months ago, your grandfather started touching your five-year-old sister Karen all over her body and this made her cry. You told your teacher about this the next day because you wanted to help Karen and you didn't know what else to do. You also told the teacher that your grandfather had been touching you like this all of your life. You begged your teacher to do something to protect your sister. She contacted the school principal, who then called Children and Youth Services (CYS). A case manager from this agency came over to talk to you at school. After talking to you, she called your mother from the principal's office and said she was bringing you home from school and would want to talk with her and with Karen. When you and the CYS worker got to your house, no one was there. There were signs of a hurried packing up. You rushed to the room you shared with Karen. She was not there; all signs of her having been there were gone. You were placed in emergency foster care. Children and Youth Services is searching for your family but has had no luck to date. They have sent you to this appointment to get help, but you don't really understand what they mean by this.

If asked about what your grandfather did to you, say he just has to touch you all over and stick things in you. He, and three of your adult male cousins, have done this to you for as long as you can remember. You want to stop talking at this point. If pressed gently by the interviewer, you provide more details. You say that these men taught you how to suck on them and how to lie quietly while they put their things into you. When it first started, you begged them to leave you alone but after awhile, you gave this up because it never worked. These individuals repeatedly threatened to take your mom away if you ever told anyone about the abuse. You were so worried about your sister that you took a risk and told your teacher. You may feel very overwhelmed by feelings as you say this. They did steal your mom away from you; just like they had always threatened. If asked whether your mom knew about your sexual activities, say that she never talked to you about it. She must have known something because she would just leave the room if someone started to touch you.

If asked what you want, say you want to be reunited with your family. If asked how you are doing in foster care, say that you are having trouble sleeping and are wetting the bed each night. This wetting problem is new and started when you went to foster care. If asked if you know why this is happening, say that your foster father keeps coming in to kiss you goodnight after he turns off your light at night. This terrifies you. You are sure he is kissing you because he wants to have sex with you. You hate him for this. If asked about your foster mother, you say you like her. She makes meals for you and encourages you to call her "mom." You would never talk about your foster dad with this new mom. You loved your mother, yet she immediately abandoned you when you revealed the sexual abuse to your teacher. This was just what your abusers had threatened. Thus, you are not going to risk losing this foster "mom" by telling her about your fears concerning your foster "dad." If asked how you will handle this problem with your foster dad, say that your mom has lived with many different men. You expect that your foster mother will change partners often too. You hope that it won't be long before there is a new "foster dad" in the home and you additionally hope that this "dad" won't be interested in you.

If asked about prior treatment, you say this is your first time and you don't know what will happen.

4. How do you feel?

You are terrified that you will be kicked out of your foster home because you have no place to go. You are also terrified that you will have to start having sex with your foster dad if you stay at this house. You try not to think about your mom. When you do, you lose control and cry for hours. You are also very worried about your sister. Will your mother take care of her for you? Will your sister remember how to make peanut butter and jelly sandwiches for herself if mom doesn't feed her? When you don't think about your family, you just feel all alone and hopeless.

5. How do you think?

You view yourself as incompetent and stupid. Your poor grades in school further reinforce your feelings that you are "dumb as a stone," as your grandfather used to say. You don't trust your ability to think or solve problems because, after all, when you told of your abuse to protect your sister, you ended up being separated from her. Now she is off somewhere without anyone who will bathe, feed, or clothe her. In your attempt to protect her, you have left her without yourself—her sole protector. You expect that all men want to have sex with you. You perceive all nurturance from males as a prelude to sex. You like women because they don't hurt you, but you don't expect them to protect you either.

6. What do you like about yourself?

If asked about this, you become very quiet and start to cry. If pressed further by the interviewer, you say you have been a loser since birth. You can't please anyone except by having sex with them, and you hate having sex. If given support and encouraged to think more, you say that you liked the fact that you have been able to teach yourself how to adequately clean, clothe, and feed yourself. No one helped or encouraged you to learn these things. You have actively used these skills to provide care for your younger sister. Your younger sister loves you for this, and this makes you feel good.

8. How have you been doing in school?

You never got to learn much at school because your mom moved you and your sister around so much. You are currently at the bottom of the class in the fifth grade. All the other students in your reading and math groups seem to have serious problems talking and thinking. You figure you must be like them because you are in their group and your grandfather has told you how stupid you are. You have made superficial friends with a group of three girls at your newest school who include you at lunch and recess. You have never seen them outside of school.

9. How is your health?

You have never in your life seen a pediatrician or a dentist. Your foster mother has scheduled exams for you and this makes you anxious because you don't know what to expect. You are not sick now, but whenever you were sick in the past, you gave yourself Tylenol and Pepto Bismol. You are confused about why your foster mom is concerned about your health, but it feels good to you when she fusses over you just because you are coughing.

10. How do you relate to others?

You really want to be close to female adults and children. Your general style is to be a people pleaser. You are passive and compliant. You never assert yourself in any way, and you become very anxious when you do not know how people want you to behave. Surprises of any kind fill you with fear because you don't know how you are supposed to react. You are a good listener and know how to compliment people so they like to have you around.

You prefer to avoid males of any age. You assume that adult males will want you to suck on them and do other stuff you don't like; anything nice a male does just means he is going to want this other stuff from you. You aren't exactly scared of boys your own age, but you are aware that they have the same private parts as your grandfather and adult cousins.

How do you relate to teachers? In school, you just sit quietly and try not to make the teachers angry. Your current teacher has yelled at you for not paying attention in class and for performing poorly on homework. You try to hide it from your teacher that you often don't understand the work she is giving you to do because you are afraid she would dislike you because of it. Your poor performance is also because memories of your abusive experiences often come back to you when you are trying to do school work so you can't really concentrate. Whenever teachers or other adults praise you, you are filled with a mixture of elation and fear: elation that anyone would like you and fear that they will either want you to engage in sex with them or that they will be repulsed by you once they know of your sexual behavior. These fears make it difficult for you to accept help from teachers, CYS workers, and other nonabusive adults. You have seen other children being praised by parents and teachers and wish that you were not such a terrible person so that adults would really like you and want to care for you.

How do you relate to peers? Your only real friend has been your younger sister Karen. You have tried to take good care of her by making her sandwiches and helping her with homework. She often has told you how much she loves and depends on you. You have always shared everything you have with her. Karen knows how much you hate having sex. She cries when grandfather makes her leave the room because she knows what will happen to you. You are scared that Karen is being forced to take your "place" now that you are gone.

Your relationships with peers in school have also been generally positive. You are friendly and compliant, and this had led you to develop "school friendships" in each school you have attended. You have never told any of these friends what has happened to you.

11. How do you view your life?

You desperately want to find a way to get back with your mom and your sister. You don't want to be involved in sex again, but you think the only way to get to see Karen and protect her is to "put up" with it. You are very sorry now that you told your teacher about your problem.

EXERCISES FOR THE INTERVIEWER

Exercise 1: Develop a diagnosis for Cathy

A. What criteria does Cathy meet for an Axis I diagnosis of Posttraumatic Stress Disorder or Sexual Abuse of Child?

_____

_____

_____

_____

Name two other Axis I diagnoses that you might want to rule out for Cathy and indicate what additional information might be needed to differentiate between the diagnostic choices for her.

_____

_____

_____

_____

Does Cathy meet all the criteria for an Axis I disorder? Should the diagnosis be deferred, or is a diagnosis not needed?

_____

_____

_____

_____

B. What criteria does Cathy meet for an Axis II diagnosis (Personality Disorders and Mental Retardation)? Should the diagnosis be deferred, or is a diagnosis not needed? Explain and be as specific as possible.

_____

_____

_____

_____

C. Is there anything you might report for Cathy on Axis III (General Medical Conditions that are potentially relevant to the client's mental disorder)?

_____

_____

_____

_____

D. List all specific psychosocial and environmental stressors that are influencing Cathy at this time for Axis IV? Indicate if each stressor is mild, moderate, or severe.

_____

_____

_____

_____

E. What is your global assessment of Cathy's functioning for Axis V (current and highest in past year)?

_____

_____

_____

_____

F. Double-check your diagnostic choices starting at Axis V and proceeding backward through Axis I to determine if you may have overestimated or underestimated the impact of the situational, biological, or individual psychological factors on Cathy's current functioning. Should you change anything? Be specific in describing why or why not.

_____

_____

_____

_____

G. Review your diagnostic choices again from Cathy's point of view. Do your choices support the discussions you have had with her? Would she be disturbed by your choices? Be specific in discussing why or why not.

_____

_____

_____

_____

Exercise 2: Practice deepening interview with Cathy

A. Cathy makes many comments indicating that she is afraid that her foster father will molest her. Write an empathetic comment, in response to each of her remarks, that validates her reactions to her life experiences, that lets her know you understand how she feels about her experiences, or that helps her regain emotional control. Use the information in the case history to help you develop your comments. Use simple vocabulary words in your comments to insure that an eleven-year-old can understand them. An example is provided of using empathy to demonstrate to Cathy that she is understood.

Cathy: My foster mom will leave if I tell her I am scared of my foster dad.

Your mother left you when you told your teacher about your grandfather. You are afraid your foster mom will leave you too.

Cathy: Maybe, if I just say nothing, my foster dad will get tired of coming in since I ignore him.

_____

_____

_____

_____

Cathy: I can't tell my foster dad to stop coming in and touching me because that never works.

_____

_____

_____

_____

Cathy: He wouldn't come in if he didn't want sex from me.

_____

_____

_____

_____

B. Cathy's safety has been compromised many times by different men. Make summarizing statements in response to her concerns about her foster dad. You can summarize to demonstrate listening, to highlight a theme, to transition into some other topic, or to decrease her emotional intensity. An example is provided using summarizing to highlight a theme.

Cathy: I hate it when he comes in my room at night. This is how it always started. It was always night. At first I would ask them to go away. That never worked. Then, I would cry. They didn't care. I would try to wear a lot of clothes. Nothing ever helped. I hate my foster father. I wish he would drop dead.

Theme: She can't protect herself.

You didn't want them to touch you but they always did. You can't protect yourself. You tried so hard, but it never worked. You asked them to go away. You cried. You tried to protect your body by wearing lots of clothes. Nothing ever worked, so you feel helpless to protect yourself now from your foster dad. You think you can't be safe from him unless he is dead.

Cathy: Why does my foster dad have to touch me all the time? Touching is gross. My skin crawls when he touches me. Yesterday, I fell off my new bicycle, and he rushed over and picked me up. He carried me into the house. It was so horrible. He spent the day patting my arm and asking me if I was still hurting. He always finds reasons to touch me.

_____

_____

_____

_____

_____

Cathy: Every night when my foster mom tells me to brush my teeth, my heart begins to pound because HE will come soon. I am supposed to brush my teeth and get into bed. He knocks on the door but then comes in even though I never say "Come in." He walks toward me and says, "I hope you have sweet dreams." Then he pulls the covers around my neck. He's gross!

_____

_____

_____

_____

_____

C. Cathy has been socialized to be sexual with adults; however, she avoids sexual behavior as much as she possibly can. Assume that you are seeing Marissa, a girl with a very similar history to Cathy, but who has responded differently to her victimization. Marissa tries to get what she wants from both male and female adults by approaching them sexually. Assume Marissa has repeatedly made sexual advances to you during your interview including: rubbing the sides of her body suggestively, undoing the first three buttons on her blouse and leaning dramatically forward, and making pelvic tilts in the chair while saying she is ready if you "want some," and so forth. These behaviors erupt on the three attempts you have made to discuss her family relationships. This didn't happen when you were discussing her school work or her relationships with friends.

Make a process comment to Marissa pointing out the pattern in her behavior.

_____

_____

_____

_____

Make an empathetic comment to Marissa that indicates that you understand why she would be confused about what you, and other adults, want from her.

_____

_____

_____

_____

Exercise 3: Thought questions related to Cathy

A. Consider who you are as an interviewer and write down what you think might be most difficult about establishing rapport with Cathy based on your age, ethnicity, gender, socioeconomic status, sexual orientation, religion, physical characteristics, and personality style. What specifically might happen?

_____

_____

_____

_____

_____

B. Is there anything you could do to enhance your ability to establish an effective working relationship with Cathy? Be specific and detailed in describing your ideas.

_____

_____

_____

_____

_____

C. What might change about your reaction to this client if it was a Carl not a Cathy who has been sexually abused by male relatives? Eleven-year-old Carl has not gone through puberty yet. Is Carl's abuse relevant in any way to his future sexual orientation?

_____

_____

_____

_____

_____

D. Assume that you are interviewing Marissa again. Imagine that Marissa has just said, "Do you want to have sex now?" How might you respond internally and what might you need to do within and outside of the session to keep your interactions with her therapeutic?

_____

_____

_____

_____

_____

References

American Psychiatric Association. (2000). *Diagnostic and statistical manual of mental disorders* (4th ed., text revision). Washington, DC: Author.

American Psychological Association. (2000). Guidelines for psychotherapy with lesbian, gay and bisexual clients. *American Psychologist, 55*(12), 1440–1451.

American Psychological Association. (2002). *Getting ready for HIPAA: What you need to know now. A primer for psychologists.* Washington, DC: Author.

American Psychological Association. (2003). Guidelines on multicultural education, training, research, practice and organizational change for psychologists. *American Psychologist, 58*(5), 377–402.

Beutler, L., Machado, P., & Neufeldt, S. (1994). Therapist variables. In A. Bergin & G. Garfield (Eds.), *Handbook of psychotherapy and behavior change* (4th ed., pp. 229–269). New York: Wiley.

Boat, B., & Everson, M. (1986). *Using anatomical dolls: Guidelines for interviewing young children in sexual abuse investigations.* Chapel Hill: University of North Carolina at Chapel Hill.

Cardemil, E., & Battle, C. (2003). Guess who's coming to therapy? Getting comfortable with conversations about race and ethnicity in psychotherapy. *Professional Psychology: Research and Practice, 34*(3), 278–286.

Egan, G. (1994). *The skilled helper: A problem-management approach to helping* (5th ed.). Pacific Grove, CA: Brooks/Cole.

Feminist Therapy Institute, Inc. (1995). Feminist therapy code of ethics. In E. Rave & C. Larsen (Eds.), *Ethical decision making in therapy: Feminist perspectives* (pp. 38–44). New York: Guilford Press.

Grencavage, M., & Norcross, J. (1990). Where are the commonalities among the therapeutic common factors? *Professional Psychology: Research and Practice, 21*(5), 372–378.

Hays, P. A. (2001). *Addressing cultural complexities in practice: A framework for clinicians and counselors.* Washington, DC: American Psychological Association.

House, A. E. (2000). *DSM-IV diagnosis in the schools.* New York: Guilford Press.

Ivey, A., Gluckstern, N., & Ivey, M. (1997). *Basic attending skills* (3rd ed.). North Amherst, MA: Microtraining Associates.

Lambert, M., & Bergin, A. (1994). The effectiveness of psychotherapy. In A. Bergin & G. Garfield (Eds.), *Handbook of psychotherapy and behavior change* (pp. 143–189). New York: Wiley.

Langer, I. J., & Abelson, R. P. (1974). A patient by any other name . . . : Clinician group differences in labeling bias. *Journal of Consulting and Clinical Psychology, 42,* 4–9.

Langer, I. J., & Imber, L. (1980). The role of mindlessness in the perception of deviance. *Journal of Personality and Social Psychology, 39,* 360–367.

Miller, W. R., & Rollnick, S. (1992). *Motivational interviewing: Preparing people to change addictive behavior.* New York: Guilford Press.

Morrison, J. (1995). *The first interview: A guide for clinicians.* New York: Guilford Press.

Newman, R. (2003). The whys of HIPAA compliance. *Monitor on Psychology, 34*(1), 29–31.

Piaget, J. (1952). *The origins of intelligence in children* (M. Cook, Trans.). New York: International Universities Press.

Prochaska, J., & DiClemente, C. (1986). The transtheoretical approach. In J. Norcross (Ed.), *Handbook of eclectic psychotherapy.* New York: Brunner/Mazel.

Prochaska, J., DiClemente, C., & Norcross, J. (1992). In search of how people change. *American Psychologist, 47*(9), 1102–1114.

Rapoport, J. L., & Ismond, D. R. (1996). *DSM-IV training guide: For diagnosis of childhood disorders* (4th ed.). New York: Brunner/Mazel.

Reid, W. H., & Wise, M. G. (1995). *DSM-IV training guide.* New York: Brunner/Mazel.

Rosenhan, D. L. (1973). On being sane in insane places. *Science, 179,* 250–258.

Saywitz, K. J. (1995). Improving children's testimony: The question, the answer, and the environment. In M. Zaragoza, J. Graham, G. Hall, R. Hirschman, & Y. Ben-Porath (Eds.), *Memory and testimony in the child witness* (pp. 113–140). Thousand Oaks, CA: Sage.

Slattery, J. M. (2004). *Counseling diverse clients: Bringing context into therapy.* Belmont, CA: Brooks/Cole.

Snyder, M. (1984). When belief creates reality. In L. Berkowitz (Ed.), *Advances in experimental social psychology* (Vol. 18). New York: Academic Press.

Sue, D. W., & Sue, D. (2002). *Counseling the culturally diverse: Theory and practice* (4th ed.). New York: Wiley.

Teyber, E. (1997). *Interpersonal process in psychotherapy: A relational approach* (3rd ed.). Pacific Grove, CA: Brooks/Cole.

Whiston, S., & Sexton, T. (1993). An overview of psychotherapy outcome research: Implications for practice. *Professional Psychology: Research and Practice, 24*(1), 43–51.

Suggestions for Further Reading

DIAGNOSIS

American Psychiatric Association. (2000). *Diagnostic and statistical manual of mental disorders* (4th ed., text revision). Washington, DC: Author.

House, A. E. (2000). *DSM-IV diagnosis in the schools*. New York: Guilford Press.

Rapoport, J. L., & Ismond, D. R. (1996). *DSM-IV training guide: For diagnosis of childhood disorders* (4th ed.). New York: Brunner/Mazel.

Reid, W. H., & Wise, M. G. (1995). *DSM-IV training guide*. New York: Brunner/Mazel.

DIVERSITY ISSUES IN INTERVIEWING

American Psychological Association. (2000). Guidelines for psychotherapy with lesbian, gay and bisexual clients. *American Psychologist, 55*(12), 1440–1451.

American Psychological Association. (2003). Guidelines on multicultural education, training, research, practice, and organizational change for psychologists. *American Psychologist, 58*(5), 377–402.

Gibbs, J. T., & Huang, L. N. (1998). *Children of color: Psychological interventions with culturally diverse youth*. San Francisco: Jossey-Bass.

Hays, P. A. (2001). *Addressing cultural complexities in practice: A framework for clinicians and counselors*. Washington, DC: American Psychological Association.

Perez, R. M., DeBord, K. A., & Bieschke, K. J. (2000). *Handbook of counseling and psychotherapy with lesbian, gay, and bisexual clients*. Washington, DC: American Psychological Association.

Sue, D. W., & Sue, D. (2002). *Counseling the culturally diverse: Theory and practice* (4th ed.). New York: Wiley.

INTERVIEWING SKILLS FOR ADULT CASES

Brems, C. (2001). *Basic skills in psychotherapy and counseling*. Belmont, CA: Wadsworth/Cole.

Egan, G. (1994). *The skilled helper: A problem-management and opportunity-development approach to helping* (5th ed.). Pacific Grove, CA: Brooks/Cole.

Hill, C. E., & O'Brien, K. M. (1999). *Helping skills: Facilitating exploration, insight and action*. Washington, DC: American Psychological Association.

Ivey, A., Gluckstern, N., & Ivey, M. (1997). *Basic attending skills* (3rd ed.). North Amherst, MA: Microtraining Associates.

Morrison, J. (1995). *The first interview: A guide for clinicians*. New York: Guilford Press.

INTERVIEWING SKILLS FOR CHILD AND TEEN CASES

Brems, C. (1993). *A comprehensive guide to child psychotherapy*. Boston: Allyn & Bacon.

Kratochwill, T. R., & Morris, R. J. (1991). *The practice of child therapy* (2nd ed.). Elmsford, NY: Pergamon Press.

Orton, G. (1997). *Strategies for counseling with children and their parents*. Pacific Grove, CA: Brooks/Cole.

Sattler, J. (1998). *Clinical and forensic interviewing of children and families*. San Diego, CA: Author.

Wachtel, E. (1994). *Treating troubled children and their families*. New York: Guilford Press.

MENTAL STATUS EVALUATIONS

Morrison, J. (1995). *The first interview: A guide for clinicians*. New York: Guilford Press.

SUBSTANCE ABUSE EVALUATIONS

Miller, W. R., & Rollnick, S. (1992). *Motivational interviewing: Preparing people to change addictive behavior*. New York: Guilford Press.

National Clearinghouse for Alcohol and Drug Information (NCADI) TIP 35. (2001). *Enhancing motivation for change in substance abuse treatment* (BKD342). Rockville, MD: U.S. Department of Health and Human Services.

SUICIDE ASSESSMENT

Berman, A. L., & Jobes, D. A. (1991). *Youth suicide: Assessment and intervention*. Washington, DC: American Psychological Association.

Jobes, D. *How to work effectively with suicidal clients*. Eau Claire, WI: Health Education Network, LLC (to order call 800-839-4584 or fax a request to 715-839-8680).

Jobes, D. CAMS-Revised Suicide Status Form-II (SSF-II) Assessment, Treatment Planning, Tracking, and Outcome Forms. Eau Claire, WI: Health Education Network (to order call 800-839-4584 or fax a request to 715-839-8680).

Kleespies, P., Deleppo, J., Gallagher, P., & Niles, B. (1999). Managing suicidal emergencies: Recommendations for the practitioner. *Professional Psychology: Research and Practice, 30*(5), 454–463.

VIOLENCE ISSUES

American Psychological Association. (1996). *Violence and the family*. Washington, DC: Author.

Eron, L., Gentry, J., & Schlegel, P. (1994). *Reason to hope: A psychosocial perspective on violence and youth*. Washington, DC: American Psychological Association.

Wolfe, D. A., Wekerle, C., & Scott, K. (1997). *Alternatives to violence: Empowering youth to develop healthy relationships*. Thousand Oaks, CA: Sage.

Quinsey, V., Harris, G., Rice, M., & Cormier, C. (1998). *Violent offenders: Appraising and managing risk*. Washington, DC: American Psychological Association.

Supervisory Feedback Worksheet

Student Interviewer: Date:

Supervisor:

Skills in training: *Attending, open-ended questions, closed questions, comments on nonverbal behavior, summarizing, reflective listening, empathetic comments, redirecting, supportive confrontation, process comments.*

1. Interviewer strengths observed during interview

2. Areas for interviewer growth observed during interview

3. Client observations (Mental Status Evaluation, Presenting Problem, Observed Behavior, Feelings, Cognitions, Relationships, and Situations)

4. Areas to cover with client in further sessions

5. Treatment recommendations (Does client need insight? Does client need to think more? Does client need to feel more? Does client need to stop or start taking action steps?)

1. Interviewer attended to material using appropriate nonverbals (leaning forward, head nods, etc.).

0 . . . . . . 1 . . . . . . 2 . . . . . . 3 . . . . . . 4 5
None   Sometimes   Frequent   N/A

2. Interviewer used open-ended questions to draw information out of client.

0 . . . . . . 1 . . . . . . 2 . . . . . . 3 . . . . . . 4 5
None   Sometimes   Frequent   N/A

3. Interviewer used closed questions as appropriate to draw out specific information.

0 . . . . . . 1 . . . . . . 2 . . . . . . 3 . . . . . . 4 5
None   Sometimes   Frequent   N/A

4. Interviewer made comments on client nonverbal behavior when appropriate.

0 . . . . . . 1 . . . . . . 2 . . . . . . 3 . . . . . . 4 5
None   Sometimes   Frequent   N/A

5. Interviewer used summary statements to resonate with client concerns, thoughts, and experiences.

0 . . . . . . 1 . . . . . . 2 . . . . . . 3 . . . . . . 4 5
None   Sometimes   Frequent   N/A

6. Interviewer used reflective listening skills to pinpoint client feelings.

0 . . . . . . 1 . . . . . . 2 . . . . . . 3 . . . . . . 4 5
None   Sometimes   Frequent   N/A

7. Interviewer made empathetic comments to show understanding and validation of client feelings.

0 . . . . . . 1 . . . . . . 2 . . . . . . 3 . . . . . . 4 5
None   Sometimes   Frequent   N/A

8. Interviewer used redirecting when appropriate.

0 . . . . . . 1 . . . . . . 2 . . . . . . 3 . . . . . . 4 5
None   Sometimes   Frequent   N/A

9. Interviewer used supportive confrontation skills when appropriate.

0 . . . . . . 1 . . . . . . 2 . . . . . . 3 . . . . . . 4 5
None   Sometimes   Frequent   N/A

10. Interviewer made process comments when appropriate.

0 . . . . . . 1 . . . . . . 2 . . . . . . 3 . . . . . . 4 5
None   Sometimes   Frequent   N/A

Appendix:
Interviewing Skills Worksheets

WORKSHEET 1: Nonverbal Attending 1

Instructions: Use the following brief scenarios to enhance your awareness of how nonverbal behavior can affect you at the gut level and influence your attending behavior. One person should take on the interviewer role and one the client role. After you have done the brief role play, discuss the questions that follow the scenario with your partner.

Scenario 1. The client is male and a lot larger than the interviewer. When the interviewer comes to greet this man, he looms over the interviewer, shakes the interviewer's hand very forcefully, and when sitting down, pulls his chair in so close to the interviewer that their knees touch.

1. How did each of you feel at the gut level in response to this interaction? How might this be reflected in your nonverbal attending behavior?

_____

_____

_____

2. How did each of you react externally to the nonverbal behavior of the other? Behaviors to consider include eye contact, body orientation, body posture, facial expression, and autonomic behavior.

_____

_____

_____

3. If one or both of you had a negative gut response to the other, what might you say to discuss this gut response openly? How might this influence the course of the interview?

_____

_____

_____

4. If one or both of you had a negative gut response to the other, what do you think might specifically happen over the course of the interview if you try to ignore this?

_____

_____

_____

5. Assume the interviewer felt intimidated by the behavior of the client. What comment might the interviewer make in an attempt to open up communication with the client about this? Make sure this comment does not sound like a criticism.

_____

_____

_____

Scenario 2. The client is a great deal older than the interviewer. As the interviewer greets the client, he or she says, "You remind me so much of my grandchild who is living in California." As you sit down to begin the interview the client says, "How did you ever decide you wanted to do this with your life?"

1. How did each of you feel at the gut level in response to this interaction? How might this be reflected in your nonverbal attending behavior?

_____

_____

_____

2. How did each of you react externally to the nonverbal behavior of the other? Behaviors to consider include eye contact, body orientation, body posture, facial expression, and autonomic behavior.

_____

_____

_____

3. If one or both of you had a negative gut response to the other, what might you say to discuss this gut reaction openly? How might this influence the course of the interview?

_____

_____

_____

4. If one or both of you had a negative gut response to the other, what do you think might specifically happen over the course of the interview if you try to ignore this?

_____

_____

_____

5. Assume the client made the interviewer feel "child-like." What comment might the interviewer make in an attempt to open up communication with the client about this? Make sure this comment does not sound like a criticism.

_____

_____

_____

Scenario 3. The interviewer has a terrible cold and took a strong decongestant before coming to the session. The client has come in to get help quitting smoking. The client has a very soft voice and keeps going off on numerous tangents about other people he or she knows who have problems with smoking. During these comments, the interviewer keeps sniffing and coughing.

1. How did each of you feel at the gut level in response to this interaction? How might this be reflected in your nonverbal attending behavior?

_____

_____

_____

2. How did each of you react externally to the nonverbal behavior of the other? Behaviors to consider include eye contact, body orientation, body posture, facial expression, and autonomic behavior.

_____

_____

_____

3. If one or both of you had a negative gut response to the other, what might you say to discuss this gut reaction openly? How might this influence the course of the interview?

_____

_____

_____

4. If one or both of you had a negative gut response to the other, what do you think might specifically happen over the course of the interview if you try to ignore this?

_____

_____

_____

5. Assume the interviewer is having trouble listening to the client because of feeling ill. What comment might the interviewer make in an attempt to open up communication about this? Make sure the comment does not sound like a criticism or make the client feel responsible for the interviewer's welfare.

_____

_____

_____

WORKSHEET 2: Nonverbal Attending 2

General Instructions: With a partner, practice becoming aware of your nonverbal behavior using the following scenarios. Take turns taking on the role of client or interviewer. Sit opposite each other so that you can easily observe the other's nonverbal behavior. Try to use nonverbal attending to enhance rapport.

Client Instructions: Read a scenario and then take on the role of a client during an intake or initial interview. In response to intake questions, you are to tell the interviewer what has just happened to you. Try and make your tone of voice, body posture, and so forth emit your mood as you relate the information from the scenario to the interviewer.

Interviewer Instructions: You start by asking the client why he or she is here. As the client tells you about his or her life, respond as you would during an intake or initial interview. After a few minutes of interviewing, stop the role play and discuss the effects of any nonverbal behavior on both you and the client.

Scenario 1. Andre is very angry because he has recently been fired by his boss. The nephew of his boss had been his assistant and had been repeatedly late for work. Last week, Andre told the nephew that he either had to come to work on time or look for a new job. The nephew immediately complained to his uncle, and Andre was fired. Adding insult to injury, Andre's ex-boss gave his nephew Andre's old job.

1. Were there any indications of nonverbal mirroring? If so, how did it influence the interaction?

_____

_____

_____

2. Did you or the client show opposite nonverbal behavior? If so, how did it influence the interaction?

_____

_____

_____

3. Did you or the client perceive anything positive or negative from the nonverbal behavior of the other? Behaviors to consider include eye contact, body orientation, body posture, facial expression, autonomic behavior, and attire.

_____

_____

_____

Scenario 2. Caroline is feeling very hostile toward you and the agency because she was reprimanded by the financial officer of your mental health agency for not having paid her bills from the last time she was in treatment. She believes that if you truly cared about her, you would tell the financial officer to stop being concerned about her paying her prior bill. She doesn't have the money to pay the bill and this agency is supposed to help people not yell at them. She is tired of people saying they care about her and then showing that they do not really care. She wants you to prove you care before she opens up her heart to you about her current problems.

1. Were there any indications of nonverbal mirroring? If so, how did it influence the interaction?

   _____

   _____

   _____

2. Did you or the client show opposite nonverbal behavior? If so, how did it influence the
   interaction?

   _____

   _____

   _____

3. Did you or the client perceive anything positive or negative from the nonverbal behavior
   of the other? Behaviors to consider include eye contact, body orientation, body posture,
   facial expression, autonomic behavior, and attire.

   _____

   _____

   _____

Scenario 3. Jose's wife died suddenly from undiagnosed cervical cancer. They had been married for 15 years and had four children together. Jose comes in feeling very depressed, hopeless about the future, and fearful about his ability to care for his children without the help of
his beloved wife, Consuela.

1. Were there any indications of nonverbal mirroring? If so, how did it influence the interaction?

   _____

   _____

   _____

2. Did you or the client show opposite nonverbal behavior? If so, how did it influence the
   interaction?

   _____

   _____

   _____

3. Did you or the client perceive anything positive or negative from the nonverbal behavior
   of the other? Behaviors to consider include eye contact, body orientation, body posture,
   facial expression, autonomic behavior, and attire.

   _____

   _____

   _____

Scenario 4. Marta is afraid that she will be deported back to Colombia because of some ir-
regularity in her green card. She must attend a court hearing next week. The judge at this
hearing will decide if she will be deported from the United States. She doesn't understand
why she is in this trouble. She is currently working as a child-care provider for three young
children on a ranch in New Mexico. Her employer has hired an attorney for her to fight this
deportation threat and has sent her to you to get help calming down. She has been so nervous lately that she can't sleep. She tries to watch the children but keeps going off in a daze.
Marta is very grateful to her employer for his assistance. However, the attorney he selected

frightens her. He stares at her when she is with him, and he does not explain what is going to happen when they go to court.

1. Were there any indications of nonverbal mirroring? If so, how did it influence the interaction?

   _____

   _____

   _____

2. Did you or the client show opposite nonverbal behavior? If so, how did it influence the interaction?

   _____

   _____

   _____

3. Did you or the client perceive anything positive or negative from the nonverbal behavior of the other? Behaviors to consider include eye contact, body orientation, body posture, facial expression, autonomic behavior, and attire.

   _____

   _____

   _____

WORKSHEET 3: Responding to Nonverbal Behavior

Background: It is the beginning of your intake interview with Tommy, a nine-year-old boy. He has a learning disability and shows mildly disobedient behavior at school. Right now, he is behaving in a very withdrawn manner and is responding to you only in monosyllables. You know he is currently in danger of being retained, for the second time, in the fourth grade. He has lived in three different foster homes since being severely abused by his father when he was in the first grade. He hasn't seen his father in two years. Children and Youth Services is having this family situation evaluated to see if termination of parental rights is appropriate. If termination is considered appropriate, Tommy can be made available for adoption and have a permanent home.

Instructions: Use information from Tommy's nonverbal cues to help him become more aware of his nonverbal behavior and what it might mean. Make one comment that relies solely on sense data. In the second comment, tie the nonverbal cue to a possible feeling state. When you identify a feeling, state it in a tentative way so that Tommy can consider whether it is accurate or not. Use the background information to help you judge what his feeling state might be.

Scenario 1. You ask Tommy to talk about his dad. Tommy is staring at the clenched fists in his lap and saying nothing. His face is red.

1. _____

_____

2. _____

_____

Scenario 2. You ask Tommy if he knows about Children and Youth Services' plan to terminate his father's rights so that he can be made eligible for adoption. Tommy's face looks pained. He responds to your comments by sinking more deeply into his chair.

1. _____

_____

2. _____

_____

Scenario 3. Tommy is silent. His face is white as a sheet in response to your question about how he would feel if his father tries to regain custody of him.

1. _____

_____

2. _____

_____

Scenario 4. You tell Tommy that he might be asked to testify in court if the judge wants his opinion about terminating his father's parental rights. The judge may ask him if he wants to return to his dad. He has curled up in the chair, and no part of his face is visible.

1. _____

_____

2. _____

_____

WORKSHEET 4: Open-Ended and Closed Questions

Instructions: You are at the beginning of an interview and need to gain a lot of information from a client. Starting with a closed question is a mistake. Turn the following closed questions into two open-ended ones. Have the first open-ended question be extremely broad. Imagine the client makes a response to this that is very vague. Create a second, more specific, open-ended question to use as a follow-up to help you gain a greater understanding of the client's experiences. Finally, imagine the client responds to your last open-ended question in a way that makes it important for you to follow-up with a highly specific closed question.

1. Do you like living alone?

_____

_____

_____

2. Was it hard to adjust to life in a small town after living in a big city?

_____

_____

_____

3. Are you close to your parents?

_____

_____

_____

4. Are you nervous about being here?

_____

_____

_____

5. Have you ever experienced symptoms of withdrawal?

_____

_____

_____

6. Are you doing okay since you were released from jail?

_____

_____

_____

7. Is life outside the detoxification center much different than you expected it to be?

_____

_____

_____

8. Do you get along with your children?

_____

_____

_____

9. Was your family pleased to see you come home?

_____

_____

_____

10. Were you angry when your boyfriend broke up with you?

_____

_____

_____

11. I know we come from different backgrounds. Is it okay with you to work with me?

_____

_____

_____

12. I know you have been in treatment before and have not been satisfied. Do you think it will work this time?

_____

_____

_____

WORKSHEET 5: Reflective Listening

Instructions: Respond to the following client statements with a reflective listening comment to show the client that you are listening. Remember you can reflect the content of what the client says, the feeling the client expresses, or both. If the client expresses ambivalence, or more than one feeling, make sure your comment includes this also.

1. I feel on top of the world. I know that I am supposed to take my Lithium, but I just don't want to give up this fantastic feeling.

   _____

   _____

   _____

2. I hate that woman. She is always in my face trying to annoy me. She always demands that I do such ridiculous and time-consuming things.

   _____

   _____

   _____

3. I don't get it. I try and try, but he is never satisfied. I have spent so much time trying to figure out what he wants from me, but it doesn't seem like I ever will. I don't know if I want to try harder or give up all together.

   _____

   _____

   _____

4. It will make you think I am crazy, but I just feel as light as air. I know it is only an exam, but I got an "A"! I studied so hard! It was so important for me to do well and prove to myself that I could do it. Now I can't keep myself from just staring at the grade and smiling.

   _____

   _____

   _____

5. I don't know if I'm happy or sad. Things are changing so fast. I've graduated. I have a new job and a new apartment. How am I supposed to feel?

   _____

   _____

   _____

6. Always, always, I get dumped on. I am so sick and tired of people taking advantage of me. I can barely stand even looking at people at work because I can just see it in their eyes that they view me as a sucker. On the other hand, I don't want to let them get the better of me, so I guess I have to keep trying.

   _____

   _____

   _____

7. Will I ever get through this divorce horror and be happy again? Every day I feel more and more trapped by the legal proceedings. My husband keeps threatening me. He says that if I try to remain in the house and get a share of our savings account, he will fight me for custody of our children. He has always been the one in charge. He always told me what to do. Now I am on my own and I just don't know what I should do. I feel stuck and unable to move forward. When he comes by and finds me crying, he uses this against me and says I am an unfit mother. My friends tell me to fight him but I am so tired. I can't seem to do anything but cry.

_____

_____

_____

WORKSHEET 6: Empathetic Comments

Instructions: Read the following scenarios and then practice making three types of empathetic comments in response to each one. The goal of each comment is to emotionally support the client and demonstrate that you understand what he or she is going through.

Scenario 1. You were very ill last week so you had to cancel all your client appointments.

Henry: People are always letting me down and leaving me in a jam. Take last week: My probation officer screamed at me because he said I was not working hard enough with you on my alleged hostility problem. My boss called him and said I had just been fired for yelling at a customer. I know that working was a condition of my parole, but does that mean I have to let a customer treat me like dirt? That customer who got me fired had interrupted me when I was helping someone else. I said to him, "I'll be with you in just a moment," and the guy said he was not going to wait and if I didn't help him right now, he would complain to my boss. What was I supposed to do? Just dump one customer for another? My boss dressed me down in front of both customers without even giving me a chance to explain. So, I am the one with a hostility problem? And how am I going to make progress when I get stuck with an idiot for a boss and you just up and won't take the time to see me when it is not convenient for you?

1. Make an empathetic statement that shows Henry you understand his situation.

_____

_____

_____

2. Make an empathetic statement that validates the reality of what Henry is experiencing.

_____

_____

_____

3. Assume that Henry's level of emotion is so high that it precludes his thinking carefully about his situation. Make a series of empathetic comments to help him feel emotionally supported enough to calm down and be ready to think.

_____

_____

_____

Scenario 2. Your client is being investigated by Child Protective Services because her son went to school covered in bruises.

Latisha: I don't know what I am going to do. My man is threatening to walk out on me. I know I complain a lot about him not coming home at night and wasting all his money on gambling, but I need him. He is so important to me. Everyone nags me to leave him. No one seems to get it that I know we belong together. I just need to help him stop drinking and get his act together so we can take good care of our two kids. The kids need him too. Sure, I am not a fool. I know he overdoes it sometimes and has really hurt them. But kids need their father. His being there is just more important than the fact that he loses it sometime. I know I can do something about that. I know I can help him if people will just take the pressure off of me. What I don't need to hear from other people is that I need to walk out. Walking out on him is not what I want to do right now. I married him for better or for worse, in sickness and in health.

1. Make an empathetic statement that shows Latisha that you understand her situation.

_____
_____
_____

2. Make an empathetic statement that validates the reality of what Latisha is experiencing.

_____
_____
_____

3. Assume Latisha's level of emotion is so high that it precludes her thinking carefully about her situation. Make a series of empathetic comments to help her feel emotionally supported enough to calm down and be ready to think.

_____
_____
_____

Scenario 3. Your client expressed a lot of suicidal ideation last week and you worked with her to design a "no suicide" pact; both of you signed this agreement.

Katarina: Everything is out of control. My roommates are threatening to kick me out of our apartment because I am not paying my share of the bills. My tuition check bounced because I forgot to put my last paycheck into my checking account. I have gotten threatening phone calls from the university saying my academic schedule will be cancelled if I don't come in and pay up right now. My boyfriend says he is tired of me holding back on him and that I have to prove to him, once and for all, that I love him. He doesn't seem to understand or care that it is against my religious beliefs to have sex before marriage. It seems that I can't please anyone. I do everything wrong and no one wants to give me a break. I don't think I can go on anymore; it is so hopeless. Those suicidal thoughts I told you about last week seem to come to me more and more often. Maybe it is just what I need right now; it's a fast way out of all this trouble.

1. Make an empathetic statement that shows Katarina that you understand her situation.

_____
_____
_____

2. Make an empathetic statement that validates the reality of what Katarina is experiencing.

_____
_____
_____

3. Assume Katarina's level of emotion is so high that it precludes her thinking carefully about her situation. Make a series of empathetic comments to help her feel emotionally supported enough to calm down and be ready to think.

_____
_____
_____

WORKSHEET 7: Summarizing

Instructions: Respond to the following client remarks with a summarizing comment. Remember you are paraphrasing the client, in a succinct manner, to show that you have listened and understood the client's point of view.

Client 1. I am so confused about what I want. I've been dating the same guy, Bill, for two years and it was going great until he broke his parole and was sent back to jail for six months. I planned to be faithful to him and I was for the first two months. But I got so lonely that I just needed to start going out to the bars again. I didn't plan anything to happen, but then I met someone at a bar last week and I was really attracted him. We talked and drank till the bar closed. It was great and he asked me to meet him at the bar again the next day. I went and it was good again. I'd really like to keep going out with him, but I feel like I'm cheating on Bill. On the other hand, Bill is in prison so he wouldn't have to know. I could just keep going out with this guy for a while before I decide what to do. I just don't know what to do.

1. Write a summarizing comment that demonstrates you are listening.

   _____

   _____

   _____

2. Write a summarizing comment that will serve as a transition from this topic of how she is relating to her significant "others" to the topic of how she is relating to her family members.

   _____

   _____

   _____

Client 2. Well, I'm a freshman psychology major. I come from a town that's about two hours away from school. I can get home on weekends twice a month. I'm pretty close to my family. I have two younger sisters. I feel a little lonely at school because I haven't made any real friends yet. I guess I'm pretty shy and it is hard for me to make new contacts. College is a lot harder than I expected. I used to be a straight "A" student in high school, but even though I study a lot, I haven't gotten a single "A" since I came here. Most of the people in my dorm are drinkers and I don't enjoy getting drunk.

1. What theme might represent the client's experience in college?

   _____

   _____

   _____

2. Write a summarizing comment to highlight this theme.

   _____

   _____

   _____

Client 3. I have a big family wedding coming up and I know everyone is going to be drinking. You told me I had to stay abstinent and I understand what you're saying about relapse. But I am the only one in the family who is not married and every time we have one of these occasions, everyone puts me on the spot with jokes and stuff. It really helps me take the heat off if I have a few beers. And also, there are going to be toasts to the new couple and I was asked to give one. If I don't drink the toast, everyone is going to notice and wonder what my problem is. I haven't told anyone at home about my drinking problem because I just don't want them to know. They think I am doing great. I was thinking that maybe I could just drink at this wedding and then go back to abstinence.

1. What theme might represent the client's concerns about drinking?

_____
_____
_____

2. Write a summarizing comment to highlight the theme.

_____
_____
_____

Client 4. Everyone is on my back about the cocaine. Okay, I know that it has gotten out of hand. I will quit but I can't do it overnight. My wife is screaming because I used the mortgage payment to pay for my last binge. My kids are screaming because I didn't buy them bikes for Christmas like I promised. Even my mother is berating me and saying I am a bad father. She is treating me like a baby and telling me what to do. I just hate this. Why can't everyone realize that I need time to beat cocaine?

1. Assume this client's comments show he is experiencing a high level of rage. Make a summarizing comment that might help decrease his emotional intensity so that he can think more carefully about his experiences.

_____
_____
_____

WORKSHEET 8: Redirecting

Instructions: Practice using redirecting in response to each of the following scenarios. The goal of redirecting is to politely interrupt clients and redirect them back to a topic or issue that needs to be discussed further, help them clarify their remarks, or redirect them to a new area that needs to be discussed. Redirecting should start with a supportive or respectful comment and end by changing the direction of the conversation.

Scenario 1.

Interviewer: What problems has cocaine caused in your life?

Client: So many of my friends and family have told me that cocaine has caused me so many problems. Of course, the person in my family with the biggest problems is my cousin Lucille. Lucille has been in nothing but trouble since she was about eleven years old. The first thing she got into was smoking. No matter what I said or what anyone else said, she was not convinced that smoking was bad for her. Why my uncle even showed her his fingers and how yellow they were. She hears him coughing all night long because he's got emphysema but will she listen to reason?

(The client has gone off on a tangent rather than discussing her use of cocaine.)

1. What comment might the interviewer make to redirect the client back to her own cocaine use?

_____

_____

_____

Scenario 2.

Interviewer: Tell me about your heroin habit.

Client: When I was fourteen, the whole thing started. My teachers noticed it and I did not know what to do about that. Every time my teachers approached me, I knew something was up. I told my parents I was going to drop out of school, but they forced me to stay in. Now, they didn't physically hurt me or anything; they just woke me up every day like parents do from time to time when they think of it. Now, I definitely have developed some bad habits. Everyone I have met here says heroin is one, smoking is one, and probably the way I drive is another. You seem to be sensible people, but I don't know how I am going to break these habits since they make me feel good. I don't know if my teachers ever tried heroin. If they did, they never told me.

(The client keeps going off on confusing tangents.)

1. What statement might you make to signal to the client that you are confused and redirect him back to talk in detail about his use of heroin?

_____

_____

_____

2. What might need to be assessed if this client still goes off on tangents rather than focusing in on your questions?

_____

_____

_____

Scenario 3.

Interviewer: Tell me how you are coping with your husband's death?

Client: That reminds me of something important I wanted to ask you. Remember how I told you that my daughter actually had to take a leave of absence from work because she was just so depressed about her dad's death? Well, over the weekend, she called me and said she was crying all the time at home even when she was playing with her children. She said they are getting scared and just clinging to her all the time. I told her that she needed to call you up and make her own appointment. I promised I would come over and babysit during her appointment so she didn't need to worry about a thing.

(Based on her past behavior, you believe the client is trying to avoid discussing her own reactions to the death.)

1. What redirecting statement, to prevent this avoidance, might you as the interviewer make to return the conversation back to the woman's own reactions to her husband's death?

_____

_____

_____

Scenario 4.

Interviewer: What led to your decision to seek a divorce?

Client: It probably started even as early as our honeymoon. He seemed more interested in Hawaii than in talking to me. I remember our first dinner. We had a Polynesian feast that consisted of roast pig, three kinds of strange new vegetables, a huge pineapple dessert piled high with those cute paper umbrellas. Then, we watched some hula dancers who must have danced for four hours. I was amazed at their endurance. They must practice a great deal to be so strong. After this entertainment, my husband seemed so tired. That was the first time I thought to myself that, if he was really in love with me, he would have had more energy for romance.

(The client is being very talkative. While she is open to relating her experiences, she is giving details about things that are unlikely to be helpful in resolving her current relationship problems.)

1. What redirecting statement might you, as the interviewer, make that would communicate appreciation for this client's openness but which would then encourage the client to talk specifically about her current divorce?

_____

_____

_____

WORKSHEET 9: Supportive Confrontation

Instructions: Write a supportive confrontation in response to each of the following scenarios. Remember to include both an affirmation or supportive comment as well as a confrontation in your remarks. Select one or more of the four styles of supportive confrontation: (1) De-emphasize labeling. (2) Emphasize personal choice and responsibility. (3) Demonstrate that you listened to what the client needs. (4) Be honest with the client about problem behaviors in terms of the likelihood they will bring the client positive or negative consequences. Remember that the goal of supportive confrontation is to get the client to consider the need for change.

Scenario 1. Your sixteen-year-old client says to you, "Drinking and driving is no problem for me. In fact, it's a blast and I do it every weekend. The police are idiots. They never catch anyone for drinking and driving and if by some miracle they caught me, my folks would get me out of it."

_____
_____
_____
_____

Scenario 2. A parent of a teenager says to you, "I couldn't help myself. I had such a splitting headache last Sunday and my kid was blaring his stereo so loud I thought I would die. I didn't mean to break his arm, but I had told him many times before to keep it down. He needed a lesson that he would learn. If he hadn't tried to keep me from throwing his stereo out the window, he wouldn't have gotten hurt in the first place. It is not just me; lots of neighbors have complained about his music and the landlord has threatened to kick us out of our apartment."

_____
_____
_____
_____

Scenario 3. A forty-year-old, female client says to you, "I know that you wanted me to follow up with my gynecologist about that breast lump I found. But I just didn't do it and I don't want to discuss it. I listened to what you had to say, but I don't want to deal with it now. I hate going in and having my insides prodded; it is uncomfortable and embarrassing. I just know that I will get sent in for a mammogram or some other intrusive medical test, and I just don't need the stress of this right now."

_____
_____
_____
_____

Scenario 4. A thirty-year-old client says to you, "Men always do it. They lie about being married and go off and have as much sex as they want. My father was such a pig in that way. My mother was a fool. She would just cry and cry about it. I said to myself when I got married that I was not going to wait around for my husband to cheat. If I saw something good, I would go after it. What's fair for men is fair for woman. No one will get hurt. My husband doesn't ever have to know, and my kids are too young to notice anything."

_____
_____
_____

Scenario 5. The client is of the opposite sex to you. When this client first came through the door and the two of you shook hands, the client held onto your hand too long and looked you up and down. The client then moved a chair very close to where you were sitting. The client brushed against you in sitting down. As you are trying to conduct the interview, the client keeps shifting the focus of the conversation to be a discussion of you. The client has asked you many personal questions. You have tried several times to get control of the situation and return to appropriate intake questions, but the client persists in foiling your efforts.

_____

_____

_____

_____

Scenario 6. Your client is a mandatory referral from the court system. He has received probation, after assaulting a coworker, on the condition that he receives treatment to gain control of his temper and alcohol use. Many of his past conflicts with others have involved physical assaults. Throughout the first thirty minutes of your interview, the client has reacted to all of your questions about these assaults, and his alcohol use, with verbally threatening behavior. These threats have not stopped even though you have tried to apologize for disturbing him and then tried to clarify in detail why you need to ask him those questions in order to be of help to him.

_____

_____

_____

_____

WORKSHEET 10: Process Comments

Instructions: Practice making a content-to-process shift for each of the following scenarios. The goal of a process comment is to shift the focus in the interview from the content of what is happening in the client's life to a focus on the process that is going on between the client and the interviewer or significant others.

Scenario 1. You are interviewing a woman who consistently responds to all of your questions by saying, "Why is this question relevant?" After you explain your reasoning, she will respond vaguely and not clearly address your question. Twenty minutes have gone by, and you haven't learned much about her life or why she has come in for the interview. You find yourself feeling quite exhausted and resentful in your attempts to conduct an intake interview.

1. What comment might you make about the interpersonal process occurring between you and the client? Encourage the client to turn inward and consider the meaning of this pattern, being careful not to sound disrespectful or critical.

_____

_____

_____

_____

Scenario 2. You are interviewing a man who has come through your agency three times in the past three years and has a record of canceling appointments frequently, coming late to the appointments he attends, and not paying his bills. Your agency has told you that this client is getting "one more chance." If this client shows the same pattern as before, he will be barred from the agency's services. This client was informed about this "last chance" by your supervisor before he was given this appointment with you. He is now complaining bitterly about the unfeeling nature of your supervisor's comments and assuring you that any problems he had before were because of the poor quality of care he received in the past. He insists that his first counselor had misled him about the billing policies because he had just been hired and was still wet behind the ears. He said his second counselor was burned out and didn't care about any of his clients. He said his third counselor had been sexually provocative toward him. When he had rejected her advances, she terminated him. You are thirty minutes into this interview, and the client has consistently rephrased your questions before answering them. You perceive this to be an attempt to "subtly" tell you that you are not a clear communicator.

1. What comment might you make about the interpersonal process occurring between you and the client? Encourage the client to turn inward and consider the meaning of this pattern; be careful not to sound disrespectful or critical.

_____

_____

_____

_____

Scenario 3. You are interviewing a woman who keeps looking to you for reassurance and advice about how to deal with her boss, her teenage son, and her ex-husband. All of these relationship problems seem to revolve around her allowing someone with a stronger will to dictate to her how to handle every situation. You are trying to help her learn to be assertive and take charge of her own life. While discussing each of these relationship problems, she seems to avoid making a decision about what steps she wants to take by criticizing her own ability to choose an appropriate course of action.

1. What process comment might you make to help the client explore her pattern of relating to others? Encourage the client to turn inward and consider the meaning of this pattern; be careful not to sound disrespectful or critical.

_____

_____

_____

_____

WORKSHEET 11: Supportive Confrontation Versus Process Comments

Instructions: Read the following scenario and then practice making both a supportive confrontation and a content-to-process shift. Then, compare what the results might be of choosing one type of comment over the other for this specific client.

Scenario 1. You are interviewing a forty-two-year-old client who is now working after five years of unemployment. In his youth, he dropped out of high school because he hated the way the teachers would order him around. He joined his father and two uncles working in the coal mines. When the coal mines in his community closed down, his family encouraged him to study for the GED exam so he could become eligible for more job opportunities. He had refused to do so saying he always hated school and was too old to let anyone pressure him into doing something he hated. While he was unemployed, he applied for a lot of jobs but always lost them to other applicants who had their high school diplomas. He had spent almost all of his savings. Then, a family friend got him a job stocking shelves at a local grocery store. The client was initially very grateful about having gained employment. However, he has now told you that his boss threatened to fire him last week for insubordination. Your client says to you, "I know it was a lucky break that I got this job. Lots of people I know are still out of work. But I am not going to let my boss walk all over me by telling me when I have to get to work, what I have to wear, and how I have to talk to customers. The next thing I know, this guy is going to be telling me how to piss in the bathroom."

1. Use supportive confrontation in response to this client.

_____

_____

_____

_____

_____

2. Use a content-to-process shift with this client and point out the interpersonal pattern that often seems to crop up when he is relating to an authority figure. Ask him to turn inward and explore the possible meaning of this pattern without judging or criticizing him.

_____

_____

_____

_____

_____

3. What are the pros and cons of choosing to make a process comment versus making a supportive confrontation to this particular client? Describe in detail what you think the differential impact will be on the client and on the interviewer–client relationship of each of these types of interviewer comments.

_____

_____

_____

_____

_____